The Acquisition of Library Materials

STEPHEN
FORD

The Acquisition of Library Materials

AMERICAN
LIBRARY
ASSOCIATION

Chicago 1973

Library of Congress Cataloging in Publication Data

Ford, Stephen.
  The acquisition of library materials.

  Includes bibliographies.
  1. Acquisitions (Libraries) I. American Library
Association. II. Title.
Z689.F74   025.2   73-9896
ISBN 0-8389-0145-X

Printed in the United States of America

CONTENTS

PREFACE

In 1969 an Ad Hoc Committee of the Acquisitions Section of the Resources and Technical Services Division and of the Library Education Division of the American Library Association recommended that ALA develop and publish a book on acquisitions work that could be used both as a text for library science courses and as a reference book by those actively engaged in the work. This book is a direct result of that recommendation.

Because the committee proposed that the book be addressed to a large audience, stress has been placed on topics that are of concern to all libraries regardless of size. The scope of acquisitions work, outlined in the Introduction, acknowledges the importance of selection policy, serials recording, and other topics kindred to acquisitions. These topics are discussed in this book only as they relate to obtaining library materials. They are examined thoroughly in books and papers that are cited in the references and the bibliographic note.

Centralized acquisitions and automation of order routines are of major importance in order work and they are reviewed as chapters in this book. These chapters are introductions to the concepts and problems of centralization and automation, not manuals of practice. For treatment of these topics in particular and in depth the reader is referred to the references cited. For automation these references are only a modest selection from an enormous literature.

References are presented in three ways in this book. Those at the end of each chapter are specific and give full bibliographical details. Those in chapter 4, "Bibliographies Used in Searching," also are specific and most of them give full bibliographical details. Some, however, are continuing series, some of them long-standing, and for these, entries have been condensed or simplified, on the assumption that the user will turn to Winchell, Walford, or one of the other guides for complete details. Those references cited in the text are done with only edition, publisher, and date or frequency. Most of the latter are directories, guides, indexes, and other items published periodically with changes in format, description, publisher, place, or other features that make it advisable for the user to seek out the latest information about them from standard sources.

I wish to acknowledge here my indebtedness to the Grand Valley State Colleges for the sabbatical leave of absence that permitted me to do most of the work on this book. I am also indebted to the acquisitions staffs in several libraries for help given me, particularly at the University of Chicago and the University of Michigan. I am especially grateful to Lawrence Auld, who has been very generous with his help in the chapter on automation. My colleagues in the library at Grand Valley have unfailingly supported my efforts and I want especially to note the assistance of Betty Jones, M. Nancy Terry, Robert Beasecker, and Marlene VanNoller.

INTRODUCTION

The increase in publications of all kinds, in all subject areas, throughout the world, will be an important and challenging feature of the last third of this century. Each year, half a billion dollars are spent by American libraries for books and other library materials. College and university libraries, alone, add thirty million volumes a year to their holdings. There is an excitement peculiar to acquisitions work which is related to or arises from collection building and the acquisition of books. It may come from as simple but skill-demanding a task as buying and processing fiction titles to have them available to patrons as soon as they read a notice or review of them, or from as complex a job as the pursuit of issues of a journal irregularly published in Baghdad or Bangkok. For many librarians this work is the most interesting phase of librarianship.

SCOPE

Acquisitions work is concerned with obtaining books and other library materials for a library or group of libraries. In addition to books, the term "library materials" includes periodicals and other serials, government publications, pamphlets, technical and research reports, microforms, music scores, and audiovisual materials. It does not include supplies or equipment or other items that are not parts of a library's collections for informational, research, instruction, or leisure use.

Acquisitions work includes obtaining materials by purchase, gift, or exchange; paying for or acknowledging receipt; and maintaining appropriate records. The acquisitions department is a resource for the library and its community for information about publishing, publications, and book dealers. The work may also include the selection of materials, the formulation of selection policy, collection evaluation and weeding, work related to binding and rebinding, the recording of serials, precataloging and allied operations.

The service of acquiring books is among the oldest of librarianship. Acquisitions work was done by the head librarian with the assistance of his office staff, and it was not until well into this century that recognizable acquisitions departments appeared in American libraries, along with the development of large collections and budgets. It is interesting to note that many of the best known figures in the history of American librarianship were collection builders. Scholarship has a deep indebtedness to such librarians as William Warner Bishop and Lawrence Clark Powell, whose wide influence in many areas of librarianship is eclipsed by their gathering of great library collections. As separate acquisitions departments were slow to emerge, so too was our chief professional organization, the American Library Association, slow to recognize acquisitions as a major library activity. Although there had been many committees, boards, and similar units concerned with aspects of acquisitions, it was not until the reorganization of the mid-1950s that acquisitions interests were unified as the Acquisitions Section of the Resources and Technical Services Division, renamed the Resources Section in 1973.

The terms "acquisitions work" and "order work" are sometimes used interchangeably. Usually, however, order work applies to purchasing, while acquisitions work includes obtaining material by exchange and gift, processing material for binding and, in some libraries, book selection, as well as purchasing.

RELATION TO LIBRARY STRUCTURE

The work of the acquisitions unit must mesh with that of almost every other library operation. It is essentially a service unit for the public services and it must treat public services departments and staff as customers to be satisfied. It obtains the materials they require for their service to patrons as quickly as possible. It informs them of new materials being published, new materials available in the library, and, in many libraries, the status of book funds. The acquisitions unit works with the circulation unit in the preservation of the collection through binding and rebinding, and in replacing lost, damaged, and wornout materials. Acquisitions, in its establishing of priorities for searching, ordering, and processing, has a direct influence upon the satisfaction of library users. In academic libraries the unit may work directly with many of these patrons, especially the faculty.

Relationships with the processing or technical services units are close and critical. Acquisitions and cataloging operations must work together to process books and other library materials as quickly as possible at the least possible cost. They share records and bibliographic tools, transfer information to prevent duplication of effort, and share personnel to accommodate peak loads and special projects. The bibliographic record which ultimately makes the publication available to the user is begun by the selector, developed by the acquisitions staff, and completed in the cataloging department. This work must be continually examined and revised to ensure that it is being done to the best possible advantage of the library and its users. It is important for new librarians to understand this coordination of library functions and for new and old alike to understand that library departments are parts of a team with the same goals, not adversaries.

THE ACQUISITIONS LIBRARIAN

The acquisitions librarian needs special skills. Chief among these is book knowledge and other media knowledge, combined with an understanding of the ways books and other library materials are published and distributed and an awareness of the history and current state of the book trade.

The person who comes to library acquisitions with a knowledge of books and the trade has the chief element for success, but not all new librarians have this knowledge. It can, however, be learned. An acquisitions librarian should be completely familiar with cataloging, including the rules for entry and description in the library's catalog and the rules and methods used in constructing other tools in cataloging, such as the shelf list. Linguistic ability is a prerequisite for acquisitions work in a library where foreign language material is acquired. In many acquisitions positions the librarian also must have some managerial skills and business competence. The satisfactions of working in acquisitions lie in developing collections and serving others, satisfactions that can be the most rewarding of librarianship. The field needs people who are caught up in the excitement of the world of books and the book trade.

1

PLANNING
FOR ACQUISITIONS

Acquisitions planning includes the establishment and acknowledgment of book selection policies and practices, budgeting for the purchase of materials, and budgeting for the costs of acquiring and processing these materials.

SELECTION POLICIES

Planning for acquisitions begins with plans for the selection of books and other library materials. The chief manifestation of selection plans is a written policy statement. According to the Public Library Standards, 1966:

> All materials should be selected and retained or discarded in keeping with stated objectives of each system. . . . Every system and every library within the system should have a written statement of policy, covering the selection and maintenance of its collection.

Most of the other standards for libraries cite the need for selection policy statements and it is a common admonition in the literature of librarianship. The fact is that most libraries do not have written statements, probably more from inertia or the difficulty of forming and writing a policy than from opposition to the idea of a policy.

A statement of policy is needed not only because it publicly expresses the relationship of collection development to the objectives of the institution but also because of the need for practical guidance in everyday selection problems and for support and assistance in justifying the selections made for the library, that is, in the defense of intellectual freedom. Almost every library has an acquisitions policy whether or not it is written; books and other library materials are not chosen at random. The selection agents use some principles, stated or unstated, good or even bad. Selection will be better if it is backed by a policy statement and guidelines that are based upon library objectives and the needs of its users. These can be discovered and stated for every library, although the complexity of the exercise will vary greatly between a public library in a homogenous community and a special library serving a utilitarian information function or a major research library with diverse clientele and goals.

Public libraries have a firmer tradition for the formulation and articulation of selection policy than others. Not only do their standards offer specific recommendations but many libraries have published their policies, thus providing models for other institutions. Academic libraries, on the other hand, are not so favored, although the institutions they serve often have statements of programs of instruction and research that are translated into library selection programs instead of policy statements. The selection of materials cannot be automatic even with the most detailed policy statement because no library can purchase without limit and all must depend upon the judgment of the person who does the selection.

SELECTION PRACTICES

The ultimate responsibility for selection should rest with the head of the library under authority delegated by its governing body. In small libraries the head librarian usually is the prime selector, and he is more likely to keep this nonadministrative role than any other as the library grows in size and complexity. In public libraries selection is done almost entirely by staff members as contrasted to other types of libraries where a significant portion of selection may be done by people outside the library. Selection for a medium-size public library usually involves the whole professional staff, either by assignment of subject specialities based upon each selector's background and interest or by assignment of the selection tools. The greater complexity of the larger public library is reflected in more highly organized procedures for selection. There is usually a clear development of responsibility for subject selection by the library staff, although branch heads also may play important roles in selection. In some instances book selection departments have evolved as central agencies for selection and for the coordination of selection.

They may check published reviews and copies of books received on approval from publishers or jobbers, write reviews, make referrals to other staff members, and compile lists for purchase or for recommendations to others for purchase. In some larger public libraries a selection committee performs all or part of this work.

In academic libraries selection usually involves many people outside the library. Ideally, selection is a cooperative venture of the library staff and the faculty. In small colleges all of these people may be involved in building the library's collection. In larger institutions selection requires more formal organization: faculty participation in selection may proceed through departmental chairmen or departmental library representatives or, in large departments, even library committees. In the library the acquisitions librarian and the public service staff may do selection. Many larger libraries have established selection units or specialized bibliographic staff to do selection and to coordinate selection done by others in the library and on the faculty.

The debate on who should do book selection for an academic library is complex and not susceptible to a widely accepted solution. On the one hand, faculty members are the experts in their subject fields and can make better selections than librarians who are generalists. On the other hand, librarians are better able to see the overall collection needs of the library and will take the long-range needs of the institution into greater consideration than will faculty members who may be concerned only for the instruction that must be supported immediately or for their narrow areas of research. Many trends in recent years have resulted in more selection responsibility being left in hands of librarians. The trends include increased student enrollments, increased scholarly publication, and other increases in demands upon the time of faculty members, along with the creation of many new institutions of higher education and the introduction of better financial support for all academic libraries. When book funds are short the debate is renewed.

In special libraries selection of materials usually rests with the librarian or library staff, perhaps with the help of the staff outside the library or the assistance of a library committee. As part of the selection process the acquisitions department may play a referral role by informing others of what has been published. Referral usually includes routing selection tools, advertisements, and catalogs to the appropriate selection agents, inviting their recommendations for purchase.

Acquisitions librarians are more apt to play a role in selection today than they did in the past, and it is increasingly common for there to be bibliographers or subject specialists in libraries who are usually in or closely allied to the acquisitions department.

BUDGETING

One of the most important exercises a librarian is called upon to perform is the preparation of a budget for a forthcoming period, usually a year although sometimes a two-year period. Occasionally an institution will prepare a long-range budget for five, ten, or more years. The conventional approach to budgeting has been to build a request upon the current or past year's experience, requesting a little more for next year's needs, such as more money for postage because of anticipated increases in the cost of postage or for another assistant to help keep abreast of current searching. In colleges and universities, budgeting by formula has been used, the best-known and most-used formulas being the percentage of total institutional expenditures, number of volumes per student enrolled, and amount spent per student. A library allocation that equals 5 percent of a university's total expenditure may be completely inadequate for a library in an institution rapidly expanding its graduate program, while that percentage may be generous for a library in a long-established, stable institution.

Most public libraries have line-item budgets, a type of budget that lists expenditures separately by type or function. For acquisition of materials there might be line-items for books, periodicals, and nonprint materials. Some line-item budgets are extremely detailed and may be quite restrictive if money cannot be transferred from one line to another.

Program Budgets

These approaches to budgeting are not necessarily unreasonable, but the agencies of which most libraries are a part are moving to budget requests that are made in terms of programs and are based upon performance, both past and anticipated. A college library is asked to prepare a budget aimed at the college's educative goals; an industrial library writes a budget based upon the company's research goals. At the same time, librarians are discovering that the competition for funds is increasing from new services of government and education, and in this competition the library has no secure place which will permit it to ask for and receive increased allocations without justifying its requests and proving that it is making efficient use of the resources it has.

No special insight or training is required to understand or prepare a program budget for a library. It is simply a statement of what the library will do with the money it is requesting and a statement of how much money is required for these goals. In acquisitions, for example, the need for new materials, their number, kind, and source accompanied by a statement of the amount of staff, supplies, and equipment necessary to acquire these materials might constitute a program budget. The budget should describe the acquisitions programs so that a legislator, alderman, or corporation board member can understand them and their utility. It is good practice to present a budget that differentiates between maintenance of the existing level of acquisitions and expansion of acquisitions. This permits the appropriating body an overview that it needs to make intelligent decisions and helps identify how much of a requested increase in appropriations is for increases in costs of materials and staff and how much for new programs.

An acquisitions budget should include the following:

1. The number of volumes required for acquisition to maintain the current level of acquisitions, including a defense of the continuance of the current level of acquiring, or modification downwards if that is possible.
2. The number of volumes required for the support of new programs or expansion of existing programs, with descriptions of the programs outlining what each of its expansions will achieve and what the consequences will be if the programs are not supported.
3. An estimate of the cost of each volume to be acquired.
4. An estimate of the cost of acquiring each volume.
5. Modifications of each of the above or additional requests prepared in the same manner for periodical subscriptions and other serials and services, sound recordings, tapes, films, and other nonbook materials.
6. Analyses of other costs not reflected in purchase acquisitions: gift and exchange programs, binding, withdrawals, and related acquisitions programs.

The budget should be developed with the understanding that programs cut across organizational structure. A budget for an acquisitions department is not necessarily the same as a budget for acquisitions although both are incorporated in the above acquisitions budget. Statements that a program will improve something are unlikely to find support unless they are accompanied by statements of why improvements are desirable and how they are to be achieved. The librarian should remember and should always be careful to point out to others that a budget tends to be an assessment of quantity rather than quality.

In the pursuit of funds for library materials it may be important and even necessary to use formulas such as those in the several ALA standards or those developed by statewide agencies or others. These quantitative recommendations are usually for minimum collection levels and may limit the library that already has a good collection. There are more poor than rich library collections, and the application of a formula in a budget request for a poor library can be effective in defense of the request. Nevertheless, formulas should not be applied without qualitative plans for collection growth and without the support of statements of performance.

PPBS

The most recent change in budgeting is the introduction of the PPBS, Planning-Program-Budgeting System. This method, frequently modified by other budgeting procedures, is being instituted by many governmental bodies. The PPBS method differs from other budgeting in a number of ways, among the most fundamental being the development of planning objectives and alternatives. In planning objectives it may not be adequate to assume the library's unique role in, for instance, a college or university; the library may be presented as a part of a group of services supporting instruction with information flow, along with the television production facilities, the bookstore, and other information services. Stating objectives for a PPBS budget may be very difficult for a librarian, requiring a radically different approach in budget preparation. A PPBS budget usually requires alternative presentations for which the extreme might be what are the alternatives to a library, that is, what would happen if the library were discontinued and, perhaps, sold. It is believed that those people evaluating budgets receive the best information from a PPBS budget because it assists them in developing support for the best benefit at the least cost. PPBS budgets are usually made for five-year periods, renewed each year with the subtraction of the current year, the addition of the fifth year, and reassessment of the other years.

COSTS

Materials

Budget preparation requires the maintenance of appropriate records. The record of first importance to an acquisitions librarian in preparing a budget is the price of books and other materials the library acquires with a view to translating this information into estimates of costs for the prospective budget period. Each year since World War II prices have risen, and projecting price changes is an important feature of budgeting for acquisitions. The presentation of statistical evidence of price changes is used not only to justify increases in total allocations but also to determine the distribution of funds within a library's budget for materials. Fortunately, librarians have sources of information about prices in the price indexes that have grown, primarily, from the work of the Library Materials Price Index Committee of the Acquisition Section of ALA's Resources and Technical Services Division.

A price index is obtained by dividing the average cost of the group of materials published or released in a year by the average cost of the same group of materials in a base period. The resultant index figure is the percentage increase over the base period. Indexes are made both for form of material and for subjects. Base periods tend to vary according to the agency preparing the index and this can cause some confusion, but the essential exercise, projection of costs for budgeting, can be done satisfactorily irrespective of the base period. The figure lost by not having a common base period is the single index for all library materials; one must be satisfied with the several indexes by form of publication.

The index of prices of hard-cover books, subdivided by subject, is prepared by the R. R. Bowker Company and includes all hard-cover books listed in the "Weekly Record" given in *Publishers Weekly*. This index appears in *Publishers Weekly* soon after the end of the calendar year, usually early in February. It used the same bases as those for serials, described below, until producing the figures for 1970, when a change to a one-year base was made. At the same time, Bowker presents information on prices of paperbacks and average prices over a longer period of time for novels, biography, and history.

The price indexes for U.S. periodicals and for serial services are prepared by the Library Materials Price Index Committee and have been published in the July issues of the *Library Journal*. They originally used the three-year period 1947–49 as a base, then 1957–59 and in 1971 moved to 1967–69. Price indexes for British publications are a cooperative effort of the Library Association and in recent years have appeared in the August issues of the *Library Association Record*. Figures are based upon publications listed in the *British National Bibliography*. Price indexes for library microfilm appear in *Library Resources & Technical Services,* compiled from editions of the *Directory of Institutional Photocopying Services* (University of Chicago Library) supplemented by data secured directly from the libraries included in the index. Preparation is by the Library Materials Price Index Committee.

For an example of a use that a library can make of a price index, assume the need for a budget figure for periodicals for the next budget year for a liberal arts college library. Exclude those subject areas outside its interests, such as medicine, industrial arts, and engineering. The price index for the appropriate U.S. periodicals for the current year is 214 (114 percent increase over the base years) and for last year it was 195. Periodicals increased in price 19 percent in the most recent year for which statistics are available. In twelve years since the base period, prices have increased an average of 9.5 percent each year. For the new budget year it is unlikely that increases will be less than 9.5 percent and highly probable that they will be 19 percent or more since the rate of increase is rising each year. The librarian has no alternative to requesting an increase in allocation of 19 percent to pay the renewal bill for current subscriptions.

A subcommittee of the American National Standards Institute Z39 Committee is responsible for a USA Standard for price indexes for selected library materials. It probably will provide criteria for the construction of price indexes for books, periodicals, serial services, and microfilm.

Other statistics of publication are relevant in planning for acquisitions. Book titles published in the United States each year are recorded in the issue of *Publishers Weekly* that contains the price indexes. The number of titles published can be of importance to a library in budgeting especially when exceptional changes in the number of books published might change the amount of money required to keep pace with current publication. For instance, 1971 showed an increase in gross total output over 1970 from 36,071 to 37,692. One of the reasons for recent increases has been the growth in reprint publishing, which constitutes a growth factor of importance to many libraries. The standardization of publication statistics is now a USA Standard (ANSI Z39.8-1968) and is under consideration as an international standard.

The available price indexes are primarily for American and British materials. More than one-half of the books and periodicals purchased by a large university or research library may be in languages other than English and published outside America and Britain. It is necessary for such libraries to establish their own cost figures based upon local experience and possibly upon the experiences of other libraries purchasing similar materials.

Processing

In budget preparation it is necessary also to know the costs of acquisitions work. The clearest and most useful cost that can be presented for budget purposes is the unit cost. A unit cost may be formed by taking the total cost of an operation and dividing it by the number of units produced. A unit might be any aspect of acquisitions work. How much it costs an acquisitions department to acquire a book can be determined, in rough form, by dividing the total costs of the department for staff, supplies, overhead, and so forth, by the number of volumes acquired:

Cost of department for the year	Volumes acquired for the year	Cost of acquiring one volume
$50,000	25,000	$2.00

To illustrate the use of this cost figure, a book budget that is to be increased $20,000 for the ensuing year to increase the rate of collection growth might produce, at $9.56 anticipated average cost per volume, 2,092 additional volumes. At $2.00 cost per volume acquired, the library would have to provide $4,184 for the acquisitions department, plus factors, of course, for cataloging and preparation. The figure $2.00 may require restudying and adjusting to the expected cost of operation of the department for the year being budgeted. If the cost of living index rose 5.5 percent in the most recent calendar year, it is reasonable to expect that at least this percentage increase should be added to the $2.00 unit cost, and many libraries study anticipated costs in some depth to determine the level of support with greater accuracy.

The computation made above to illustrate the cost of acquiring one volume would be an unrefined figure for most acquisitions departments: Are materials received by gifts and exchange included? What of volumes received on subscription? Does the acquisitions materials receiving unit receive, sort, and distribute mail for the whole library or perform other duties not directly arising from acquisition? The actual cost of acquisitions usually will be determined by a more careful analysis based upon unit costs of the several aspects of acquisitions work.

Staff

The major part of acquisitions costs is for staff. Staff cost can be arrived at by dividing the salary paid for a position by the units produced. In this calculation it is necessary to remember that employee benefits beyond salary must be taken into consideration. Let us say that an acquisitions bibliographer performing preorder searching in a large research library earns $10,000 a year. Add to this the value of benefits for social security, retirement, and insurance plans contributed by the employer equal to 15 percent of the salary, or $1,500. The cost of the searcher is $11,500. If he searches 29,000 preorder requests each year, each search costs about 40 cents:

$11,500   29,000 titles $0.396

If his work results in placing 15,000 orders, assuming he discovered the library already owned 14,000 of the title requests he searched, the preorder searching cost of each title ordered is about 77 cents:

$11,500   15,000 titles $0.766

If, as compared to titles, his efforts produced the addition of 16,800 volumes to the library's collections, the preorder searching cost for adding a volume is 68 cents:

$11,500   16,800 volumes $0.684

Cost per Productive Hour Worked. Rarely, however, will a library have a position so neatly compartmented. Even some of the largest libraries with highly specialized jobs will attempt to vary the duties of a preorder searcher with selection work or training and revising the work of other searchers or some other responsibilities that do not fit into the above fomula. It should be possible, however, to make an estimate or even a tally that says what percentage of his time a searcher spends at one task or another. The time percentage can then be applied to salary percentage to arrive at unit cost as illustrated. Estimates and tallies probably will not be as accurate as analyses based upon labor cost per *productive* hour worked.

In the determination of unit costs based upon productive hour worked, it might be discovered through study that the preorder searcher searches 20.1 titles per hour. This is fixed after actual time study over a sufficiently long period of time to ensure that the entire range of complexity of searches is encompassed: from simple monographs to complex serials and government documents.

The next step is to determine how much each hour of the searcher's time costs. The library pays for a 37½-hour week, 52 weeks a year, or 1,950 hours a year. The searcher receives the ubiquitous "month's vacation," or 22 working days at 7½ hours each, or 165 hours. He is entitled to 12 days' sick leave each year and, on an average, uses 6 of them, or 45 hours. The library observes 10 holidays a year for which the searcher is paid, or 75 hours. The searcher is allowed two "coffee breaks" a day of 20 minutes each and another 20 minutes for personal needs, or one hour each day that he is on the job, or 223 hours each year. He works a total of 1,442 hours each year, and at his salary plus benefits of $11,500, each of these hours costs $7.97. With 20.1 titles searched each hour, each title costs $0.396 to search.

Other Unit Costs

The unit of cost of each step in the acquisitions process can be established in this manner, including the cost of supplies. The costs of supervision, training, and administration are units of production that vary in difficulty and may require a larger unit of measurement such as a month or even a year. A completely accurate picture will be presented only if it includes costs of equipment amortized over a suitable period and overhead costs, including building cost, heating, lighting, and all the features of costing that a business would use. Most libraries, however, stop their cost analysis somewhere before overhead costs when preparing a budget request. Government and educational units, for example, do not prepare for the replacement of buildings by earmarking funds ahead of time, however much we might wish they did.

In budgeting for acquisitions attention must be given to the *kinds* of materials that are to be acquired. An increase in the book budget may not mean that the additional materials to be acquired are exactly the same as the materials currently being acquired. The ratio of fiction to nonfiction to children's books and the attending degrees of difficulty in acquisitions may change, especially when a budget increase is intended to strengthen the collection in a specialized area. If a library receives an increase to establish a Latin American business and economics collection, unit costing will have to be studied to weight it in favor of the increased complexity of searching a higher proportion of nonfiction and material in Spanish and Portuguese. In this context, larger libraries probably will want to establish unit costs for diverse forms of materials: monographs, serials, technical reports, government publications, materials in languages other than English, and out-of-print books. A preorder searcher's production will be many times greater when working with in-print trade books than when working to verify and determine the availability of government documents from the remoter parts of the world.

COSTS AND STANDARDIZATION

The unit cost analysis of acquisitions costs made by comparing cost per hour to production per hour probably is most useful in evaluating job economy and performance. Moving aside from budgeting, there has long been need for standards for library work that would permit a comparison of performance in one library with that in others. The value of such standards could be immense, ranging from assistance to the librarian in determining budget structure to convincing a board of trustees that the library it views as a bottomless financial pit is at least not different from other libraries of similar purpose and support.

Although many studies have been made, there are no standards for acquisitions costs. TSCOR (Technical Services Costs Ratio), a concept for measuring the total cost of technical services, was developed by the RTSD Technical Services Costs Ratio Committee (now disbanded). The TSCOR figure is arrived at by adding the costs of salaries for technical services personnel and dividing the total by the amounts spent for library materials for the same period of time. The result is a dollar statement of how much it costs to add a book to the library for every dollar spent for materials. A library may, for example, be required to spend $10 for salaries for each $10 that it spends for materials. It is not certain that TSCOR answers can be compared between libraries, but they can be of great assistance to a library that figures its TSCOR over a period of years, especially in predicting the real costs of increases in the materials budget. Experience seems to indicate that the larger the library the larger the TSCOR; that is, it costs more to add materials to a large library than to a small library. This does not hold for public libraries. In fact, an inverse ratio for public libraries is reported in the article by Helen Welch in *Library Resources & Technical Services* cited in the References to this chapter.

The establishment and acceptance of a standard list of technical services functions would provide an important tool for comparative cost studies. The development of standard time units for acquisitions operations offers promise for comparative cost studies. Where costs might vary greatly between libraries, the times to perform clerical routines do not have as great a potential for variance. The time required to place an ownership mark on the outside of a book will be more nearly the same among libraries than the cost of doing so. The bits of information acquired through the use of standard times may be very difficult for an administrator to manage, but they will let him understand how much it costs to deviate from standard procedures.

ALLOCATIONS

All libraries have some allocation or subdivision of the funds budgeted for materials. The head librarian plays the principal role in determining how funds are distributed, in accordance with an approved budget, but the acquisitions librarian will have an important role even if it is limited to an advisory one. He should be the person best able to provide and interpret the records of expenditures for previous years and should be most familiar with changes in the book market. In addition, he should be aware of needs for new materials and capable of weighing the demands for changes in selection policies and procedures.

A library may limit its allocations to only three or four. Money may be set aside to renew subscriptions, to continue payment for standing orders, to sustain programs of cooperative purchasing with other libraries, and to replace worn out or missing volumes and pay for needed binding and rebinding, with the balance in a general fund from which all other purchases are made. In research libraries the amount required for obligations already incurred may be as high as 50 percent of the total budget for materials and in some special libraries it will be even higher because of their limited dependence upon monographic materials. Theoretically, any divisions or allocations should be made on the basis of responses to a program budget.

Where allocations are made, public libraries may divide funds by departments (such as reference, children's, branches), or by subjects, or by a combination of both form and subject. Separate allotments usually are made for adult and juvenile books. In the past, library book funds in academic institutions were distributed directly to teaching departments. Although this unwieldy arrangement has vanished, the majority of academic libraries make allocations for the use of departments, schools, and colleges, while retaining funds for standing orders, serials, replacements, and other obligations and for general purchases such as for reference and bibliography and for materials not attributable to any one department or school. A university library may have dozens of book allocations. Some academic libraries do not allocate funds to departments, and others have control over allocations that permits library staff members to make purchases from them. In other institutions, allocations to faculty units are small and a large general fund gives the library faculty extensive responsibility for collection development.

It is not the object of this discussion to present the extensive arguments for and against the allocation of funds in academic libraries but to point to the existence and problems of allocations because they have a significant effect on the work of acquisitions departments in selection as well as in the maintenance of records and accounting. Some allocations are based upon elaborate formulas which attempt to take into consideration every variable that might apply, beginning with the number of books published annually in a subject field and enrollment in the corresponding instructional department, and ending with the number of references to the subject in pertinent abstracts. Care should be taken to be sure that allocations are related to the needs' of the collection as expressed in budgeting and not used as a method of controlling the selection activities of faculty members. Familiarity with allocation rationale and methods is a necessity for the librarians in academic acquisitions work.

Other allocations of funds will arise from gifts and endowments and from grants from government or other agencies. Separate accounts usually will have to be maintained for these funds, sometimes to the specifications of the grant, as is the case with federal funds, and selection of materials may be governed by the terms of the gift or grant.

In the structure of fund distribution it is important to provide resources to allow the acquisitions librarian to meet unexpected demands. These might include the offer of a scarce but much-needed set that has not been budgeted, or prepublication offers that could not be anticipated and that provide substantial savings for order or payment before publication.

Some libraries, or the agencies of which they are a part, control expenditures through the periodic release of funds. This is most commonly done quarterly so that an allocation for children's books of $10,000 for a fiscal year will allow the encumbrance of $2,500 at the beginning of each quarterly period in the year. This is usually a device to assure that there will be sufficient funds to provide for purchases throughout the year or to protect against overly zealous selectors. For a library to have encumbered all of its funds within a few months of the beginning of a fiscal year is an indication of either extreme undersupport or poor management or, most probably, both.

An interesting variation in allocations is practiced in some public libraries and has potential for all libraries. This is the allocation of units instead of dollars. A unit may be the average cost per volume or other predetermined translation of dollars into rough equivalents. For instance, each five dollars or a part thereof may be one unit, based upon a determination of average volume costs. The advantage is in record keeping. A children's department can maintain a simple record of the number of units it has used and know how many more it can use during a budget period. No elaborate system of accounting is necessary and frequent statements of balances from the library's order or finance department are not necessary. Usually, under the unit system, the agency responsible for accounting makes an actual financial reckoning each quarter for each allocation and adjusts the available units accordingly.

REFERENCES

Selection Policies and Practices

Boyer, Calvin J., and Eaton, Nancy L. *Book Selection Policies in American Libraries, an Anthology of Policies from College, Public, and School Libraries.* Austin, Tex.: Armadillo Pr., 1971. 222p.

Carter, Mary D., and Bonk, Wallace J. *Building Library Collections.* 3d ed. Metuchen, N.J.: Scarecrow, 1969. 319p.

Gaver, Mary V. *Background Readings in Building Library Collections.* Metuchen, N.J.: Scarecrow, 1969. 2v.

Lane, David O. "Selection of Academic Library Materials, a Literature Survey." *College & Research Libraries* 29:364–72 (Sept. 1968).

Merritt, LeRoy C. *Book Selection and Intellectual Freedom.* Bronx, N.Y.: Wilson, 1970. 100p.

Budgeting

Fazar, Willard. "Program Planning and Budgeting Theory: Improved Library Effectiveness by Use of the Planning-Programming-Budgeting System." *Special Libraries* 60:423–33 (Sept. 1969).

Jenkins, Harold R. "The ABC's of PPB." *Library Journal* 96:3089–93 (Oct. 1, 1971).

Maybury, Catherine. "Performance Budgeting for Libraries." *ALA Bulletin* 55:46–53 (Jan. 1961).

Price, Paxton. "Budgeting and Financial Control." In *Encyclopedia of Library and Information Science* 3: 430–41. New York: Marcel Dekker, 1968.

Summers, William. "A Change in Budgetary Thinking." *American Libraries* 2:1174–80 (Dec. 1971).

Costs

Brutcher, Constance, and others. "Cost Accounting for the Library." *Library Resources & Technical Services* 8:413–31 (Fall 1964).

Dougherty, Richard M., and Leonard, Lawrence E. *Management and Costs of Technical Processes: A Bibliographical Review, 1876–1969.* Metuchen, N.J.: Scarecrow, 1970. 145p.

Kountz, John. "Library Cost Analysis: A Recipe," *Library Journal* 97:459–64 (Feb. 1, 1972).

Leimkuhler, Ferdinand F., and Cooper, Michael D. "Cost Accounting and Analysis for University Libraries." *College & Research Libraries* 32:449–64 (Nov. 1971).

"Prices of U.S. and Foreign Published Materials." In *Bowker Annual of Library and Book Trade Information.* New York: Bowker, 1956–   . Annual.

Tuttle, Helen Welch. "Standards for Technical Service Cost Studies." In *Advances in Librarianship,* ed. by Melvin J. Voigt, p. 95–111. New York: Academic Pr., 1970.

Tuttle, Helen Welch. "TSCOR: The Technical Services Cost Ratio." *Southeastern Librarian* 19:15–25 (Spring 1969).

Voos, Henry. "Standard Times for Certain Clerical Activities in Technical Processing." *Library Resources & Technical Services* 10:223–27 (Spring 1966).

Welch, Helen M. "Technical Service Costs, Statistics and Standards." *Library Resources & Technical Services* 11:436–42 (Fall 1967).

Wynar, Bohdan S. "Cost Analysis in a Technical Services Division." *Library Resources & Technical Services* 7:312–26 (Fall 1963).

Allocations

Bach, Harry. "Why Allocate?" *Library Resources & Technical Services* 8:161–65 (Spring 1964).

Ladenson, Alex. "Budget Control of Book Purchases and Binding Expenditures in Large Public Libraries." *Library Resources & Technical Services* 4:47–58 (Winter 1960).

Lane, David O. "The Selection of Academic Library Materials, a Literature Survey." *College & Research Libraries* 29:364–72 (Sept. 1968).

McGrath, William E., and others. "Allocation Formula Derived From a Factor Analysis of Academic Departments." *College & Research Libraries* 30:51–62 (Jan. 1969).

Schad, Jasper G. "Allocating Book Funds: Control or Planning." *College & Research Libraries* 31:155–59 (May 1970).

2

THE ORGANIZATION OF ACQUISITIONS WORK

The importance of good organization and management in library operations is self-evident. We live in a time of increasing demands for money for a wide array of services and of increases in both number and diversity of publications. Because much of it is routine and repetitive, acquisitions work lends itself to organizational scrutiny as much as any work in libraries. A poorly functioning acquisitions operation can affect the well-being of a library seriously. Although not a public-service operation, acquisitions work has an important effect upon the view that patrons have of the library. It may be the fault of the acquisitions unit if a popular new book is not available for borrowing immediately after publication or if an instructor's request for an uncommon item does not get filled promptly and accurately.

The organization and management of acquisitions work are basically the same in all libraries although there will be variations by type of library. The acquisitions unit must be responsive to the goals of the institution in its policies and procedures. If a library order unit in a liberal arts college is forced to establish priorities for searching and ordering books, it will give first priority to books required for course reserves. In a special library, under similar circumstances, priorities may be given to materials that are published in limited quantities and will be out of print if the order is delayed. Where an order unit in one library might stress a careful balancing of the best possible service with the lowest possible cost, another might find that the importance of speed in ordering transcended that of economy.

RESPONSIBILITY DESCRIPTIONS AND PROCEDURES MANUALS

The acquisitions unit should have a statement of responsibilities that includes the functions for which it is responsible and explains its relationships with other library departments. For instance, a part of a statement of responsibilities might be:

> *Periodicals.* The Acquisitions Department is responsible for the selection of vendors for the library's subscriptions, based upon economy and service. The Periodicals Unit in the Reference Department prepares and submits the subscription list to the Acquisitions Department, records issues received, claims missing issues, approves invoices to confirm that subscriptions are in effect, and submits approved invoices to the Acquisitions Department for payment. The Acquisitions Department maintains records of fund balances and encumbrances and submits monthly statements to the Periodicals Unit.

In addition to the statement of responsibilities for the unit, each position in acquisitions should be described in writing. A position description defines a job so all will know what to expect of the person occupying it and assists in easing communication with others working in the department and in the library. It is also an important tool in recruitment, informing the personnel agency of the library's needs and prospective employees of the nature of the job. Another use for the position description is in analyses to improve or change the work of a unit.

Manuals and job instructions are other tools that should be features of every acquisitions unit. A manual spells out procedures to which more than one person may contribute, such as placing orders or receiving books and approving invoices. A manual for bibliographic searching will be a common tool in every order unit and one of the published manuals may be suitable, perhaps with modifications for local circumstances. A job instruction goes into depth beyond the position description, giving details on how a job is to be done. Function statements, position descriptions, manuals, and instructions must be kept up-to-date if they are to be useful, and keeping them up-to-date requires the assumption or assignment of responsibility.

An additional and seemingly contradictory prescription is required for successful work in acquisitions: preserve the ability to operate flexibly, knowing when to break the rules. For example, a college library learned of the existence of a copy for sale of a great foreign-language dictionary in publication for a hundred years and unobtainable complete from any commercial source. The library had not budgeted the hundreds of dollars asked for the set and it was owned by a gentleman five hundred miles away who was not interested in the details of invoicing or packing and shipping. An appeal was made to the president and the money was found outside the library allocations. A special courier was sent, with a check for payment, to pack and bring back the set. All of these steps ran against routine procedures for acquisitions, but the college could not have had this important set without circumventing standard procedures.

FUNCTIONS OF AN ACQUISITIONS DEPARTMENT

The following list is a compilation of the functions characteristic of an acquisitions department:

1. Providing and maintaining up-to-date order tools appropriate to the needs of the library, including publishers' catalogs, trade bibliographies, and other bibliographies as required.
2. Maintaining lists (files) of books and other library materials on order and in process in a manner that will permit all staff members to use them with ease.
3. Performing preorder bibliographic searching to prevent unwanted duplication, to obtain sufficient information to permit an order to be placed, and to establish the main entry that probably will be used when the material is cataloged.
4. Selecting dealers or other sources for the purchase of materials, typing and mailing orders, and ordering Library of Congress cards or making other provision for the preparation of cataloging copy.
5. Receiving, unpacking, sorting, and checking in books; determining that items received correspond to items ordered, that the material is in appropriate condition, and that the price and discount or surcharge are in accordance with the purchase agreement.
6. Approving invoices for payment and forwarding them to the appropriate office for payment; maintaining records of payment and encumbrance if this is done in the acquisitions department.

7. Placing ownership marks and accession numbers or other markings on library materials as required by library procedures.
8. Forwarding materials for cataloging.
9. Entering subscription orders, receiving and recording periodicals and other serials, placing ownership marks on them, and forwarding them.
10. Claiming unfilled orders.
11. Informing originators of orders of the receipt of materials or the status of orders; issuing lists of books and other library materials added to the library.
12. Searching for out-of-print materials.
13. Selecting books and other library materials for purchase; acting as a clearing house for information about new or newly available publications, appropriate bibliographies, and other information pertinent to collection development.
14. Soliciting gifts and establishing exchange agreements, maintaining appropriate records, receiving materials and forwarding them the same as other library materials. Sending exchange shipments to exchange partners.

Other functions may come into the sphere of the acquisitions department. Many departments provide messenger or courier service for the library, operate receiving and shipping departments, and order supplies, equipment, and services for the whole library. Sometimes the assignment of these responsibilities is defended on the basis that the acquisitions department has the business knowledge necessary to manage them properly. At other times the chief reason is to keep them from the head librarian's overburdened administrative payroll. It is better to allow the acquisitions department to concentrate on the acquisition of books and other library materials, cultivating an expertness that must be diluted if other responsibilities are assigned or assumed.

ORGANIZATION BY TYPE OF LIBRARY

The place of acquisitions in the organization of the library varies according to the type and size of the library. In small libraries it may not form a separate department or unit and in the smallest the librarian and a part-time clerical assistant may do all the order work.

In the small to medium-size public library order work is often supervised by the head librarian with clerical assistants. Many public libraries use no professional librarians in order work. In medium-size to large public libraries there often will be a technical services department which includes acquisitions, cataloging, preparation, and binding and mending. The head or coordinator of the technical services department then replaces the head librarian as the professional supervisor of acquisitions. The size of a public library acquisitions unit depends in great part upon its responsibilities. It will be larger and have professional librarians if it has selection responsibility. If, as is the case in some medium-size libraries, all selection and preorder searching is done by public service units, the order unit may need only a part-time clerk for order typing, filing, and receiving. The largest public libraries usually have acquisitions departments similar in size and responsibility to those in large academic and research libraries.

The smallest academic libraries also may depend upon arrangements for acquisitions which use part of the time of the head librarian or another professional librarian. It is more common for an academic library than for a public library with a similar total operating budget to have an acquisitions department because academic libraries assign a larger proportion of total library funds to the purchase of materials than do public libraries. Furthermore, they do little multiple-copy buying and more of their purchases are obscure, hard to find, out-of-print, or otherwise time-consuming for staff members. It requires considerably less staff time to do preorder searching, place orders, and do the receiving for $10,000 worth of in-print trade books than it does to perform the same tasks in spending the same amount for the publications of associations, government agencies, colloquia, conferences, and the like. Academic libraries also have less control over selection sources than do public libraries, and this adds to the complexity of their work. The selection for a public library is done by the staff of the library, who can be expected to transmit complete and accurate order information to the acquisitions unit, and the greatest part of the selection is done from standard selection sources that offer complete or reasonably complete bibliographic information. Selection for an academic library will be more widely based, much of it by staff that the library does not "control." Faculty members, for example, can only be coaxed to give all of the information they have about prospective purchases. In addition, the sources are more diversified and may be less reliable, such as badly made footnotes offering misleading information. No preorder searcher of more than six months' experience in an academic library has avoided spending half-an-hour trying to verify a faculty order for a book only to discover it is a magazine article. The size of acquisitions departments in college, university, and research libraries will vary also depending upon their duties, but they occur as identifiable and fully organized operating units more often than they do in public libraries.

The special library acquisitions operation will be similar to that of an academic library, its size depending upon the size of the library and the responsibilities assigned to it. Several features set the special library apart from the others. It does not usually rely on books as much as other libraries and consequently its order unit will spend more time on subscriptions to periodicals and other serials. A higher proportion of the materials it requires are obscure or ephemeral in nature and, because such materials generally are published in small runs, great speed is needed to be sure the publisher receives an order before the supply is exhausted. Many special libraries will spend more acquisitions time on securing free materials than on purchases.

Technical Services

Most medium-size and large libraries organize technical services or processing in one of two ways: either with acquisitions and cataloging and, possibly, serials departments reporting to the director of the library or with these units as parts of a technical services department whose head is the chief of processing. The head may be an assistant or associate director of the library or may report to a person with that title. Combining processing units in one department draws attention to their unity of purpose in acquiring and processing materials and may promote the cooperation between them that is essential to their smooth functioning. Supporters of the pattern in which the acquisitions and cataloging departments report directly to the head librarian believe that this organization emphasizes and capitalizes upon the unique characteristics of these operations and that cooperation can be affected by coordination between units without the interposition of an administrative layer. The choices depend, in large degree, upon the size of the library, the span of control of the director of the library, and the talents and attitudes of the people working in processing and administration.

Organization within processing takes many forms. Some of these are: acquisitions and cataloging; acquisitions, serials, and cataloging; acquisitions, cataloging, preparations, and binding and mending; book selection, ordering, preorder and precataloging searching, serials, cataloging, binding, and photo-reproduction. It is possible to expand and ring the changes on processing organization to a dozen or more without repetition. Whatever method of organization is selected it is important to emphasize the necessity of coordination between processing units. Work done in one unit should never be repeated in another; and, if work done in one unit cannot be used with ease in another, consultation should be made to be sure that the reasons for this are sound and in the interests of the total processing operation.

ORGANIZATION IN ACQUISITIONS

Organization within an acquisitions unit can be effected in several ways. Perhaps the most common is by type of activity, that is, by the method of acquisition: purchase, gift, and exchange. Many variations may be developed on this theme: preorder searching, book selection, and the acquisition receipt of serials may be added as part of each of the three types of activity. Gifts and exchanges may be combined, a common arrangement in libraries. In very large libraries gifts and exchanges may be such important operations that they are formed into a separate division, parallel to the acquisitions division. Another common organization of acquisitions work is by type of material: books, serials, documents, etc. Here, too, variations occur. For example, most documents are serials and work on both documents and serials may be combined into an operating unit. A library may be of a size to provide a specialist in acquiring maps and documents but cannot afford specialists in each of these areas. In this case, a maps and documents acquisitions unit may be a practical and effective organizational feature.

Serials Acquisitions

Serials represent a major area for consideration in the organization of acquisitions work. The acquisition of serials is closely related to their recording since serial recording confirms the receipt of materials and gives the acquisitions librarian authority to renew subscriptions and standing orders and pay invoices. The recording of serials is also an extension of the library's catalog. A serial record usually is separate from the catalog because it is not economical to enter the receipt of each issue in a card catalog. Consequently, most libraries are presented with a difficulty because the serial holdings and recording file is an acquisitions tool as well as a cataloging and public record. Interdepartmental cooperation is relied upon to solve the difficulty.

A serials record may be kept in the acquisitions department or in the technical services department, midway between acquisitions and cataloging, where it can be available for continuing and heavy use by the processing staff. In either of these locations it may be difficult for the reference staff and the library's patrons to use, especially during evenings and weekends when the processing staff is gone and the record inaccessible. One frequently observed solution is the provision of some kind of a duplicate file, usually simplified, adjacent to the public card catalog or the reference desk. This is almost inevitably a questionable practice because of the duplication of effort such a file represents. When the serial record is moved to a public area, and this has happened in many libraries in recent years, the processing staff is confronted with time lost in consultation of the file, and duplicate records appear in technical services areas. One of the happiest prospects of automation in the library is the provision of a complete serial record at more than one location in the library. Not many libraries can afford this luxury yet, and, among those that can, the usual offering is a printout record of serial holdings that is too expensive to keep up-to-date each day as must be done with a proper serial record.

Some librarians have for many years promoted the idea of a separate serials department which combines acquisitions, recording, and cataloging. Some libraries have moved to establish such departments but they tend to incorporate serials acquisitions and recording, but not cataloging. The most common organization is assignment of serials acquisitions and recording to the acquisitions department and cataloging of serials to the catalog department. Second is the placement of serials functions, exclusive of cataloging, in a separate department. There also are libraries in which serials are decentralized and acquisition and recording is done in more than one unit by subject division or by type of material.

Documents and Maps in Acquisitions

Documents acquisitions is another kind of acquisitions work that is sometimes done outside the acquisitions department. This occurs for four reasons. First, documents are fairly easy to identify when they are received in the library and routing them to the proper place for the recording of receipt can be done quickly and without much risk of error. Second, most United States and United Nations documents are classified and arranged according to the Superintendent of Documents and United Nations classification schemes, with principal bibliographical approaches other than the library's catalog. Third, documents are subject to and best served by a specialized reference service, and are identified by librarians and patrons as different from other library materials. Fourth, most libraries with extensive collections of United States government documents are depository libraries. The receipt of materials on deposit is unique in libraries as far as acquisitions are concerned and outside the mainstream of purchasing in the acquisitions department. A documents department may be responsible for the acquisition of documents. Coordination of this work with the acquisitions department may require extensive effort because there remain many national, state, and local documents that must be purchased in the same way as other library materials, and not all United States documents are available on deposit or in duplicate, causing even the largest depository libraries to acquire them by purchase.

Maps also may be handled completely separately for much the same reasons as documents. They are easy to identify upon receipt, their preorder identification and handling upon receipt require special training, and they, too, are often items of deposit or gift outside the usual purchase procedures. Again, however, some maps are purchased and methods for purchase require coordination with procedures in the acquisitions department.

Book Selection and Searching in Acquisitions

Book selection may or may not be a part of acquisitions as discussed in chapter 1, "Planning for Acquisitions." Book selection units exist most often in public libraries but a significant number of university and research libraries are developing bibliographic staff for book selection. Some libraries have combined the work of book selection and preorder searching, providing or training people with subject or area specialties. The idea of the bibliographic specialist has meaning primarily in the largest libraries with huge and still expanding collections.

Another function of acquisitions that may leave the acquisitions department is preorder searching. In addition to the instance mentioned above where public service staff does preorder searching, there is some indication in larger libraries of the combination of preorder searching with precataloging searching. We have long recognized that the work done and the training required to do it are very similar. Combining these searching units not only may be an economical utilization of staff but also may provide better precataloging information.

Nonbook Materials in Acquisitions

The ordering of some nonbook materials may also fall outside the responsibility of the acquisitions department or require the larger acquisitions department to develop people with highly specialized skills. Phonograph records, tapes, scores, films, filmstrips, and other nonbook materials are controlled with specialized acquisitions tools and sources.

A characteristic arrangement of duties in libraries is to have the public service staff member who is responsible for these materials do the selection, search to prevent duplication, and deliver all information, including source, to the acquisitions department for the placement of orders.

CENTRALIZATION OF ORDERING

In this discussion of organization it has been taken for granted that centralization of ordering functions is desirable. If all of the public service departments of a public or university library purchased their own materials, the duplication in materials and in time and records would be excessive. A centralized operation can provide assembly-line processing and specialists who can perform the work faster, do better work, and achieve a coordination of effort that would be impossible in a decentralized situation. There is a case for decentralization, however, in larger libraries where an acquisitions department ordering as much as a million dollars' worth of books and serials a year may become ponderous and unable to provide the quick and personal service that a smaller library is able to give. In addition, central libraries on large campuses may be remote from some college or departmental libraries. It is common practice for law and medical libraries on university campuses to do their own purchasing and some universities have highly decentralized purchasing procedures. These more often occur because of peculiarities of funding than for desire to give good service, but the latter may be the overriding reason for their continued independence. Of course, measures for coordination must be maintained to prevent indefensible duplication of materials and effort.

STATISTICS

Statistics of acquisition for the official records of the library are the chief statistical responsibility of the acquisitions department. They are a function of the receipt of materials and are discussed in chapter 14, on order routines. Other statistics form important records of performance for the library and should be maintained. Their variety is as great as the functions of the acquisitions department: number of orders placed, performance of dealers, average discounts, unintentional duplicates, and similar information. Many statistics should be kept only for the period that an operation is being studied or for short intervals throughout the year to form a body of samples. Processing departments must be on guard to be sure they do not keep statistics that are not really needed.

PERSONNEL

Considerations of staffing for acquisitions vary from staffing in other parts of a library only by the higher proportion of clerical or nonprofessional staff. In acquisitions, as in circulation, most of the staff may be clerical, and in even the largest library the ratio of professional to nonprofessional staff in acquisitions would not exceed one to one. Large libraries have professionals at the head of the several units in the acquisitions department: gifts, exchanges, serials, documents, and bibliographic searching. In some cases, there will also be professionally trained assistants.

There are many points in acquisitions work where professionally trained librarians may inadvertently do clerical work. Special care must be maintained to be sure that acquisitions staff members do work that is appropriate to their training and skills. One of the more familiar points of confusion between professional and clerical work is in the performance of "important" jobs. For example, an important job in acquisitions is the approval of invoices; that is, being sure the proper materials are received and the purchase terms are observed correctly. A business office likes to have a responsible or important person's signature before it writes a check, but approving invoices is not a task requiring the attention of a professional librarian. A properly trained, reliable clerk will be able to do the work as well if not better, find greater satisfaction in it, and cost the library less money.

In the assignment of clerical duties care also must be taken to be sure that the people performing them are not overqualified or underqualified. When the job market is in the favor of the employer, it is not unusual to hire the most highly qualified person rather than the person best qualified for the vacant position. A high school graduate who is a good typist should do better work at typing orders than a college graduate who is a good typist. The latter may become bored more quickly and his or her dissatisfaction with the work may mean poor performance or an unnecessarily early resignation. Similarly, some work is so routine that no one should be required to do it exclusively.

For example, a large acquisitions department may have an employee who types one kind of order form all day long; but, for job satisfaction and good performance, this job should be assigned to two people who also share another kind of work with similar intellectual requirements, or part-time assistants should be used. In academic libraries there are many tasks that part-time student assistants can do better than full-time workers, despite the temporary and sometimes evanescent nature of student help.

Wherever there is a large clerical staff in a library, there may be a high turnover in that staff. Position descriptions, manuals of procedures, and job instructions provide important assistance in compensating for this turnover by reducing the supervisory time required for training and by assuring that routines will be carried on without change. Technical services departments should give consideration to using people with library technician training and should assist in the development of training programs wherever possible.

The bibliographic searching done in acquisitions work poses a complex problem in the recognition and assignment of professional and nonprofessional duties. The small to medium-size library may use only nonprofessional staff for its bibliographic work except for searching difficult items or solving problems. The larger library may use professional staff or nonprofessional staff with special skills such as language or subject knowledge for searching the high proportion of foreign, obscure, or difficult-to-identify publications with which it must deal, as well as to work with a complex library catalog and large files and a wide range of bibliographies. Good training, supervision, and assignment of material requiring searching are the keys to the successful division of work between professional and nonprofessional staff, and success depends largely upon the skill of the supervisor of searching.

In addition to the standard professional journals an order librarian will want to see *Publishers Weekly* and *AB Bookman's Weekly* regularly, possibly also the *Bookseller,* and the several excellent house organs from publishers and dealers as well as catalogs, brochures, and advertisements. In addition to knowledge of media the acquisitions librarian needs managerial skills. Beyond common sense and good judgment, these may have to be learned on the job since most librarians will not have had formal management training. The literature of librarianship in the last ten years contains some good material on the management of technical processes. Knowledge of the steps taken in cataloging and processing materials allows the acquisitions librarian to make informed analyses and decisions relating the work done in acquisitions to cataloging.

The work of the professional associations is important in the support of acquisitions work. Chief among these is the ALA Resources and Technical Services Division and its sections. In addition to their activities related to processing, resources, selection, and preservation, they provide formal liaison with publishers and booksellers and publish the key professional journal for acquisitions librarians, *Library Resources & Technical Services*.

Librarians in processing work, usually divorced from service to the public, may feel isolated from their institution's purpose and policy making. For librarians working in processing departments the case for participatory management can be supported as easily as elsewhere in the library. They should be involved in the formulation of policies and procedures not only for their own units but also for the whole library.

WORK SIMPLIFICATION AND SYSTEMS ANALYSIS

A substantial portion of the work done in libraries is routine and repetitive and can be subjected to quantitative analysis. Some jobs in acquisitions are more forthrightly mechanical than others, but even book selection can to some extent be measured quantitatively.

Frequently, simply asking why a job is performed or a file maintained leads to simplification and possible improvement in operations. Eliminating a step or a file on a temporary basis as an experiment has often been successful in demonstrating the worth of the step or file, and experiments in rearranging the sequence in which a job is performed may reveal opportunities for improvements without risk of sacrificing the quality of the job.

Operations that are not moving smoothly should be selected for study. Those that are repeated most often and are the most routine should be studied because even a small saving in time or material may prove to be quite significant if the operation is performed often enough. Dougherty and Heinritz in *Scientific Management of Library Operations* cite a hypothetical routine that saves one minute per book in the process of ordering 10,000 books a year. The result is a saving of 167 hours or a month's labor by a full-time employee each year. The authors admit that circumstances are rarely this neat but the illustration dramatizes the possibilities for operations like acquisitions where typing, filing, form separation, arranging, and similar steps are such a large part of the total effort. Although many of the problems in acquisitions work can be solved by the use of logic, common sense, and observation of procedures in other libraries, we now have new and important literature on systems analysis and scientific management for libraries, part of which is cited in the references for this chapter. There is also a vast literature on systems analysis in general. "Systems analysis" is now identified with computer technology, but the term is used here without that connotation. It is acknowledged that an automated system may be the end result of a system analysis, but this is not necessarily so in a library where automation may be economically unrealistic.

The ideal person to conduct the analysis of a library's systems is one who has background in both scientific management and librarianship. Some management firms have developed an expertness in the analysis of library work, but the most satisfactory arrangement for most libraries is to employ as a consultant or as a member of the staff a librarian who is acquainted with the principles of good management. A management firm or a consultant librarian can bring an objectivity to a problem that might not be possible for a member of the library staff. On the other hand, the library staff member has a familiarity with the library's operations that might take an outsider a long time to acquire. Most studies of acquisitions procedures can be done by a librarian who is familiar with the principles of scientific management; usually this person should be the department head.

It should be remembered that work simplification and systems analysis will not solve all of the problems of an organization. They are tools that can aid a library in using its resources efficiently and intelligently. Care must be taken to assure that quality of services is not sacrificed for cost. Librarians have a responsibility for providing services at reasonable cost at the level of quality required.

REFERENCES

Bolles, Shirley W. "The Use of Flow Charts in the Analysis of Library Operations." *Special Libraries* 58:95–98 (Feb. 1967).

Chapman, Edward A., and others. *Library Systems Analysis Guidelines*. New York: Wiley, 1970. 226p.

Dougherty, Richard M., and Heinritz, Fred J. *Scientific Management of Library Operations*. Metuchen, N.J.: Scarecrow, 1966. 258p.

Dougherty, Richard M., and Leonard, Lawrence E. *Management and Costs of Technical Processes: A Bibliographical Review, 1876–1969*. Metuchen, N.J.: Scarecrow, 1970. 145p.

Heinritz, Fred J. "Quantitative Management in Libraries." *College & Research Libraries* 31:232–38 (July 1970).

Kipp, Laurence J. "Management Literature for Librarians." *Library Journal* 97:158–60 (Jan. 15, 1972).

Melcher, Daniel. *Melcher on Acquisition.* Chicago: American Library Assn., 1971. 169p.

Moore, Edythe. "Systems Analysis: An Overview." *Special Libraries* 58:87–90 (Feb. 1967).

Tuttle, Helen W. "Operating an Effective Acquisition Department." Paper prepared for the Institute on Acquisitions Procedures in Academic Libraries sponsored by the University Library, University of California, San Diego, August 25–September 5, 1969. ERIC Document ED 043 344. 22p.

3

ACQUISITIONS SEARCHING

Acquisitions searching is done to prevent unwanted duplication of books and other library materials and to obtain enough information to permit placing a purchase order. It may also be done as the first step in cataloging to establish information about a title which will advance its processing when it is received in the library.

ORDER REQUESTS

Requests for orders are received in the acquisitions department from the selector in one of several modes according to the procedures of the library. Many libraries provide printed order-request forms that are completed by the selector. The order-request form attempts to draw from the user as much information as he or she has about the title being requested. The form may include instructions for its use and may provide for recording completed searching as well as for reporting to the selector the status of his request.

Many libraries accept requests for purchase in any mode that is legible. These requests may be in the form of brochures or publication announcements, marked publishers' catalogs, marked catalogs of out-of-print and antiquarian dealers, and bibliographies, either published or specially prepared for expansion of the library's holdings. Other libraries require completed order-request forms for every item requested for purchase. Order-request forms provide many advantages in addition to eliciting information about selections that the selector might not consider important. Ease of arrangement for searching is their chief advantage: they can be arranged alphabetically by main entry for searches in the library's catalog and order and in-process files, and rearranged by title or editor for continued search. They can be arranged by language or country or date of publication for searching in printed bibliographies, or by form of publication for searching as series or government documents. Approaching a large card catalog in its order of arrangement can be demonstrated to be far more efficient than searching it in the arrangement of a publisher's catalog or a subject bibliography. A searcher also can be expected to make fewer errors if he or she can arrange and rearrange the work as it is moved through the searching sequence.

Libraries that require completed forms or prepare them in the acquisitions department before searching do so for entirely defensible reasons of economy of operation. Libraries that accept requests for purchase in any fashion do so for good reasons as well. The chief of these is to encourage selection activity. The order-request form is seen as a deterrent to selection. A faculty member or a library subject division specialist who has little or no clerical assistance may not have time to fill out forms and yet his or her subject knowledge and interest may be exceptionally important to the library. To encourage such a person to send an initialled advertisement or a checked copy of a catalog or a bibliography to the acquisitions department may be in the best interests of the library and far more important than the economies that can be realized from the use of order-request forms. The speed with which out-of-print and antiquarian catalogs should be handled in selection and in the order process precludes typing order-request forms unless the level of clerical staffing is substantial.

If the selector or the supervisor of preorder searching recognizes that much of the material selected may already be owned by the library, he may not have order-request forms filled out or may defer their preparation until searching of the library's catalog has been completed. This situation occurs most often in retrospective searching where use is made of printed bibliographies with entries the same as or near the entries in the library's catalog and arranged in the order of the catalog. The best policy for most libraries is to use forms where possible but not to require their use if doing so will handicap operations or slow selection of acquisitions. Preparation of order-request forms as source documents for the preparation of purchase orders is sometimes done by the searcher after search in the library's catalog, where the proper entry can be identified as well as relevant associated information.

STEPS IN PREORDER SEARCHING

Sorting

An important step preliminary to preorder searching is the sorting of order requests by the supervisor if there is more than one searcher. In the smaller library the head librarian or the person in charge of ordering holds for his or her own work the more difficult searching. In libraries where there is more than one searcher the work is sorted according to the difficulty of the searching involved and the experience or skills of the searchers. Language and subject knowledge, types of materials, source of publication, and tools to be used are taken into consideration in sorting. It is also important for searchers to have work that gives them job satisfaction and sense of worth. It may be necessary to sort searching to assure sufficient challenge and variety for searchers. In addition to making work interesting the quality and quantity of searching will be better if boredom can be minimized or eliminated.

It may also be necessary to sort searching to establish priorities. Few libraries have an even flow of material for searching because publishing and the issuing of out-of-print catalogs are seasonal and the people doing selection may not do it regularly. For example, the beginning of the fall term in most colleges and universities is a time when there will be overloads in searching. The reason is the return of faculty and the up-swing in publishing. Many items require "rush" handling because the need for them was not anticipated far enough in advance of the beginning of classes. Establishing priorities for searching and ordering can be an extremely sensitive task since it involves deciding which materials are most important for the library. The selector whose work receives a low priority may not agree. It is well to establish and state policies on priorities for searching and ordering. This policy formulation should involve the counsel of people outside the order department. Characteristically, in a college or university library requests from faculty members take precedence over those from library staff members, but it might be decided that library-originated selections are of more importance to a larger group of people than faculty selections and deserve higher priority. Some searching must be given the highest priority to take advantage of the availability of the material requested. This includes the searching of out-of-print dealers' catalogs and specialized lists of materials that are published in limited quantities, such as the items in the annual list of curriculum materials from the Association for Supervision and Curriculum Development. When there are serious temporary overloads in preorder searching, it may be necessary to have all searchers working on requests arranged by priority rather than by the skills and specialties of the searchers.

In order to obtain as much economy of movement as possible, the searcher will sort the searching to be done according to the tools to be searched and according to the internal arrangement of these tools.

Library Catalog

The usual first step is to check the library's catalog under the entry presented on the order request. If it appears that the library already owns the title, the searcher will determine whether or not the request is for a new edition or for an edition different from the one the library owns. If it is clear from the request that the selector wants the title with characteristics other than those of the one owned by the library, such as a different edition or translator or illustrator or a special preface or introduction or notes, the searcher will record that the title requested is not in the card catalog. If it is not clear that the selector wants an edition with features different from those of the copy owned by the library, the request should be returned to the supervisor of searching and possibly to the selector. There is inherent in searching and searching supervision the need for book knowledge. For example, the return of an order request for the major new multivolume edition of Pepys' *Diary* with the note that the library already owns six editions of the *Diary* will not earn the order department any credits for perspicacity.

At the library's catalog the searcher also will try to discover if the title requested is part of another work already owned by the library, such as a complete set of an author's works; whether the title is part of a series that is catalogued under the series rather than under the names of the authors of the volumes in the series; and if the work is the same as another work published under a different title. In a library having subject divisions or departmental or collegiate libraries, it is necessary in searching to note the location of a copy or copies already owned by the library and report this to the searching supervisor or the selector. This would not be necessary if the order request specifies the need for an additional copy in the same or another location.

Use of the library's catalog requires the searcher to be thoroughly knowledgeable of the filing rules used in the catalog and the library's system for recording multiple copies and locations of copies.

Outstanding-Order File

All libraries have a file listing materials the library has ordered and has in process but that are not yet in the library's catalog. They may be in a single file of on-order and in-process items or they may be in two files, and a library may have additional files for continuations or for special forms of materials, such as government documents or music. Most commonly, the outstanding-order file will incorporate materials in process and include cards for continuations, or cross-references to them; gifts; exchanges; and out-of-print books advertised or placed in the hands of dealers. It is usually wise practice to reduce the number of files to one although some libraries have internal organizational reasons for preferring more than one file.

The major difference between the approach to the outstanding-order file and that to the library's catalog is that there is only one entry for each title in the file. The care with which the outstanding-order file is made is not comparable to that used for the catalog so there is greater possibility for errors in typing and filing. There may be form entries in the outstanding-order file for such materials as maps, atlases, and dictionaries.

In preorder searching it sometimes may be economical to search the outstanding-order file before going to the library's catalog. Groups of requests for newly published books may be searched there first if in the judgment of the searcher or the searching supervisor this is a wise step. A widely announced new book may be requested by many selectors working in and for medium- and large-size libraries.

Some libraries temporarily file copies of outstanding orders and in-process slips in their catalogs. This may make preorder searching easier because it can be done in only one file, the catalog. It also permits the arrangement of the outstanding-order/in-process file by title, making the file easier for the nonprofessional to use and offering a second approach to a publication if the entry is in question. In a large library, however, cards for books on order and in process will probably be found more quickly in a separate file than in a large and complex card catalog. The introduction of these cards or slips into the library's catalog is primarily for the information of users of the library.

Series

The arrangement of series in libraries varies widely. For the purposes of preorder searching the series usually will be listed in the library's catalog, but in most libraries the details of the library's holdings of the series will be in the serial file. Outstanding orders for books in series may be in the outstanding-order file or in the serial file and they may be cross-referenced from one to the other. The searcher must establish a searching sequence that assures the examination of the library's catalog and files to prevent unwanted duplication. New series require special attention since it may not be known they will be handled as series in the library until after they are received or after they are cataloged.

Verification

Verification means determining that a title submitted as an order request by a selector exists and that the description offered is accurate. If an item selected for purchase is not found in a search of the library's catalog and in its files of items on order and in process or waiting for cataloging, most libraries will require or attempt verification for most materials. If the selector used and submitted a Library of Congress catalog card as the purchase recommendation, the item is already verified, as are most selections from the "Weekly Record" in *Publishers Weekly* or from any of a number of other reliable selection tools that may be, in themselves, verification tools as well. In verification the searcher will use one or more of the standard tools, as appropriate and according to the verification standards of the library in which he or she is working. The searcher usually will be able to verify the item. If in verifying an item additional information about a title is discovered or if it appears that the information on the order request was incorrect, it will be necessary to return to the library's catalog and the on-order and in-process file for researching, considering the new information that has been found, to see if the library has the item.

For the librarian to know where an order should be placed and how much money should be encumbered, it is usually necessary to discover the name of the publisher, the price and, sometimes, the series, and whether or not the book is in print.

There are sequences for verification that searchers must follow if they are to make good use of their time. Sequences will vary with the amount of verification required by a library. Foremost in establishing sequences is understanding of the bibliographic tools used for verification. Some libraries have fixed searching sequences and have reported them (see the references for this chapter), but no one sequence is desirable for all items searched for even one library and there will be differences between libraries.

Another aspect of verification is the question of when a library might order materials without verification. An order request that appears to contain enough information to permit placing an order may not be verified in some libraries if the cost of the item is near the cost of verification. Some libraries decide that no item costing less than two dollars will be verified, feeling that it is cheaper to duplicate the item than it is to search it. In many libraries if the information at hand appears to be reliable, that is, the dealer or publisher is known for giving complete and accurate information, and the item is not expensive, an order will be placed without verification. Similarly, if a book is not yet published but is needed in the library as soon as it is published it will be ordered even though it cannot be verified.

The question of the amount of verification given to order requests calls for the use of good judgment on the part of the searcher or the searching supervisor. Inadequate verification may produce not only unwanted duplicates but also complex problems in post-ordering operations where duplication is discovered only after expensive steps in cataloging have been taken. Inadequate verification may also result in the purchase of the wrong book. Conversely, order departments that insist upon complete verification for each item are more expensive to operate and may lose time in obtaining materials.

Searching Record

The searcher must record where searching was done and what was found. This permits keeping track of the steps that were taken and serves as a reminder of where re-searching should be done if new information is discovered. It also provides information for the supervision of searching either in revising searching or training a new searcher. The searching record may be preserved and forwarded to the catalog department along with the book when it is received to share with the catalogers all of the information the preorder searcher has found. Of course, if precataloging is being done at the time of preorder searching, the amount and detail of information will be more complete.

The record may be maintained quite simply with symbols. In many libraries circles or checks showing negative or positive results are noted along with the tool consulted. BIP plus a zero means that *Books in Print* was consulted without success; OOF plus a check means that the item is on order and a copy of the order is in the outstanding-order file. Many libraries use preprinted forms, usually as part of the order-request form, containing printed symbols for frequently used tools against which checks are made by the searcher to record the searching done.

PRECATALOGING

Preorder and precataloging searching are similar; they require the same skills in use and interpretation of the library's catalog and of many of the bibliographies, and the training and supervision given for both kinds of searching is similar. Preorder verification establishes what the entry for a title will be. The performance of precataloging makes several further steps: determining whether or not the main entry and the added name and subject entries have already been used in the catalog and whether cataloging copy for the books is in the library or can be obtained as printed cards. In most libraries this searching is done by the catalog department after the book is received, but in some it is done in the acquisitions department with preorder searching or preorder and precataloging searching combined in a separate unit or in the catalog department. There can be significant economies in combining order and cataloging searching, but critics contend that placing the extra work of determining entries upon the preorder searching unit will slow the placing of orders and that precataloging searching can be done more effectively with the book in hand.

ISBD

The idea of universal bibliographic control is reflected in the International Standard Bibliographic Description (ISBD) adopted by many national bibliographies in 1972 and 1973. ISBD provides for the compatability of the descriptive cataloging performed in each country by a national agency.

REFERENCES

Fristoe, Ashby J. "Bitter End: the Searching Process." *Library Resources & Technical Services* 10:91–95 (Winter 1966). Comment by Frances Ann Simonsen, with rejoinder. *Library Resources & Technical Services* 10:492–94 (Fall 1966).

Lazoreck, Gerald J., and Minder, Thomas L. "A Least Cost Searching Sequence." *College & Research Libraries* 25:126–28 (March 1964).

Lowy, George. *A Searcher's Manual*. Hamden, Conn.: Shoe String, 1965. 104p.

Tauber, Maurice F., and others. *Technical Services in Libraries: Acquisitions, Cataloging, Classification, Binding, Photographic Reproduction, and Circulation Operations*. New York: Columbia University Pr., 1954. 487p.

4

BIBLIOGRAPHIES USED IN SEARCHING

In acquisitions work bibliographies are used to verify an item and to obtain enough information to permit placing a purchase order. A third purpose may be precataloging.

The bibliographic tools listed and partially described in this section are a modest selection from dozens of national, trade, and general bibliographies that might be used in acquisitions work. This group represents those bibliographies that are most often found in or near the acquisitions department of a large university library, with the exclusion of bibliographies in languages that require a specialist for their use. The model of the large university library is used, for its scope should include the bibliographic tools that would appear in any general library. The listing of certain special bibliographies, such as those of government documents and nonbook materials, is incorporated in the discussion of those materials rather than in this section.

For discussion of additional bibliographies the following titles might be consulted:

> Besterman, Theodore. World bibliography of bibliographies. 4th ed. Lausanne, Societas Bibliographica, 1965–66. 4v. and index.
>
> Malclès, Louise-Noëlle. Les sources du travail bibliographique. Genève, Droz, 1950–58. 3v. in 4.
>
> U.S. Library of Congress. General Reference and Bibliography Division. Current national bibliographies. Government Printing Office, 1955. 132p.
>
> Walford, A. J. Guide to reference material. London, The Library Association, 1966–70. 3v.

40

Winchell, Constance. Guide to reference books. 8th ed. American Library Association, 1967. First supplement, 1965–66; Second supplement, 1967–68; Third supplement, 1969–70.

Zimmerman, Irene. Current national bibliographies of Latin America. University of Florida, 1971. 139p.

Robert Greer's "National Bibliography" in *Library Trends* (15:366–77 [Jan. 1967]) offers an excellent table, "Charactistics of Current National and Trade Bibliographical Services," outlining bibliographical services for 87 nations.

For acquisitions purposes there are three kinds of bibliographies: national, trade, and general. A national bibliography may incorporate all of the books published in a country or books written in the language of a country or it may represent all of the books written about a country. The perfect national bibliography for acquisitions purposes would list all materials published in and about a country and in its language, including pamphlets, government publications, periodicals, dissertations, music scores, films, filmstrips, phonograph records, tapes, and any other form of publication that might interest a library. There is no perfect national bibliography.

Trade bibliographies list books, usually by country, available in the regular book trade; that is, books that can be purchased in a bookstore. Trade bibliographies usually are based on book-trade advertising and therefore may not be reliable, as details important to libraries, such as those relating to series and edition, may be missing. Trade bibliographies usually do not list government publications, the publications of scholarly societies and associations, most pamphlets, and many other items of importance to libraries. In the United States and in most other countries there are many more nontrade publications than trade publications released each year. Trade bibliographies are extraordinarily important in acquisitions work but except in the smallest libraries, good preorder searching requires the use of national and general bibliographies as well as trade bibliographies.

General bibliographies, for acquisitions purposes, are library catalogs like the *Library of Congress Catalog* and the *British Museum Catalog* or union lists like the *National Union Catalog*.

Using a bibliography requires understanding of its arrangement, inclusion, scope, period, indexes, and other features. Occasionally the title and subtitle offer a fair description, but the user should read the prefatory material that most bibliographies have and read about the bibliography in Winchell or one of the other annotated bibliographies. It is rarely safe for the searcher to assume that he knows how to use a bibliography. In addition to differing methods and inclusion among bibliographies, a single title still in process of publication can change coverage or method so that it is important to keep one's knowledge of a work up-to-date.

The acronym and full form follow for the bibliographies discussed in this chapter. References to other bibliographies are usually abbreviated to last names or shortened titles, such as *Sabin* or *Fichero*.

BBIP	British Books in Print
BIP	Books in Print
BM	British Museum
BN	Bibliotheque Nationale. Catalogue General
BNB	British National Bibliography
CBI	Cumulative Book Index
DB	Deutsche Bibliographie
LC	Library of Congress Catalog
NUC	National Union Catalog
PW	Publishers Weekly
PTLA	Publishers' Trade List Annual
STC	Pollard and Redgrave. Short Title Catalog

UNITED STATES

The Library of Congress and National Union Catalog series:

1. U.S. Library of Congress. A catalog of books represented by Library of Congress printed cards, issued to July 31, 1942. 167v.
2. ———— ———— Supplement: 1942–47. 42v.
3. Library of Congress author catalog. 1948–52. 24v.
   v.24 is Films.
4. National union catalog: a cumulative author list representing Library of Congress printed cards and titles reported by other American libraries, 1953–57. 28v.
   v.27 is Music and phonorecords; v.28 is Motion pictures and filmstrips.
5. ———— 1958–62. 54v.
   v.51–52 is Music and phonorecords; v. 53–54 is Motion pictures and filmstrips.
6. ———— 1963–67. 67v.

Music and phonorecords (3v.) and Motion pictures and filmstrips (2v.) are numbered separately.
7. —————— 1952–55 imprints: an author list representing Library
   of Congress printed cards and titles reported by other American
   libraries. 30v.
8. National union catalog: a cumulative author list. Library of
   Congress, Card Division. Monthly, with quarterly and annual
   cumulations.

The supplement, 1942–47, and later cumulations contain
cards issued during the periods indicated; the dates of the
cumulations do not necessarily relate to the dates of publication
of books cataloged. As with other bibliographies, the user
should consult the introductory material in the latest set to
understand what to expect of this great series.
A "master cumulation" of the LC and NUC author lists for
1942–62 has been published by Gale Research. Gale also is
publishing *English language books by title,* a catalog based on
Library of Congress depository cards arranged by title. The
base set, in twenty volumes, is for 1969 and 1970, and is
supplemented quarterly.

Library of Congress catalog. Books: subjects 1950–54, 20v.;
1955–59, 22v.; 1960–64, 25v.; and 1965–69, 42v.
Only titles with an imprint date of 1945 or later are included.
Continues with quarterly issues and annual supplements.

National union catalog. Pre-1956 imprints. A cumulative author
list representing Library of Congress printed cards and titles
reported by other American libraries. . . . London, Mansell,
1968–   . v.1–
To be complete in about 610 volumes after about ten years
of publication (1979). When complete this supersedes items 1,
2, 3, and 7 of the LC/NUC series listed above, except that it
does not include volumes for motion pictures, filmstrips, and
phonograph records.
In addition, it incorporates entries from the Union Catalog
card file at the Library of Congress and will be a record of all
pre-1956 imprints held by more than 700 American libraries
up to a year before the publication of the volume in which a
work appears.

National union catalog. 1956 through 1967. A cumulative author list representing Library of Congress printed cards and titles reported by other American libraries. . . . Rowman and Littlefield, 1970–72. 125v.

An "augmented" compilation into one alphabet of the 1958–62 and 1963–67 supplements noted above. Because of the inclusion of 1956 and 1957 imprints in the 1958–62 supplements, this set, 1956–67, is the first supplement to the *National union catalog. Pre-1956 imprints,* listed immediately above.

Sabin, Joseph. Dictionary of books relating to America, from its discovery to the present time. Begun by Joseph Sabin, and continued by Wilberforce Eames. . . . Sabin, 1868–92; Bibliographical Society of America, 1928–36. 29v. (Repr.: Amsterdam, N. Israel, 1961–62)

This set is sometimes called *Bibliotheca Americana,* its half-title.

As the title indicates, this bibliography is not confined to books published in America or inclusive of all books published in America. Sabin's dates of cut-off are not uniform. For many titles library locations are given. The person using this set should read "Sabin procedure" in volume 29. Any bibliography compiled by rules of entry with which we are not familiar or without consistent application of rules presents a special problem for the reseacher. When an item does not appear where the searcher would expect it to be, he should persist with other possible approaches.

Coverage: 1492 to mid-nineteenth century.

Evans, Charles. American bibliography; a chronological dictionary of all books, pamphlets and periodical publications printed in the United States of America from the genesis of printing in 1639 down to and including the year 1800. . . . Chicago, printed for the author, 1903–59. 14v.

Publisher varies: v.13–14 published by the American Antiquarian Society. (v.1–12 repr.: Peter Smith, 1941–42).

Evans' arrangement is by date of publication, then alphabetically by author. It includes books, periodicals, and pamphlets. Each volume has an index of authors, a classified subject index, and an index of printers and publishers. Volume 13, compiled by Clifford K. Shipton, 1955, completes the year 1799 and carries the bibliography through 1800. Volume 14, edited by Roger P. Bristol, 1959, is a cumulated author and title index.

Evans must be used with care. It is estimated that one item in ten has serious errors. It is difficult to use without accurate author or title information or date of publication. The subject approach is difficult and should be attempted only after other resources have failed.

The next two entries are important adjuncts to Evans and together with Evans they form a major part of American bibliography.

Coverage: 1639–1800.

Bristol, Roger P. Supplement to Charles Evans' American bibliography. University Press of Virginia, 1970. 636p.

Published for the Bibliographical Society of America and the Bibliographical Society of the University of Virginia. This is a chronological list, 1646–1800, of "not-in-Evans" items. This volume has 10,000 titles additional to Evans' 39,162 items. Entries are arranged alphabetically under year of publication the same as the original Evans' volumes.

Coverage: 1646–1800.

Shipton, Clifford K. National index of American imprints through 1800; the short-title Evans by Clifford K. Shipton and James F. Mooney. American Antiquarian Society, 1969. 2v.

This is a combined alphabetical index to Evans' *American bibliography,* with corrections, and Bristol's "not-in-Evans" *Supplement to Charles Evans' American bibliography.* This is a convenient entry to Evans. All of the cumulated errors and omissions have been brought together. It does not replace Evans but gives searchers more confidence in Evans.

Coverage: 1639–1800.

Shaw, Ralph Robert, and Shoemaker, Richard H. American bibliography: a preliminary checklist. Scarecrow, 1958–66. v.1–19 and addenda 3v.

Contents v.1–19: 1801–1819; Addenda: list of sources and list of library symbols; title index; author index, list of corrections.

Evans planned his bibliography to extend through 1820, but the work stopped at 1800. Shaw and Shoemaker completes Evans. It is "a preliminary checklist" compiled from printed sources such as library lists and library catalogs rather than from examination of the works listed. Entries are arranged alphabetically by main entry by year of publication. Locations of copies are shown except when no copy could be located. It includes government documents. Newspapers and periodicals are listed only once.

Coverage: 1801–19.

Shoemaker, Richard H. Checklist of American imprints. Scarecrow, 1964–73. 12v. and title and author index for 1820–29.

This is a continuation of Shaw and Shoemaker and uses the same method except that it does not list periodicals and newspapers, referring the reader to the Union List of Serials. It replaces Roorbach for the years covered.

The last volume was compiled by Gayle Cooper after Shoemaker's death in 1970.

Coverage: 1820–30.

Roorbach, Orville Augustus. Bibliotheca americana. Roorbach, 1852–61. 4v. (Repr.: Peter Smith, 1939)

This is an author-title catalog of American publications. It is very incomplete, has many inaccuracies, and lists no locations.

Coverage: 1820–61.

Kelly, James. American catalogue of books (original and reprints) published in the United States from Jan. 1861 to Jan. 1871, with date of publication, size, price, and publisher's name. Wiley, 1866–71. 2v. (Repr.: Peter Smith, 1938)

Kelly continues the main body of American bibliography from Roorbach. Its shortcomings are the same as Roorbach's, but both list material that cannot be found elsewhere and are the most general lists for their periods.

Coverage: 1861–71.

American catalogue of books. Publishers Weekly, 1876–1910. 9v. in 13 (Repr.: Peter Smith, 1941)

The first volume is a catalog of books in print July 1, 1876, arranged by author-title and subject. It is supplemented by cumulated volumes of the *Annual American catalogue,* the volumes covering various periods and including all books published in the United States that were for sale to the general public.

This information is generally reliable although it was compiled from publishers' reports as listed in *Publishers Weekly,* rather than from examination of the books.
Coverage: 1876–1910.

United States catalog; books in print. 4th ed. Wilson, 1928. 16v.
1st ed., 1899; 2d ed., 1902; 3d ed., Jan. 1, 1912.
Supplements were published for intervening years as *Cumulative book index.*

Cumulative book index. Wilson, 1898–
Published since 1898 with cumulations forming supplements to the *United States catalog.* Frequency varies. Together these form the record of American publishing from 1898 to the present. Bibliographic searching usually is concentrated in the volumes from 1928 to date, but earlier volumes will be consulted for books not in print in 1928 and for fuller information.
Inclusion has varied. Its present scope is as an international bibliography of books in the English language; works wholly in a foreign language are not listed but certain foreign language books are included if they contain some English. It is essentially a *book* list and does not include government documents, pamphlets, and publications of limited interest or distribution. For inclusion in the various volumes of this important series the searcher should consult the introductory material in each volume.
Entries are in a single alphabetical list and include author, subject, title, editor, translator, joint author, illustrator, series, etc. Author entries are more complete than others and contain full name form (including synonyms), complete title, series, edition, paging, price, date of publication, publisher, International Standard Book Number, and Library of Congress card number.
It is presently published monthly except August, cumulates through the year, and is moving to permanent annual cumulations (1969 is the first of these) in place of the multi-year volumes which have been published in the past.
Coverage: 1898–

Forthcoming books. v.1–   , 1966–   . Bowker, 1966–
Bimonthly.
Provides author and title index to books due to appear in the

coming five months plus a cumulating author-title list of books that have appeared since the last *Books in print* went to press. *Subject guide to forthcoming books* is a separate bimonthly listing.

Publishers weekly . . . 1872–   . Bowker, 1872–   . v.1–   . Weekly.
> Subtitle varies.
>
> Contains the "Weekly record" of current American book publication, arranged by author; includes LC cataloging and complete purchase information, including ISBN. Does not include government publications, subscription books, dissertations, new printings, periodicals, pamphlets under 49 pages, and specialized publications (trade catalogs, telephone books, etc.) or publications intended as advertising.

BPR: American book publishing record, v.1, 1960–   . Bowker, 1960–   . Monthly.
> This is the monthly cumulation from the "Weekly record" listings of *Publishers weekly* arranged by Dewey Decimal Classification with separate sections for juvenile and fiction books and paperbacks; author and title indexes.
>
> Cumulated into an annual volume and then cumulated into 5-year sets.

Publishers' trade list annual, 1873–   . Bowker, 1873–   . Annual.
> Publishers' catalogs bound together. In many cases they offer more complete information than *Books in print* or alternate approaches, such as series.

Books in print: an author-title-series index to the Publishers' trade list annual, 1948–   . Bowker, 1948–   . Semi-annual.
> Lists titles available from almost all American publishers, arranged by author-editor and by title. Usually includes enough information to place an order (most complete information is under author), but does not include government publications, reference sets, book club editions, free material, or material available only in limited quantities. Other titles in the *Books in print* family are *Medical books in print, Scientific and technical*

*books in print, Children's books in print, Subject guide to books
in print,* and *Paperbound books in print.*

GREAT BRITAIN

Pollard, Alfred W., and Redgrave, G. R. A short-title catalogue
of books printed in England, Scotland and Ireland, and of
English books printed abroad, 1475–1640. London, Bibliographical Society, 1926. 609p.
The most complete list for this period; includes locations of
copies in British and American libraries. A new edition is in
preparation.
Coverage: 1475–1640.

Wing, Donald. Short-title catalogue of books printed in England,
Scotland, Ireland, Wales, and British America and of English
books printed in other countries, 1641–1700. 2d ed. Modern
Language Association of America, 1972–
To be complete in three volumes. Continues Pollard and
Redgrave. Contains locations; the preface should be consulted
to facilitate its use.
Coverage: 1641–1700.

London catalogue of books . . . London, Bent, 1773–   With
supplements. 19v.
Bibliographies with this title were published over a long
period covering books published in Great Britain from 1700
to 1855.
Coverage: 1700–1855.

English catalogue of books . . . London, S. Low, 1864–1901;
Publishers' Circular, 1906–   (1801–1951, repr.: N.Y.,
Kraus, 1963)
This was the standard English trade list, published annually
and cumulated variously. The last annual volume issued is for
1968.
Coverage: 1801–

Whitaker's Cumulative book list . . . London, Whitaker,
1924–

Subtitle varies. Issued quarterly, cumulating throughout the year and forming the annual volume that cumulates periodically into larger volumes, the latest of which is 1963–67.
Coverage: 1924–

Bookseller: The organ of the booktrade. London, Whitaker, 1858–   .
Weekly since 1909. Contains the list of books published each week.

Whitaker's Books of the month and books to come. London, Whitaker. 1970–
Monthly cumulation from the *Bookseller* with list of books due to be published within the next two months. Cumulates into *Whitaker's Cumulative book list*.

British national bibliography. Council of the British National Bibliography. London, British Museum, 1950–
Weekly with four cumulations a year and an annual volume. Based upon books deposited for copyright but covers more than copyright books. Five-year cumulated subject catalogs and cumulated indexes, together superseding the annual volumes.
Coverage: 1950–

British books in print. London, Whitaker, 1965–
Formerly the *Reference Catalogue of current literature;* now published annually in October. An author-title listing.

British Museum. Department of Printed Books. General catalogue of printed books. London, Trustees, 1931–66. 263v.
Volumes 1–51 were begun in 1931 and completed in 1954. By that time only *Dezw* had been reached; each volume included entries cataloged up to the time of publication. A photolithographic edition, begun in 1959 and completed in 1966, covers books cataloged through 1955 and includes updating volumes 1–51. Annual supplements published periodically.

————. ————. Ten-year supplement, 1956–65. London, Trustees, 1968. 50v.
This is the first in a projected series of ten-year supplements.

GERMANY

Borchling, Conrad, and Claussen, Bruno. Niederdeutsche Bibliographie, Gesamtverzeichnis de niederdeutschen Drucke bis zum Jahre 1800. . . . Neumünster, Karl Wachholst, 1931–36. 2v.
> A chronological list of more than 4,700 items.
> Coverage: 1473–1800.

Heinsius, Wilhelm. Allgemeines Bücher-Lexicon, oder vollständiges alphabetisches Verzeichnis aller von 1700 bis zu Ende 1892 erschienenen Bücher. Leipzig, Brockhaus, 1812–94. 19v. (Repr.: Graz, Akademische Druck, 1963)
> Publisher varies. Periods of coverage in the volumes also vary. This compilation is based upon publishers' catalogs, which produces some inaccuracies.
> Coverage: 1700–1892.

Kayser, Christian G. Vollständiges Bücher-Lexikon. Leipzig, Tauchnitz, 1834–1911. 36v. (Repr.: Graz, Akademische Druck, 1961–62)
> Publisher varies. This compilation covers approximately the same period as Heinsius, generally with more detail. Also, it has subject indexes.
> Coverage: 1750–1910.

Hinrichs, J. C. Fünfjahres-Katalog. . . . Leipzig, Hinrichs, 1857–1913. 13v.
> Five-year cumulations of weekly and semiannual author lists.
> Coverage: 1851–1912.

Since World War II national bibliographies have been published for East Germany *(Deutsche Nationalbibliographie)* and West Germany *(Deutsche Bibliographie).* They largely duplicate each other although some titles may be found in one and not the other.

Deutsche Nationalbibliographie. . . . Leipzig, Verlag für Buch-und-Bibliothekswesen, 1931–
> Subtitle varies. This compilation covered the whole of Germany to 1945; since then it is less complete for West Germany than *Deutsche Bibliographie,* listed below. *Jahresverzeichnis des deutschen Schrifttums* is the annual cumulation, followed by

five-year cumulations *Deutsches Bücherverzeichnis,* below.
Coverage: 1931–

Deutsches Bücherverzeichnis. . . . Leipzig, Verlag für Buch-und-
Bibliothekswesen, 1915–   .
Subtitle and publisher vary. This compilation continues Hin-
richs and Kayser. Lists German-language books, periodicals,
maps, and some official publications.
Coverage: 1911–

Deutsche Bibliographie. . . . Frankfurt am Main, Buchhandler-
Vereinigung GMBH, 1947–   . Weekly.
From 1947 to 1952 the title was *Bibliographie der deutschen
Bibliothek.* Scope is all books published in Germany and all
books published in the German language elsewhere. Published
weekly, monthly, and bimonthly with cumulating indexes. Arrangement has varied. Semiannual cumulations, *Halbjahresver-
zeichnis,* and five-year cumulations, *Bücher und Karten,* are
published.
Coverage: 1947–

Verzeichnis lieferbarer Bücher. Frankfurt am Main, Verlag der
Buchhandler-Vereinigung GMBH. 1971/72–
This books-in-print from publishers in West Germany,
Austria, and Switzerland lists complete order information in-
cluding price and ISBN. Distributed in the United States by
Bowker.

FRANCE

British Museum. Department of Printed Books. Short title cata-
logue of books printed in France and of French books printed
in other countries from 1470 to 1600 now in the British
Museum. London, Trustees, 1924.
Includes many items not found in the Bibliothèque Nationale
Catalogue général.
Coverage: 1470–1600.

Quérard, Joseph Marie. La France littéraire, ou Dictionnaire bibliographique des savants, historiens et gens de lettres de la

France. . . . Paris, Didot, 1827–64. 12v. (Repr.: Paris Maison-neuve, 1964. 12v.)
Volumes 11 and 12 are supplements containing corrections and additions; authors of pseudonymous and anonymous works. Emphasizes literature and is not a "complete" national bibli-ography.
Coverage: 1700–1827.

Quérard, Joseph Marie, and others. La littérature française con-temporaine, 1827–49 . . . Dictionnaire bibliographique . . . accompagné de biographies et de notes historiques et littéraires. Paris, Daguin, 1842–57. 6v.
The continuation of the preceding title.
Coverage: 1827–49.

Catalogue général de la librairie française, 1840–1925. Paris, Lorenz, 1867–1945. v.1–34.
Usually called "Lorenz." This is the standard French list for the period and is seen as a continuation of Quérard.
Coverage: 1840–1925.

Bibliographie de la France. Paris, 1811–   . v.1–   . Weekly.
This is the standard list of French publications received for copyright, published weekly as "Bibliographie Officiel" with supplementary parts and indexes cumulating to annual.
Coverage: 1811–

"Biblio," repertoire bibliographique de tous les ouvrages en langue française parus dans le monde. Service Bibliographique Hachette, 1933–71. Monthly (10 issues a year with annual cumulations)
Subtitle varies. This trade bibliography covers books pub-lished in France and French books published elsewhere. In 1972 *Biblio* merged with *Bibliographie de la France*.
Coverage: 1933–71.

Catalogue de l'édition française. Paris, VPC Livres; Port Washington, N.Y., Paris Publications, 1970–   . Quarterly.
Attempts to list—author, title, and subject—all available books published in French throughout the world.

Répertoire des livres de langue française disponibles. Paris, France Expansion, 1971–

A books-in-print author and title list of French-language publications worldwide. Distributed in the United States by R. R. Bowker.

Paris. Bibliothèque Nationale. Catalogue général des livres imprimés. Auteurs. Paris, Imprimerie Nationale, 1900– v.1–

Includes only entries under names of personal authors with appropriate cross-references. The Bibliothèque Nationale receives books for deposit, making its catalog the most complete list of French publications. Each volume includes works published up to the time the volume was published, making the earlier volumes in the alphabet very out-of-date. Beginning with volume 189, no entries published after 1959 are included.

The first quinquennial supplement is *Auteurs,* 1960–64, in 12 volumes, which contains books added to the library's catalogs from 1960 to 1964. For French works it includes books registered in *Bibliographie de la France,* 1960–64.

ITALY

Pagliaini, Attilio. Catalogo generale della libreria italiana. Milano, Associazione Tipografico-Libraria Italiana, 1901–22. 6v.

Continued with decennial supplements through 1940.

Coverage: 1847–1940.

Florence. Biblioteca Nazionale Centrale. Catalogo cumulativo . . . Nendeln, Liechtenstein, Kraus Reprint, 1968. 39v.

This is a cumulation of the *Bolletino* of the Biblioteca Nazionale Centrale. Instructions for use, in English and German as well as Italian, should be consulted to understand use and limitations of this important set.

Coverage: 1886–1957.

Bibliografia nazionale italiana; nuova serie del Bollettino delle pubblicazioni italiane ricevute per diritto di stampa. Firenze, 1958–   . Anno 1–

A national bibliography of books and pamphlets received by deposit. Monthly issues follow a classified arrangement.

Catalogo alfabetico annuale is an alphabetically arranged main-entry catalog.
Coverage: 1958–

Associazione italiana editori. Catalogo dei libri italiani in commercio. Milano, Soc. Anonima per Pubblicazioni Bibliografico-Editoriali, 1948–   .
The title of this Italian books-in-print varies. The latest edition appeared in 1970.

SPAIN AND SPANISH LATIN AMERICA

Palau y Dulcet, Antonio. Manual del librero hispano-americano . . . 2d ed. Barcelona, Librería Palau, 1948–   . v.1–   .
A comprehensive record of material published in Spain and Spanish America from the beginning of printing to the mid-twentieth century.
Coverage: 1474–

Bibliografía hispánica, año 1–16. Madrid, Instituto Nacional de Libro Español, 1942–57. Monthly.
Section 2 of each monthly issue is *Repertorio bibliográfico,* a list of books published with an annual index. Continued by *El libro español.*
Coverage: 1942–57.

El libro español . . . Madrid, Instituto Nacional del Libro Español, 1958–   . Monthly; biweekly.
Contains the monthly (biweekly since 1964) list of new books and annual indexes.
Coverage: 1958–

Bibliografía española. Madrid, Ministerio de Educación Nacional. Dirección general de archivos y Bibliotecas, Servicio Nacional de Información Bibliográfica, 1959–   . Annual.
National bibliography based upon copyright receipts.
Coverage: 1959–

Libros en venta en Hispanoamérica y España. Un servicio informativo prep. bajo la dirección de Mary C. Turner. N.Y., Bowker, 1964. With supplements.

A books-in-print for Spain and most of Latin America.

Fichero bibliográfico hispanoamericano. Buenos Aires, Bowker Editores Argentina, 1961–   . v.1–   . Quarterly; monthly, Sept. 1964–

Fichero attempts to list all new books published in Spanish in the Americas and includes many published in Spain.

5

DOMESTIC BOOK
PURCHASING

After searching, a source for the purchase of materials is selected. For books published in the United States and reported or assumed to be in print three factors are taken into consideration when selecting a source; they are price, service, and the rules and regulations of the institution of which a library is a part. It is important that none of these is sacrificed to another; that pursuit of discounts should not override good service and the regulations imposed by a purchasing agent should not be so stringent that a library is prevented from securing new books quickly and efficiently. There are some libraries where service transcends all other considerations, but they are exceptional. Most libraries must seek to combine service, discount, and fiscal responsibility to achieve the best blend that is possible for their circumstances.

SOURCES OF U.S. BOOKS IN PRINT

There are two sources for the purchase of in-print U.S. books: publishers and wholesalers. In many cases we may seem to be using other sources, but for this discussion any source other than a publisher, such as a bookstore, is considered a wholesaler since he is a middleman between the publisher and the library and is used as a source because he offers the services of a wholesaler, no matter how they may be disguised. Similarly, we may not always recognize publishers unless we recall that they include not only trade book publishers grouped in New York and the other publishing centers but also museums, professional associations, societies with itinerant offices in departments of colleges and universities, and other little-known or difficult-to-locate producers of books.

Wholesalers

Most books purchased by libraries are obtained through wholesalers or jobbers, designations that are interchangeable for library acquisitions purposes, although there is some preference in the industry for being called wholesalers.

A wholesaler buys books newly published in the United States in large quantities from publishers. He sells to buyers, chiefly bookstores and libraries, who require the books of many publishers. Libraries buy through wholesalers because by so doing they can avoid the cost in time and materials of preparing and mailing orders to many publishers and also the cost of receiving many shipments and invoices in a wide variety of forms requiring the writing and mailing of many checks. Follow-up on orders and the communication necessitated by errors in the order process are easier with several wholesalers than with several hundred or, for larger public or academic libraries, several thousand publishers. In addition, some publishers will not deal directly with libraries or are so reluctant to handle direct orders that their service is poor.

Wholesalers' Services. Wholesalers should be able to supply any book that is in print and that is available through regular channels available to them. This includes trade, text, and technical titles. A large wholesaler may be able to offer the output of as many as three thousand publishers. A trade book is a book of general interest, such as one might expect to find in a good general nontechnical bookstore, including fiction and nonfiction, classics, biographies, guidebooks, and similar works. Technical books are practical works of a scientific or technical nature, including business books. Textbooks are educational books, including books for schools and colleges and most professional books. These terms are important in selecting and dealing with wholesalers and in determining and interpreting the prices of books.

The minimum service that should be expected from a wholesaler is that he be able to supply recently published trade books from U.S. publishers in 30 to 60 days and older in-print books that are, presumably, not in his stock, in from 60 to 90 days. Nontrade U.S. publications should be supplied in 90 days for the most recent titles to 120 days for older in-print titles. The service expected from a wholesaler varies by type of library and should be agreed upon with the wholesaler either informally or formally where a contract is required or considered desirable. For service in respect to time, some libraries require delivery or a report in 30 days, others in 60 or 90 days, and still others, six months. Some automatically cancel orders at the end of one of these periods or have the option of cancelling if they so desire. Other libraries have the wholesaler ship only those titles he has in stock when he receives the order; all other orders, called "shorts" in this case, are cancelled and placed directly with the publisher.

A wholesaler should secure and maintain a stock large enough to fill the greater part of a library's order. This amount will vary by type of library, but a wholesaler should be able to supply from stock 50 percent to 70 percent of the order of a medium-size public library, taking into consideration that a typical order will contain prepublication and older in-print titles. If a library does its ordering promptly and most of its orders are for recently published trade books the percentage available in stock should be higher.

Time is not the only consideration in service from a wholesaler. The promptness and quality of his reporting is important. He should be able to report the status of an order in a reasonable time and accurately. He is, of course, dependent upon the publisher for information in many instances and this limits his performance. Some libraries have special requirements for invoicing, such as invoicing on special forms or in multiple copies or invoices by funds or allocations. Shipment may be required in unusual ways or other special services may be required, such as the rebinding of juvenile books. These are among the important reasons for dealing with a wholesaler who offers special services that a publisher may be unable or unwilling to provide. Of course, the librarian must realize that special services may be reflected in a lower discount schedule.

One of the chief problems both for libraries and for wholesalers is the batching of orders. A wholesaler gets a better discount from a publisher by sending a large order, especially of multiple copies. Also, the wholesaler is not enthusiastic about sending an order to a publisher for one book on one form, in one envelope with sufficient postage. It is in his interest to arrange or batch orders from all of his customers by publisher and send them periodically, thereby achieving economies for his own operation that he can then pass on to his customers. Batching can be a severe problem if the wholesaler is small or if the publisher is small or if for any other reason the wholesaler delays ordering books that he does not have in stock. The library should have an agreement with the wholesaler citing how long orders will be held for forwarding to publishers if they are held at all.

Shipments to the library from the wholesaler should be on a regular, agreed-upon schedule. Holding books for shipment to achieve economies in handling and shipping costs may cause undesirable delays in the receipt of books. The library has correlative responsibilities to prepare, send, claim, cancel, receive, and pay for orders in a fashion that will assist the wholesaler to perform well. These, too, should be agreed upon with the wholesaler and most of them are detailed later in this chapter under Ordering.

Choosing a Wholesaler. The *American Book Trade Directory* (Bowker, biennial) lists wholesalers. Most libraries choose wholesalers upon the basis of reputation and the recommendations of other libraries. Where this is not possible or where a library wishes to pursue evaluation in greater depth, several aspects of the business of wholesaling books should be considered. Obtaining books for libraries and, possibly, bookstores, should be the wholesaler's chief business, not a sideline. He should have a stock of new books appropriate to the needs of the library considering his services. His service will be unsatisfactory if he has only an office and no capital investment in books. Such an entrepreneur is called a "drop shipper"; he is a middleman who orders books for libraries from publishers and his offer to libraries may be tempting because his costs are so low that he can give a large discount. Clearly, without a stock he cannot give adequate service. Generally, a wholesaler can be expected to have a stock of 80,000 to 85,000 titles and 1 to 2 million volumes, as well as adequate physical facilities and staff to fulfill a library's needs.

Many libraries use more than one wholesaler, taking advantage of the services that are each one's specialty. Often, technical and scientific books are purchased from one wholesaler, other books from another. Medical books may be ordered from one wholesaler and other kinds of books from others. Experience leads libraries to these arrangements whereby they capitalize upon the best from several wholesalers. In recent years, mergers and corporate purchases in wholesaling have brought specialties together under one umbrella to offer all services to libraries from one source.

An important exception to the recommendations regarding wholesalers is bookstores acting as wholesalers. They may be able to give extraordinarily good service as middlemen because of the special book knowledge of their staffs and because they usually offer their services only to one or a few libraries. Special libraries often make good use of bookstores and some college and university libraries have had excellent experiences with them. Discounts may be lower, but this may be offset by the value of the special services.

Publishers

It is possible, of course, to bypass wholesalers and order all books directly from their publishers. Not all publishers wish to deal directly with libraries, but the number that do has increased in the last fifteen years. Many publishers seek direct orders and have sales staff calling upon librarians. Obviously, their stock is superior to that of a wholesaler and they require less time to fill an order than would be needed if a book is out of stock at the wholesaler. Some libraries rely heavily on ordering directly from publishers, especially for scientific and technical books. They receive good service and discounts and prefer the many packages and invoices received daily from many publishers to the massive shipments and multi-paged bills that come from wholesalers. The advantage remains in favor of the wholesaler, especially for the small to medium-size library, most of whose orders can be supplied from stock. It is also in favor of the wholesaler for the bulk of in-print U.S. book orders from large public, academic, and research libraries.

There are many times when libraries should place orders with publishers. Chief among these is when publishers encourage direct orders and offer special inducements to get them, such as a better discount than can be obtained elsewhere. Frequently, publishers make special offers in conjunction with standing-order plans, and these may be very favorable to libraries. Another situation calling for direct order is when material is required from one of the several publishers who will not deal with wholesalers or a particular wholesaler or when experience indicates that the publisher is so reluctant to sell this way that his service is exceptionally slow. Frequently a library knows that while a wholesaler will obtain the publications of a certain publisher he does not stock them. The library may prefer to try to speed receipt of the material with a direct order. Similarly, the publications of many societies, associations, museums, and other nontrade publications should be ordered directly. If an order librarian is trying to acquire a book of poetry published in a limited edition in a basement in Omaha, he probably is well advised to place the order directly, preferably enclosing a check, rather than wait for a wholesaler to obtain the book and put a charge on his service when he receives no discount.

Orders for books the acquisitions librarian knows have not yet been published and may not be published soon may be placed with the publisher with some expectation that he is more likely to supply them upon publication than would a wholesaler. Many libraries make a practice of ordering from the publisher books that they need quickly and that they know or suspect are not in stock at the wholesaler. Service from the publisher may be slow, but if there is a problem in nondelivery or reporting the librarian can work directly with the publisher rather than through a third party, and a faculty member, irate at nonreceipt of his urgently needed book, is more easily placated if he sees the library is working to obtain it through the publisher rather than through some agent he does not recognize. A publisher may require prepayment, especially for books costing less than ten dollars. When it is difficult for a library to arrange for payments with orders, a rush order may be substantially delayed by placing it with the publisher. Publishers' addresses are listed in *Books in Print,* the *Cumulative Book Index,* and the *Literary Market Place* (Bowker, annual).

On balance, the acquisitions librarian will use both wholesalers and publishers, refining his skill at dealer selection to achieve the best possible service for the library. There should be continuing evaluation of the performance of the sources for materials, remembering to take into consideration the quality of the orders prepared by the library and the other factors that may affect performance, such as prepublication and not-yet-published orders and the percentage of older in-print materials that may not be in stock at the wholesalers.

DISCOUNTS

Discounts have commanded much attention from libraries and institutional business management, all too frequently at the sacrifice of service. However, the importance of discounts in the selection of sources for the purchase of in-print books published in the United States should not be underestimated. A difference of a few discount percentage points can make a significant difference in the number of books a library can buy. If a library with a budget of $35,000 for U.S. in-print books receives an average overall discount of 22 percent instead of 17 percent, it can have $1,750 more for purchases. Service should never be sacrificed for discount, but a well-managed library will search for the best possible discount commensurate with good service.

Discounts received by a wholesaler from publishers vary but the trend is toward uniform discount schedules, with publishers giving the same discount to anyone who offers a book for resale. Discounts vary for different quantities of books and for kinds of books. Generally, wholesalers receive discounts of 40 percent to 60 percent on trade books, about 32 percent on technical books, and about 20 percent on texts. A library dealing directly with a publisher would never realize these discounts but might expect to receive at least the same discount as he receives from a wholesaler. In dealing with libraries the wholesaler must add his costs and profit.

The discounts a wholesaler can offer a library are based upon several elements: the amount of the library's book budget that is to be spent on in-print U.S. publications, that is, how much business the wholesaler can expect to receive; the percentage of orders in trade, technical, and text books or the percentage in popular fiction and nonfiction, reference, technical, text, and university presses; and the number of copies per title or the incidence of multi-copy orders. An offer from a wholesaler might stipulate a maximum discount of 37 percent, a high discount, but this would be for trade books only. A better statement would cite separate discounts for trade, technical, and text books or whatever classification the wholesaler uses and the library views as meaningful. It is important that a library negotiating a discount schedule not make a decision based upon maximum possible discount unless all or almost all of its books will fall into the category for which this discount is offered. An academic or special library may purchase most of its materials in nontrade categories and consequently be most interested in discounts on technical books and textbooks. Restating discounts in the subject approach familiar to libraries, books in the sciences and technology will have the smallest discount, the humanities the largest, and the social sciences a midpoint between the others. Of greatest interest to libraries is the average discount they can expect, but this only can be discovered after the purchases are made, for there is no way for a library or a wholesaler to determine in advance what the distribution of trade-technical-text purchases will be. In evaluating the prices of purchasing directly from publishers or through wholesalers, the average discount is the key figure. This can be found only through careful comparison of samples in which the distribution of trade-technical-text purchases is the same. This average discount figure also is important in controlling expenditures and in budget planning.

Librarians are dependent upon wholesalers to pass on the discount category they receive from the publisher and not let trade books slip into technical book discount levels or texts into no-discount items. Such practices will be apparent if they occur often, and the vulnerability of the librarian in this matter is still another reason for seeking and maintaining business with wholesalers who are known to deal fairly with their customers.

Service Charges

A discussion of discounts must refer to books that receive no discount or have a service charge added to their price. If a wholesaler receives 10 percent discount from a publisher and his costs and profit are 15 percent he can only lose money if he passes any discount on to his library customer. Similarly, if he receives no discount on a book he either must absorb the cost of handling the book by lowering his discounts for other materials or place a service charge on the book. More wholesalers are turning to the latter alternative and libraries are accepting it as a reasonable reflection of the cost of doing business. If a wholesaler is willing to handle no-discount items the library should be willing to pay for the service. Many libraries prefer to order books they know will have no discount directly from the publishers, thereby absorbing the service charge into their own operating costs.

Handling Charge

A few wholesalers and libraries have arrangements under which discounts are replaced by handling charges. Under these arrangements a wholesaler agrees to charge for each book a flat rate above the price he pays the publisher. This rate is calculated to include the wholesaler's costs of operation and profit. This can be a satisfactory substitute for discounts although the result for either party is not significantly different. In the case of books on which the wholesaler receives little or no discount the library will, of course, be paying more than the list price.

BIDDING

Libraries that are part of federal, state, or local governments or of school systems may be required to obtain books through competitive bidding, although this practice has become less common than it was before World War II. The requirement for bidding is justified on the basis that it protects the taxpayer from collusion between government agents and suppliers, obtains the best use of tax money, guarantees the performance of the supplier, and assures the supplier a flow of business to which he can adjust his operations for maximum benefit to himself and his customer. Those agencies that have moved away from bidding believe these advantages can be obtained with informal agreements that shed the inflexibility inherent in formal bidding.

Bids may be required for lists of books, in which case bidders show the discounts they expect to give for each title; or blanket bids may be given, covering a period of time, usually a year or more, and specifying the service and discount the buyer can expect. The latter bid may range from no discount to the maximum, net to 38 percent for instance, or, more desirably, it may specify discounts for trade and nontrade publications or some variation that reflects the differing discounts the wholesaler receives from publishers. Service bids are in the form of delivery time, methods of shipment, reporting, and other aspects of service important to a library. Bidding will specify whether or not transportation costs are additional.

Formal bidding requires that the announcement be advertised and that the bids submitted be sealed. Informal bidding need not be advertised, and may be limited to three bidders. Differences in the amount of money to be spent and in the practices of the government agency usually determine whether or not bids are formal or informal. Government units requiring bids for books usually have a level of expenditure above which bids must be sought, a level that varies from several hundreds to several thousands of dollars. The right to accept a bid other than the lowest should be firmly established to protect the library from suppliers who are unable to perform the services that are required to enable the library to fulfill its acquisitions responsibilities and serve its public efficiently and expeditiously. Provision should be made for cancellation of a contract if the supplier does not perform according to specifications.

In many government units where bidding is required for most purchases, library books have been excepted because it has been recognized that book acquisition is distinctive, in that most purchases are unique single copies with a relatively low unit price and that the number of transactions is in the thousands or tens of thousands for each library. Even where many copies of titles are being ordered it is now acknowledged that bidding delays acquisitions and consequently diminishes a library's effectiveness in providing books and information to its patrons. In many cases there is no possibility of the price of an item being reduced from list, and in others no competitive bids can be obtained. Bidding is time-consuming and counterproductive. Those librarians who must work within the bid system should consult the several relevant sections in *Purchasing Library Materials in Public and School Libraries* by Evelyn Hensel and Peter D. Veillette, and they will find help in defense of buying without bids in *Melcher on Acquisition*. Both titles are listed in the references to this chapter.

RUSH ORDERS

Every library occasionally must purchase books with great speed, bypassing routine purchasing procedures. Many possibilities exist for getting a book promptly, and the astute acquisitions librarian will experiment and establish successful sources and procedures for obtaining the different types of books that may be required quickly. First consideration should be given to the library's standard source for books, usually a wholesaler. The first questions to ask are whether or not the book is in stock and, if it is not in stock, whether the wholesaler can obtain it quickly from the publisher. Discovering the stock status of a book is done most easily with a telephone call even when the wholesaler's office is far from the library. Librarians tend to overestimate the cost of a telephone call as compared to a mail transaction; the call may be cheaper and it probably will be faster.

If the wholesaler does not have the book in stock, he may be willing to place a rush order with the publisher for delivery direct to the library. Only experience will tell whether it is faster for the library to deal with the wholesaler or directly with the publisher. Telephone calls to publishers may be successful or may be distressingly unproductive, depending upon the publisher and his desire or ability to handle direct telephone orders from libraries. The correct office and number for telephone calls may be found in the *Literary Market Place*. Established contacts with publishers who know the library making the call and want to do business directly with libraries produces very good results. Some publishers who respond well to direct orders by mail fail when telephone calls for books arrive at their switchboards. For these publishers an airmail order requesting rush service is the better choice.

Local bookstores are one of the most important sources of books needed quickly. A telephone call to the nearest bookstore that might stock a needed book, plus the use of personal pick-up or a parcel delivery service can put a "rush" book in the library in twenty-four hours or less. The librarian should not expect a discount, or, in any case, not the same discount he receives from a wholesaler, and he would be wise to cultivate the interest of the local bookstore by buying books there at times other than when he needs them quickly. Selection of many types of books is aided by the opportunity to see and handle them that the well-stocked local bookstore provides. More than one academic library has discovered a desperately needed book across the quadrangle in the college bookstore.

The variations on the theme of "rush" book ordering are many. Too frequently the book needed is a ninety-five-cent paperback or other inexpensive item. It does not require much insight to realize a publisher will lose money on an order for one copy of a cheap book, but his interest will be greater and possibly his costs will be less if the library orders five copies from him. If the book is important enough to warrant "rush" ordering it is important enough to spend five dollars for; send the four extra copies to the next sale of library duplicates.

CASH WITH ORDER

Some books require direct purchase and prepayment. The library should have a simple routine worked out with the business office that will make such transactions possible without excessive paperwork. Usually these books are relatively inexpensive and as long as the library establishes a routine of follow-up to be sure these prepaid books are received they will present no problem. Some libraries have moved to the practice of sending payment with all direct orders of modest price in an attempt to reduce the paperwork involved in purchasing by eliminating the invoicing step. An interesting related experiment is the use of blank checks (signed, good for not more than a token amount such as five dollars) that the vendor completes and cashes. The librarian will want to have some confidence the vendor is not a thief, but when one considers that most of these purchases are from established dealers, associations, societies, and agencies like libraries the need for concern is not great. Processing an invoice may cost as much as ten dollars. Prepayment reduces this work and, consequently, this cost and appears to be good practice for some library purchasing. Wholesalers who are adept at obtaining obscure titles from small and remote publishers may be able to pay cash more easily than libraries and should be considered for this kind of buying.

PROCEDURES AND POLICIES

The librarian has responsibilities to the vendor that he must recognize if he expects good service and reasonable prices. He must be sure that his procedures and policies for ordering, claiming, and payment reflect good business practice and that his requirements for delivery, invoicing, and claiming are reasonable. Most importantly, he and the vendor with whom he is working should know one another's expectations and limitations.

One of the elements of a good system for ordering books is the ability of the library to place orders directly with vendors rather than work through an institutional purchasing agent or business office. Library procedures for placing orders, forms, requirements for delivery, invoicing, and other aspects of purchasing should be developed to conform with institutional policy and practice and should be approved by the institution's business executives. The library should then have the delegated responsibility for ordering books. There are several reasons to support ordering directly by the library. Books are unique; they are unlike the supplies, equipment, and services that are the daily business of a purchasing agent; and their identification and acquisition requires special knowledge, not only of books but also of the sources of books, which are quite different from sources used for most institutional purchasing. The expertise necessary to successful acquisitions performance exists in most libraries or can be developed because of librarians' book knowledge. Duplicating this knowledge in an institutional purchasing department is either wasteful or an expression of a lack of confidence in the library staff that should be examined and corrected. The interpolation of a purchasing agent between the library and its suppliers slows the receipt of materials and impedes the communication essential to good service.

Ordering

Wholesalers and most libraries prefer a separate order slip for each title. This slip is usually a part of the multiple-copy order form and it permits flexibility in use that is not possible with the once-standard list of books. Many of those libraries who, for one reason or another, must use a list order form but prefer separate order slips for each title are able to write "list per attached order slips" on their order form and realize their preference.

Libraries must provide suppliers with complete order information. This includes the full author and title, the publisher, date of publication, edition, the library's order number, the binding required (cloth or paper, regular or library), and the number of copies wanted. If the International Standard Book Number (ISBN) is available and is cited on the purchase order, author, title, and other order information may be listed briefly. Inclusion of the Library of Congress catalog card order number may assist in the identification of a title. Orders to wholesalers also should include the address of the publisher if the publisher is not well known and further identification that would be obvious if the order went to the publisher, such as whether the library wants the American or English edition of a book.

Libraries should state their expectations on the order form. If there are special invoice requirements, such as separate billing for standing

orders and continuations or billing by fund, these should be stated, and requirements for reporting the status of the order should be listed. Some library needs should not require repeating on each form. It should be understood that invoices should include for each book the list price, the discount, and discounted price or the service charge. Costs of transportation, if they are in addition to prices shown, should be included on the
invoice, not billed separately except in the case of freight billings that
might excessively delay invoicing if the supplier were to wait for them.

Orders to wholesalers should be arranged by publisher, for this is
the way their stock is arranged. This is true of typed lists as well as
order slips. Orders should be sent out regularly, the interval depending,
in part, upon the size of the library's book budget. For most libraries
the old days of the quarterly or annual book order have passed and
books are ordered when they are needed. The wholesaler benefits from
regular receipt of orders just as the library is best served by regular
receipt of shipments. All orders for a title should be combined. This is
not always possible for a library, but better service should be possible
if the wholesaler receives all of the order from a library for one title
at one time.

Claiming

Well-organized acquisitions units will claim unfilled orders regularly.
They should claim with care, particularly with some knowledge of the
status of the book on order. Has the book been published? If the library
staff records the publication date on the order slip, there should be no
reason to claim a book not yet published. Has the supplier sent a
recent report on the book making a claim not only superfluous but
sending him to extra and unnecessary work that will slow other needed
services? In each of these cases the claims from the library usually are
the result of routine or mass claiming using low-cost assistants. Adequate
signals on cards in outstanding-order files or claim files can be set that
will prevent these unnecessary claims. When claiming, the library should
give complete information about the order. One of the most useful
claim systems sends a copy of the original order, clearly marked "claim
copy" along with space for the supplier to write a response. Multiple-
copy order forms usually have reached reasonable limits on their
number of copies before claim forms can be incorporated in the original
typing, but copying devices now available in most libraries make possible the sending of a copy of the original order at reasonable cost. Wholesalers also would like to know which claim is being sent: first claim
or second claim. Their interest, however, should be related to the

management of their internal affairs rather than being an indication that they give first claims less attention than second claims.

Cancellations and Returns

Most cancellations of orders with wholesalers occur at the end of agreed upon times as discussed earlier in this chapter. Other cancellations should be used by libraries with extreme caution. The order is a form of a contract and cancellation of items in the order process probably will mean a financial loss to the supplier. When a library must cancel orders because its financial support has changed from its expectations when the order was placed, the librarian should talk first with the supplier to explain the circumstances and to explore ways in which the cancellation might be deferred or its effects on both parties eased.

Wholesalers have policies for returning books that are worked out with their regular customers. Most wholesalers permit the return of books that do not have library markings on them. Libraries should take care to make returns as quickly as possible and to be sure that they do not abuse the return privilege by overuse. Defective books usually can be returned to wholesalers without requesting permission, but libraries usually write to publishers for instructions on returns of defective books, which is the same as requesting permission to return them.

Payment

It may appear simplistic to say libraries should pay their bills as quickly as possible, but they are notoriously slow payers. A small supplier with limited capital or a large wholesaler with whom several slow-paying libraries do tens of thousands of dollars of business a year may have to borrow money and pay interest on it to meet indebtednesses while waiting for institutions to pay their invoices. The acquisitions librarian should be sure that library operations handle invoices quickly and then should discover the practices of his institution's accounting department or invoice-paying agency to be sure library invoices are handled on a regular schedule. A few libraries are required to hold payment until an order is complete, but their number is diminishing. If not all of the material listed on an invoice has been received, the library should ask the supplier the reason rather than hold the invoice indefinitely. Similarly, suppliers should not combine on one invoice materials already sent with materials they expect to send or have ordered sent from another source.

REPORTS

The standard reports that a librarian should be able to expect from suppliers are: not yet published (NYP), with the expected date of publication if possible; temporarily out of stock (TOS) meaning out of stock at the publisher; binding or reprinting, at the publisher; and out of print (OP) at the publisher. In addition, from a wholesaler he should expect these reports: not yet received (NYR), that is, not yet received from the publisher, but already ordered; claiming from the publisher; and out of stock (OS) at the wholesaler.

There should be no misapplication of these terms. Out of print as a wholesaler's report should mean that this is the information he has received from the publisher, not that he has not had a reply from the publisher and is ready to give up or that he cannot find an address for the publisher. Some wholesalers have abused reporting, causing many librarians to suspect all reports. Uniform reporting can assist to establish confidence. Publishers are not always candid in their reporting. One practice is to report a title on which stock is low as out of print to a wholesaler. Many librarians take OPs reported from wholesalers and reorder immediately from the publisher with enough success to justify the work involved.

STANDARDIZATION

If uniform invoicing requirements could be developed, suppliers' costs would be lower and service better. Librarians and wholesalers should work together to this end. Local regulations would not allow all libraries to fit into the mold that would result, but the differences between the majority of libraries are not great and appear susceptible to adoption of uniform practices. More importantly, a standard order form should be the cooperative goal of libraries and the suppliers of books. The success of standard forms for interlibrary loan and photocopying indicates a standard order form is possible, and examination of the forms and practices of many libraries reveals more similarities than differences. Approximately the same information is needed by all suppliers and the reports libraries require are nearly standard. The design and adoption of a standard order form would be a significant advance in book purchasing.

ISBN

International Standard Book Numbers (ISBN) are assigned by publishers as their books are published, with prefixes identifying the publisher and country of publication. A unique number for each item published throughout the world has many desirable bibliographic uses and offers possibilities for the application of manual systems and computerization in acquisitions work. The obstacle to use of ISBN designations in libraries is the lack of a list of books arranged by this number. For the most part, libraries use ISBNs for the convenience of vendors and for the improvement in service that may result from easing the work of publishers and wholesalers. Many publishers make extensive use of International Standard Book Numbers for internal control. The system is now in general use in the United States and Britain, and sixteen major book publishing countries accepted it through the International Standards Organization. In the United States the numbers are applied, primarily, to the books of publishers represented in *Books in Print,* leaving as a void the equal or greater number of publications of government, societies, associations, and small publishers. The Library of Congress is studying the possibility of eventually replacing the Library of Congress catalog card number with an international standard number.

ADVERTISEMENTS

A serious and continuing problem for libraries is the identification of materials that are advertised or otherwise promoted by publishers or others who prepare and sell books and other library materials. Advertisements are more often incomplete than intentionally misleading, but in either case libraries needlessly duplicate books because they were led to believe that a publication being offered was different from one they already owned. The chief problems arise when no reference or inadequate reference is made to the series of which a publication is a part or when dates of publication infer that a new edition is being offered when the item is actually a new printing. An item frequently omitted or cited incompletely in publisher's advertising is the date of publication or availability. An American National Standard for the advertising of books (ANSI Z39. 13-1971) lists the bibliographic data to be included in market media, such as catalogs, advertisements, book jackets, and display materials, for each of four markets: trade, institutional (including libraries), educational, and consumer. The standard recommends that promotional material include, in addition to standard descriptions, both copyright and publication date, edition, International Standard Book Number, Library of Congress catalog card number, series, special physical features, prior publication record, and other information that is important to libraries both in selection of materials and in avoiding unnecessary duplication.

REFERENCES

Bromberg, Erik I. "How the Birds (Pigeons) & Bees & Butterflies Do It; Avuncular Advice to a New Librarian about How to Talk to His Purchasing Agent Who Has Already Signed a Book Buying Contract." *Special Libraries* 61:168–70 (Apr. 1970).

Dougherty, Richard M., and others. "Emerging Problems in Acquisitions." *Library Resources & Technical Services* 12:147–60 (Spring 1968).

Grannis, Chandler B. *What Happens in Book Publishing*. 2d ed. New York: Columbia Univ. Pr., 1967. 467p.

Hensel, Evelyn, and Veillette, Peter D. *Purchasing Library Materials in Public and School Libraries: A Study of Purchasing Procedures and the Relationships between Libraries and Purchasing Agencies and Dealers*. Chicago: American Library Assn., 1969. 150p.

Melcher, Daniel. *Melcher on Acquisition*. Chicago: American Library Assn., 1971. 169p.

Ruback, Martin. "We Can Get It for You Wholesale—with Help." *Library Journal* 87:730 (Feb. 15, 1962).

Saul, Margaret. "The Business of Book Buying—As Special Librarians See It." *Library Journal* 88:2636–39 (July 1963).

Tuttle, Helen Welch. "Library-Book Trade Relations." *Library Trends* 18:398–411 (Jan. 1970).

Veenstra, John, and Mai, Lois. "When Do You Use a Jobber?" *College & Research Libraries* 23:522–24 (Nov. 1962).

Wynar, Bohdan S., and others. *Cost Analysis Study, Technical Services Division, University of Denver Library*. Denver, Colo.: Graduate School of Librarianship, University of Denver, 1965. 118p.

6

PURCHASING
FOREIGN BOOKS

American libraries are purchasing more books published outside the United States than they did before the 1950s. Research in the sciences and social sciences accounts for much of the need for these books, along with the spectacular increase in area studies programs. These inter-disciplinary programs have had significant federal and private support and they are prominent features of almost every college and university. Their great dependence upon printed materials makes their support of special concern to the acquisitions librarian. At the same time, instruction in higher education has moved from heavy reliance upon textbooks to use of a variety of library materials. Concomitantly, the several national programs for acquisitions from abroad (the Farmington plan, Public Law 480, the Latin American Cooperative Acquisitions Program, and the National Program for Acquisitions and Cataloging) have stimulated the demand for new materials as they satisfied it. The American research library spends more than half its funds for materials published outside the United States and even the smaller college library supporting only one or two area studies programs and majors in several foreign languages and literatures may spend 20 percent of its budget for materials on books and periodicals published abroad. In 1969 about 400,000 titles published throughout the world were reported to UNESCO. The United States published 62,000 of these, including federal government documents and university theses, only 15 percent of the world output.

Purchasing books published abroad differs in several important ways from domestic purchasing. Libraries do not order books from publishers except in those fairly frequent instances where dealers or booksellers are also publishers. Dealers more often offer a complete in-print and out-of-print procurement service than do suppliers of books published in the United States. Discounts are not usually available to libraries whether they are in the country of origin or in the United States, although the acquisitions librarian is wise to inquire about them, especially for quantities of trade books.

The chief decision facing an acquisitions librarian is whether to order foreign books from importers in the United States or from exporters in the country or region of publication. The decision should be based upon the size of the business a library has in books published abroad. To be sure, some large libraries buy foreign books in the United States because of convenience and service; and some small libraries have successful contacts in Western Europe for their purchasing. For the most part, however, the larger the library's acquisitions from outside the United States, the more probable it is that its purchasing will be done abroad.

IMPORTERS

Importers may supply all kinds of books from throughout the world or they may have specialties. The latter is more common and examples of specialization are dealers in books published in France, or in books of French and German literature, or in art books from many countries. Prices from importers usually will be somewhat higher than from exporters. They must use expensive American staff and charge for the service of selecting, importing, and stocking books that they expect will be purchased by American libraries.

These dealers usually give good value for their slightly higher prices. Their stock selection and catalogs are tailored to the needs of many American libraries, the language of transaction is always English, claims and correspondence are easily understood, they can perform the special order and invoice procedures required by some libraries, they are paid in the same way as any other American vendor, they can be reached easily by telephone, and their representatives visit many librarians' meetings. A good importer provides a total service for in-print and out-of-print books, continuations or standing orders, and subscriptions. Some importers have offices in Europe and other parts of the world to help them provide services comparable with those of exporters. Libraries with inflexible business procedures imposed upon them may find dealing with an importer much easier than with an exporter. Smaller libraries without complete bibliographic apparatus will find an importer helpful. It frequently happens that a library cannot know whether or not a book is in print because the library cannot afford to purchase or keep up-to-date the relevant tools, or because it does not have the language competence on its staff, or because the country of origin produces no record of which books are still in print. A good importer can provide the information the library cannot get and, if he also offers an out-of-print service, will try to get the book whether it is in print or out of print.

Some importers promise a total service but are more interested in selling books from their catalogs than securing books from abroad. *Caveat emptor* applies here as elsewhere in book purchasing; the librarian can be confident of his probable success in securing materials only when he knows his dealers.

EXPORTERS

Exporters usually deal in books from the country in which they have their offices, but some exporters offer publications from several countries. In Western Europe there are many dealers, and libraries can choose an exporter who will let them develop arrangements to suit their needs best. In other parts of the world one dealer may serve a large part of a continent. For instance, in parts of the Middle East one or two dealers can best serve acquisitions from several nations. Most libraries that buy books published in England will want at least to experiment with buying books from one of the excellent exporters in England. Exporters do not always charge for mailing and can offer lower prices because of their lower overhead costs. If a book is not in stock in the warehouse of an importer in the United States, a library usually can get it more quickly with a direct order to an exporter, avoiding the delay that is almost inevitable with a middleman. Exporters usually will invoice in American dollars if asked to do so.

The language barrier is not so serious as might be imagined. Most of the dealers in Western Europe correspond in English. When one does not and a librarian learns by letter that ones *Abonnement* has expired or a *factura* remains unpaid, dictionaries usually suffice; among these are Jerrold Orne's *The Language of the Foreign Book Trade* (2d ed.; American Library Assn., 1962) and *The Bookman's Glossary,* edited by Mary C. Turner (4th ed.; Bowker, 1961). A reply in English, however, may not be entirely satisfactory, and some libraries answer such letters by the expensive practice of having them written in the appropriate language by a specialist.

In comparing a library's use of an exporter with that of an importer or vice versa, the careful librarian will watch for differences in the currency rate of exchange (that is, the value of the dollar) and whether or not a dealer charges for packing and mailing. Nurturing relations with a dealer helps to solve problems, for a dealer is more likely to handle difficult orders if he can make a profit and this can usually be done only on regular orders. Librarians should, if possible, visit both domestic and foreign dealers to gain first-hand knowledge of the people with whom they are dealing.

PURCHASING FROM NEWLY DEVELOPING COUNTRIES

Larger libraries must purchase books and other library materials from what are called, for want of a better term, newly developing countries. For the purposes of library purchasing these are countries that have no book trade or where the book trade is not organized to facilitate the reasonably easy procurement of books; they may have export restrictions and other trade limitations that make purchasing from them very difficult. Except for Latin America, most of these countries have languages with non-Roman alphabets. The expanded Farmington Plan, Public Law 480, the Latin American Cooperative Acquisitions Plan, and the National Program for Acquisitions and Cataloging, have been or are of great assistance in obtaining materials from these countries. The acquisitions librarian who has the job of buying these materials or of providing a supervisory overview will benefit from studying the excellent articles on the acquisition of library materials from newly developing areas of the world that appeared in the Winter 1963 issue of *Library Resources & Technical Services* (v. 7, no. 1) and Robert Stevens' article cited in the references for this chapter. No better assistance can be found than that from acquisitions people in other libraries who have already experienced and, perhaps, solved most of the problems the librarian venturing into a new country or area will face. He or she also can find help through special interest groups formed to share and solve problems of these acquisitions such as the Seminars on the Acquisitions of Latin American Library Materials, subcommittees of the Association for Asian Studies, and the subject sections of the Association of College and Research Libraries.

In most research libraries acquisitions of materials from many newly developing countries are linked with selection, cataloging, and, sometimes, reference service, because of the language knowledge required. Helpful as this may be, the performance and management of acquisitions from these countries requires specific skills whether it is done in these specialized units or in the central acquisitions department.

SELECTING DEALERS

As with dealer selection for other library materials, no hard and fast rules can be advanced and no list can be written down. Importers advertise in the American library journals, and dealers in foreign books and importers are listed in the *American Book Trade Directory* (Bowker, biennial). Many are listed in the *AB Bookman's Yearbook* (AB Bookman's Weekly, annual), appear at library association conferences, and issue catalogs. Many importers will be selected on the basis of their specialties. Colleagues in other libraries can provide preliminary evaluations of these dealers, and in college and university libraries faculty members will have recommendations—dealers visit professional conferences in addition to those servicing librarians! Exporters also advertise, are listed in directories, and some appear at American conferences and have representatives call at American libraries. Again, the advice coming from libraries with similar collecting interests is important. Among the more useful approaches are the lists of dealers used by several of the large research libraries in the United States.

BUYING TRIPS

A method of foreign-book purchase that is sometimes successful is the personal visit. Librarians taking the tour to buy books report that it is very difficult work. Unless he or she is hunting only for rare books or large sets or collections of books, it is probable that books can be bought more cheaply by mail through a dealer. Often a faculty member offers to buy books on a trip and it is difficult and, usually, impolitic to refuse him. The best course of action is to set an initial dollar limit on his purchases, hope that he will not follow his personal interests too narrowly, and find dealers who are willing to hold books and send lists to the library for confirming orders for titles not already held. One may also expect the faculty to suffer the same fatigue that strikes librarians.

RIGHTS AND REPUBLICATION

Some titles are published simultaneously in two countries, England and the United States for instance, or republished later in one of the countries, and the American librarian may be required to purchase the edition the publishers have agreed he can have because of their arrangements on rights. Usually this presents no problem. On some books published abroad a United States firm will have distribution rights and it behooves the American librarian to note these arrangements and order the book as he is advised or he may delay its receipt unnecessarily. Usually, books ordered from exporters will be delivered regardless of distribution rights.

IMPORT LICENSES

Purchases from certain countries are prohibited by federal law. At this time they are North Korea, North Viet-Nam, and Cuba. Libraries can obtain licenses for trade with these countries by applying to Foreign Assets Control, U.S. Treasury Department, Washington, D.C. 20220.'

DIRECTORIES

At this time the tools listed below may be of special usefulness in acquiring materials from outside the United States. All directories become quickly out-of-date; some titles are revised and new editions published regularly; others languish, and new ones appear. It is necessary to watch for these changes.

International literary market place. 1965– . Bowker, 1965– Biennial.
A directory of European publishers "considered to be among the most active and influential in the international book market" and "firms of comparable status in Africa, Australia and New Zealand, Japan, Israel and Latin America." It contains export-import information.

Publishers international directory. 4th ed. Bowker, 1969. 2v.
Published in Germany as *Internationales Verlagaddressbuch.* A list of 20,000 publishers in 144 countries in Europe, Africa, the Americas, Asia, and Oceania.

Publishers' international year book: World Directory of Book
Publishers. 1960/61– . London, A. P. Wales, 1960– .
v. 1–
Lists publishers and booksellers arranged by country. Latest
edition is 1968.

International subscription agents. 2d ed. American Library Association, 1969.
A good source for names and addresses of dealers, along with
valuable information about service. Most of the agents handle
books as well as subscriptions.

There are many other sources for addresses outside the United States:
the *Cumulative Book Index* for books within its scope, the several
"books in print" like *Libros en venta* (Bowker, 1964 and supplements);
directories like *La empresa del libro en America Latina* (Buenos Aires,
Bowker Editores Argentina, 1968); the *African Book Trade Directory*
(Munich, Verlag Dokumentation, 1971; distributed in the U.S. by
Bowker). A useful source of information to support the purchasing of
foreign books is in *The Book Trade of the World,* edited by Sigfred
Taubert (Verlag für Buchmarkt-Forschung, 1972; distributed in the
U.S. by Bowker, 3v.). It includes references to directories and other
sources of information about publishing and book selling as well as
descriptions of national bibliographies.

REFERENCES

Coppola, Dominick. "International Bookseller Looks at Acquisitions." *Library
Resources & Technical Services* 11:203–6 (Spring 1967).

Stevens, Robert D. "Acquisitions for Area Programs." *Library Trends* 18:385–
97 (Jan. 1970).

Seminar on the Acquisition of Latin American Library Materials. *Reports and
Papers.* v.1– . 1956– . Annual.

Thompson, Lawrence S. "Acquisition of Books and Pamphlets." *Library Trends*
18:280–93 (Jan. 1970).

Welch, Helen M. "Selection and Acquisition of Foreign Publications." In *Selection and Acquisitions Procedures in Medium-Sized and Large Libraries,* ed.
by Herbert Goldhor, p. 79–89. Champaign, Ill.: University of Illinois Graduate School of Library Science, 1962. (Allerton Park Institute no. 9)

7

BLANKET ORDERING AND COOPERATIVE ACQUISITIONS

Mass purchasing in place of purchasing books title-by-title is not a new feature of library operations, but it recently has taken on new dimensions. For many years libraries have had orders for monographs in series, called standing orders. Usually the items on these orders are closely related, but they may be as unlike as the items in the Johns Hopkins University Studies in Historical and Political Science or the Bollingen Series. Another kind of mass purchasing has been purchases of collections of books or whole libraries. The new dimensions in mass purchasing are blanket-order or gathering plans, approval plans, and cooperative acquisitions plans. "Blanket orders" and "gathering plans" have the same meaning. In these programs dealers or publishers select materials for libraries based upon analyses of the needs of each library. This selection, in large part, replaces the selection work done in the library. Approval plans add the privilege of approving or rejecting items sent or proposed to be sent on these plans. As most blanket orders and gathering plans also include return privileges, the names of the plans are used interchangeably. The confused librarian must discover the exact meaning of an offer from a vendor.

GREENAWAY PLAN

One of the oldest and best-known blanket-order plans is the "Greenaway Plan" named for Emerson Greenaway, for many years Director of the Free Library of Philadelphia. In the late 1950s he worked out the plan under which publishers sent all of their trade books to a library before publication, at the same time they sent out review copies. The library staff could then evaluate the books and place orders so multiple copies could be in the library on or near the day of publication and catalog records could be prepared while waiting for the books to arrive. The chief advantage of the Greenaway Plan is that it provides the ability to get books ready for public use quickly. It is particularly attractive to public libraries and is identified with them rather than with special or academic libraries. Publishers participating in the plan charge low prices for the books sent for review and there are no returns for credit, as it is cheaper to discard unwanted books than return them. Publishers depend upon multiple-copy orders to make the Greenaway Plan profitable. The plan now is used by many libraries in combination with other means of acquiring new books. The key to successful use is identification of those publishers whose output most nearly meets the selection needs of the library so there will not be excessive discards or staff time wasted reviewing books that are not likely to be wanted by the library. Evaluation also includes assessment of whether books actually are ready for use sooner than they would be ready if regular selection and acquisitions methods were used.

PUBLISHERS' BLANKET ORDERS

Many publishers offer blanket-order or approval plans for some or all of their publications. A typical plan from a major publisher will offer several dozen subject categories for acquisition either on approval or as blanket orders. Plans often take the form of submitting lists to libraries for selection rather than sending books. These publisher plans usually offer greater discounts than can be had from item-by-item direct ordering and better discounts than can be obtained from a wholesaler. They also offer the advantage of receipt of the books in the library by publication date. Many of the publishers send Library of Congress catalog cards with the books. When a publisher's blanket-order plan corresponds to the needs of a library, it provides excellent opportunities for advantageous purchasing. When a library, through misjudgment or laxity in reviewing materials, keeps books received on a blanket order that it would not have selected otherwise, the order should be discontinued. When a library has blanket orders with many publishers, the acquisitions staff may have difficulty remembering which orders the library has placed, and an extra step, potentially expensive, may be required to prevent unwanted duplication.

College, university, and research libraries buy so many of the publications of university presses that one of the oldest types of blanket orders is for all of the publications of a university press. It is now possible to have comprehensive blanket orders through the Association of American University Presses.

Approval and Gathering Plans

In the 1960s a new form of blanket order, usually called an approval or gathering plan, came into prominence and appears now to be a permanent and valued part of the acquisitions process, especially for academic and research libraries. Between the 1961/62 and the 1970/71 school years there was a 30 percent increase in the number of college and university libraries, and the number of volumes acquired each year by academic libraries rose 150 percent. During this period there was a shortage of trained professional library staff as well as a clear shift of primary responsibility for book selection from the faculty to the library. Many colleges and universities expanded instructional programs so quickly and so extensively that libraries were overwhelmed by large budgets for materials to support the programs. Blanket-order plans were an almost inevitable result of this combination of factors. The chief advantage of these plans to academic libraries was in providing a way of increasing their collections quickly.

There are important additional advantages when programs of rapid expansion no longer dominate the acquisitions scene. Speed of delivery is chief among these advantages; a well-conceived plan with a properly functioning dealer will place books in the library immediately upon publication. Savings in clerical costs also can be realized if the plan is arranged to bypass the preparation of orders for each title and the sorting and mailing of orders is avoided. Blanket orders can assure that books that go out of print quickly will be obtained. Evaluations of books on approval plans are made with the books in hand; many librarians believe they are better able to make evaluations this way than with Library of Congress proof slips or advertisements or reviews, although not all librarians agree. Finally, blanket-order plans should free the library staff members who do selection for other tasks, possibly permitting them to spend more time on the selection and acquisition of out-of-print and antiquarian books and on developing special collections.

Critics of approval and gathering plans believe librarians using them have shifted selection responsibility from themselves to their dealers. These critics claim that book selection is the base of collection development and only can be done well by staff members who are intimately involved with their libraries and the services they must support. They also believe that the review of materials received on approval and gathering plans and the analyses of materials not received, if done properly, requires much of the selection time that ostensibly is saved by the plans. Another important criticism is not a criticism of the plans but of the librarians using them; that is, through inertia or lack of staff some libraries accept everything sent to them on approval.

Many approval and gathering plans are offered to American libraries. They may be for books published in the United States although some American dealers have plans for obtaining books published outside the United States. They may be for books published abroad, from dealers abroad, either for the country in which the dealer operates or for a region or continent. Some plans are for subjects rather than areas and others are for forms of publication, such as music scores, or recordings, or contemporary fiction from Western or Southern Europe. Dealers outside the United States are unlikely to be enthusiastic about returns; by the time the books are received from a second transatlantic voyage, for instance, they can only be resold at considerable loss.

Extensive debate has centered upon what kinds of libraries should have approval and gathering plans. Some observers believe a library should have at least half a million dollars a year for materials before adopting a plan, but there are libraries with less than half of that support that have satisfactory plans. One rule of thumb is that a library should spend only one-third of its materials budget on blanket plans, reserving the balance for periodicals and serials, retrospective buying, and filling in areas the plans do not cover. If, applying this formula, a library has $75,000 to spend on a gathering plan and a dealer is both interested in an order this size and performs well on it, this then is the amount that is required. It is likely, however, that a college or university with a materials budget this size will have to be exceptionally discriminating in selection, requiring attention that only can be provided by the library staff. Similarly, a library in a newly established educational institution with a generous budget will want to spend it on retrospective purchasing to build a basic book collection, not on blanket orders for new books. The point at which blanket plans are appropriate for a library depends upon the needs and support of the library and no fixed rules can be advanced.

Establishing a Blanket Order

The first step in establishing a blanket order is to determine what material to include and what to exclude. The dealer may have a subject list for the library to check or may propose checking subjects in a standard bibliography such as *Deutsche Bibliographie* or the dealer may work out with the library a set of specifications for the order. The result is called a profile and a satisfactory profile is key to the success of a blanket order, for with it the library should get all of the books it would select if its staff did the selection and none of the books it does not want. An important aspect of most blanket orders is the initial period when the profile is being tested. The library reviews the books received and, on an approval plan, returns those it does not want. Whether it returns the books or does not have that option, the library changes its specifications or profile to try to prevent receipt of similar books in the future. Examples of on-approval and blanket-order agreements for a large research library (Stanford) are included in Rogers and Weber's *University Library Administration,* cited in the references for this chapter. Many dealers offer blanket-order plans under which checked copies of the "Weekly Record" in *Publishers Weekly,* or the *British National Bibliography,* or other standard current lists are regularly sent before the materials, permitting the library to add to and subtract from the selection made by the dealer.

In the perfectly functioning blanket plan there would be no returns; the more realistic level of return commensurate with satisfactory functioning is 2 or 3 percent; above that the plan is not working well. As important in evaluation as number of returns is an assessment of what books are not being received. During the evaluation period the library should, as a minimum, check those selection sources it used before the plan was begun to see that everything that would have been selected is being received. Theoretically, the approval or gathering plan can do a better job of selection than an overburdened library selection staff; consequently, libraries may check for broader and deeper selection than would have been their normal practice. In evaluation, libraries check Library of Congress proof slips (remembering that LC does not get and catalog all books published), the "Weekly Record" in *Publishers Weekly,* the *British National Bibliography,* and geographic, language, and subject bibliographies, as appropriate. Profiles must be under constant review to meet changing needs and programs.

The best arrangement for the benefit of the clerical operations of an acquisitions department is one in which the dealer sends a separate "order" slip with each book. This makes it unnecessary for the library to type records for its file of books in process to control duplication until the books are fully cataloged. Some dealers use the library's regular order slips. If the step of typing orders cannot be eliminated when a blanket order is begun, it is unlikely that the library will realize significant savings in clerical costs. As with publisher blanket orders, many approval and gathering plans supply catalog cards with the books. Some dealers with approval plans invoice each title separately, usually on a 3-by-5 slip, thus reducing the problem of invoice changes incurred when a book is returned. Other dealers give the library credit memoranda that they complete for returned books and attach to invoices so they can be sent directly through the payment process without return to the dealer for correction.

Special Considerations

In addition to the drawing of a good profile as a blanket order is begun, other decisions must be made. Certain types of publications are usually excluded; among them are periodicals, reprints, and, for blanket orders for books other than English language, translations. Frequently, new or rapidly expanding libraries will set date-of-original-publication limitations for reprints that may be sent automatically, but a more common practice is to have the dealer offer reprints by list rather than send them. Libraries usually set a price limit per volume that can be sent without prior approval from the library; generally fifty dollars. Some special collections maintained in depth by a library may be excepted from a blanket order. If a library collects everything by and about a twentieth-century poet, including all editions in any language, it may wish to exempt this poet from its profile for its staff probably will spend more time selecting materials and will obtain more books than would a dealer.

Series must be given careful consideration when blanket orders are placed, for all libraries will have standing orders for monographs in series that might be sent as parts of blanket orders. In many cases libraries and dealers have agreed that monographs in series should remain as separate orders. Whether or not this is the decision, the library must review all of its serial orders and let the dealer know which may be sent on a blanket order and which may not. Unless, for instance, a library has treated all numbered series as standing orders, an uncommon practice, it must identify which series are to be sent. This review is a giant task for a large library. When the decision is made that series are to be sent, special care must be taken to be sure there are no duplicates or missed volumes between the cancellation of the standing order and the beginning of the blanket order. Most specifications for blanket orders call for the dealer to send or offer the first volume of new series.

Problems

One of the problems that must be solved in using approval and gathering plans is to determine whether or not a book that is wanted by the library will be received on the blanket order. For example, if a faculty member makes a special request for a book and it is within the profile, should the library expect it to be sent automatically? Most dealers have established routines for a library to use in asking whether a title is to be sent or not. A similar problem occurs when duplicate copies are wanted by the library. One of the chief complaints about blanket orders is unintentional duplication caused when material is received by gift, exchange, or standing order. Another is poor selection work done by the dealer. These problems may be solved by refining the specifications or changing the dealer.

Librarians should recognize that discounts will not be as great for books sent on approval or gathering plans that involve dealer selection as for books they would order conventionally, title by title, based upon their own selection. The blanket-order dealer may realize a price advantage from volume buying he can do from publishers because he has guaranteed sales for the titles he selects, but this price advantage does not make up for the extra work of selection that he does for the library. If the library is to have its selection work done outside the library, it will pay for it.

DEALERS

A few dealers dominate the approval and gathering business. Most of them are also wholesalers, or importers, or exporters, and they include some of the most highly respected, long-established dealers in the world. Some of them actively promote their approval and gathering plans; others offer the plans as a convenience to the libraries they serve. The selection of a dealer should be made with great care, taking into consideration the recommendations of other libraries. Libraries should also be assured of the financial stability of a blanket-order dealer; a cancelled approval or gathering plan creates an exceptional amount of work to be sure that new titles are not missed and that series are picked up and placed again as standing orders.

Most libraries that have used blanket orders have been satisfied with them. This satisfaction appears to rest upon care in selecting the dealer, preparing a profile, and revising it upon examination of materials sent and identification of materials not sent.

COOPERATIVE ACQUISITION PLANS

LACAP

The Latin American Cooperative Acquisitions Plan (LACAP) is a blanket order that is both a commercial gathering plan and a cooperative acquisitions plan. This plan grew from the Seminars on the Acquisition of Latin American Library Materials (SALALM). The seminars were begun to try to solve the problems of getting published material from Latin America into North American libraries. The chief problem is that there has been no organized book trade in Latin America and no over-arching bibliography. The nature of publication in most Latin American countries is such that books go out of print the day they are published. SALALM and the Stechert-Hafner firm in New York worked together to establish LACAP, which was discontinued in 1973.

Farmington Plan

The history of cooperative acquisitions plans extends back many years to agreements between neighboring institutions to purchase expensive sets together or share responsibilities for collection development. The Farmington Plan was a purchase plan that arose when it was discovered during World War II that many foreign research publications were not owned by an American library. The plan, begun in 1948, was the first nationally organized cooperative effort for collection building. Its goal was to have in the United States one copy of every important book published anywhere in the world. Libraries volunteered to accept country and subject responsibilities. The selection of materials was made by dealers in the country or region of origin. The plan was reviewed and expanded in the late 1950s and operated under the aegis of the Association of Research Libraries until it was discontinued in 1972.

Public Law 480

The Farmington Plan has been overshadowed in recent years by the effects of Public Law 480, which is administered by the Library of Congress. This law provides for the use of blocked currencies gathered by the United States in countries throughout the world to purchase and send to the Library of Congress and other libraries in the United States publications from these countries. The countries involved are in Asia, the Middle East, and Eastern Europe and include areas where it has been difficult to obtain materials for libraries through conventional acquisitions methods. The Library of Congress has permanent representatives in these countries who maintain personal contacts to assure the flow of materials. Comprehensive sets of materials from these countries are distributed to about forty American research libraries and sets of materials in English are sent to over three hundred libraries. Those libraries receiving full sets pay a token charge for materials received. Cataloging is centralized at the Library of Congress, initially partly supported by contributions from participating libraries. The program has been successful in bringing into the United States and making available books and other library materials that would not otherwise have been obtained.

NPAC

The Higher Education Act of 1965, Title IIC, provides for the acquisition by the Library of Congress of library materials of scholarly and research value published throughout the world. It also provides for the cataloging of these materials and the distribution of bibliographic information about them. Full funding of this program called the National Program for Acquisitions and Cataloging (NPAC), provides for the acquisition of additional copies of materials for libraries other than the Library of Congress, a cooperative acquisitions venture without parallel. Cooperative cataloging, called in this case "shared cataloging," is part of the scheme and promises bibliographic control that ultimately will be of far-reaching importance to acquisitions operations as well as to service and cataloging functions of larger libraries. Both PL 480 and NPAC are federally funded, and the levels of their support may vary from one year to the next.

Cooperative Acquisitions Centers

Another form of cooperative acquisitions occurs at centers like the Center for Research Libraries in Chicago and the Hampshire Inter-Library Center in Massachusetts, which were formed as warehouses for storage of little-used materials. Their cooperative acquisitions functions are the purchase of less-used research materials that are jointly owned by and quickly available to the member libraries that support the centers. The Center for Research Libraries collects foreign dissertations and government publications, newspapers on film, college catalogs, state documents, scientific serials, and other materials that are needed only occasionally by member libraries.

REFERENCES

Blanket Orders

Axford, H. William. "The Economics of a Domestic Approval Plan." *College & Research Libraries* 32:368–75 (Sept. 1971).

Coffin, Lewis C. "Blanket Book Ordering." *Selection and Acquisitions Procedures in Medium Sized and Large Libraries,* ed. by Herbert Goldhor, p. 42–54. Champaign, Ill.: University of Illinois Graduate School of Library Science, 1962. (Allerton Park Institute no 9)

Dudley, Norman. "The Blanket Order." *Library Trends* 18:318–27 (Jan. 1970).

McCullough, Kathleen. "Approval Plans: Vendor Responsibility and Library Research; a Literature Survey and Discussion." *College & Research Libraries* 33:368–81 (Sept. 1972).

Morrison, Perry D., and others. "A Symposium on Approval Order Plans and the Book Selection Responsibilities of Librarians." *Library Resources & Technical Services* 12:133–45 (Spring 1968).

Spyers-Duran, Peter, ed. *Approval and Gathering Plans in Academic Libraries.* Littleton, Colo.: Libraries Unlimited, 1969. (Proceedings of the International Seminar on Approval and Gathering Plans in Large and Medium-Size Academic Libraries; held at Western Michigan University, Nov. 14, 1968)

Spyers-Duran, Peter, and Gore, Daniel, eds. *Advances in Understanding Approval and Gathering Plans in Academic Libraries.* Kalamazoo: Western Michigan University, 1970. (Proceedings of the Second International Seminar on Approval and Gathering Plans in Large and Medium-Size Academic Libraries, held at Western Michigan University on Oct. 30–31, 1969)

Stanford University. "On-Approval Agreement for Scientific and Technological Publications" and "Blanket Order Agreement." In *University Library Administration,* ed. by Rutherford D. Rogers and David C. Weber, p. 376–90. Bronx, N.Y.: Wilson, 1971.

Thom, Ian. "Some Administrative Aspects of Blanket Ordering." *Library Resources & Technical Services* 13:338–42 (Summer 1969). Comment by Harriet K. Rebuldela, with a rejoinder. *Library Resources & Technical Services* 13:342–46 (Summer 1969).

Wedgeworth, Robert. "Foreign Blanket Orders." *Library Resources & Technical Services* 14:258–68 (Spring 1970).

Wilden-Hart, Marion. "The Long Term Effects of Approval Plans." *Library Resources & Technical Services* 14:400–6 (Summer 1970).

Cooperative Acquisitions

Downs, Robert B. "Future Prospects of Library Acquisitions." *Library Trends* 18:412–21 (Jan. 1970).

Library of Congress. *PL 480 Newsletter.* 1961– . Irregular.

Savary, M. J. *The Latin American Cooperative Acquisitions Program: An Imaginative Venture.* New York: Hafner, 1968. 144p.

Shepard, Marietta Daniels. "Cooperative Acquisitions of Latin American Materials." *Library Resources & Technical Services* 13:347–60 (Summer 1969).

Skipper, James E. "National Planning for Resource Development." *Library Trends* 15:321–34 (Oct. 1966).

Vosper, Robert. "International Book Procurement; or Farmington Extended." *College & Research Libraries* 21:117–24 (Mar. 1960).

Welsh, William J. "The Processing Department of the Library of Congress in 1970." *Library Resources & Technical Services* 15:191–214 (Spring 1971).

8

PURCHASING OUT-OF-PRINT BOOKS

One of the most interesting and challenging aspects of acquisitions work is the pursuit of out-of-print books. The sense of accomplishment can be great when one has found an elusive title or built a weak section of the library to breadth or depth over a period of months or years. Despite the impressive advances in the number of titles reprinted in recent years, no adequate collection of Faulkner works and criticism or of the history of the Puritan revolution in England or of any of a thousand other topics could be gathered with only in-print books. The search for out-of-print books is particularly important for college and university libraries where new programs and courses or new faculty members teaching existing courses with new emphases require the extension of library holdings. Public libraries also need out-of-print services for replacement of lost, worn out, or damaged books; to meet changes in demand for materials; and occasionally to make up for years of poor financial support. In discussing out-of-print books reference is to the books needed for scholarly research or for the serious student whether he is in formal schooling or not. Some of these books happen to be rare collectors items and very expensive, but the quest for them is for their contents not for their form or scarcity. All too frequently libraries set aside their work on out-of-print materials until work on in-print materials, subscription renewals, and other acquisitions work is done, one day discovering their work is never done and they have built hopelessly large files of cards for out-of-print books. When book budgets are not generous libraries may believe they must concentrate on the purchase of in-print books. Under some strained circumstances it may be necessary to concentrate on the in-print, but this will be a disservice to those patrons who need books that are not in print and its effect will be cumulative so that, after several years neglect of the out-of-print, a library will be weakened.

IDENTIFYING OUT-OF-PRINT BOOKS

There are two ways in which libraries discover books to be out of print. First, the pre-order search may reveal that a book is not listed in *Books in Print,* or in one of the other tools listing materials in print or about to be published; second, a wholesaler, dealer, or publisher reports a book as out of print. As noted earlier, some libraries automatically order books reported out of print by wholesalers directly from publishers. These two sources for identifying out-of-print titles move together to make a desiderata file: out-of-print books needed by the library. A third route to the desiderata file is from reports from antiquarian and out-of-print dealers that titles the library selected from their catalogs or lists were sold to other customers before the library's order was received. Some of the titles reported sold may have come from the desiderata file; others may have been selected from the catalog or list without reference to specific desiderata titles.

In any of these cases, titles should not go automatically to a desiderata file; they always should be reviewed to determine whether or not they should be sought as out-of-print titles. The need for a book that was presumed to be in print when it was selected, and consequently easy and perhaps inexpensive to purchase, may be questioned when as an out-of-print title it will cost more in staff time to secure and probably more money to buy. Other items may have gone out of print for good reasons: a new edition is to be published or the contents are so out-of-date the book could be only of historical interest. Still other titles would be so difficult to obtain on the out-of-print market that putting them in the desiderata process is a waste of time both for the library and for the book dealers that will be approached to find the title. Many pamphlets; publications of local governments, schools, university bureaus, and institutes; and many other titles printed in small runs are already held by libraries and specialists. If they ever find their way into the used-book market, the chances of the library that wants one of them finding the dealer who has it are extremely remote. If after review it is still believed that these items should be purchased, the acquisitions department should get a microform or full-sized photographic copy.

The review of out-of-print titles before they move to the desiderata file may be done by returning them to the person who selected them. In academic libraries this is frequently a faculty member who should be informed of the status of his order and may be asked to decide if an item should be sought on the out-of-print market, copied, or its acquisition abandoned. There are some librarians who believe that once the initial step of selection has been made the acquisitions department should proceed to secure the material selected without reference back to the selector. The argument is that if selection is done by the proper people, specialists or qualified generalists, the amount of money already invested in the selection and the informed decisions that have been made preclude review, which is in itself expensive. This is a valid argument for research libraries and for the special collections of books they develop, but it should always be tempered with good judgment that allows those who are searching for out-of-print books to perform their work rationally and with some prospects of success.

SOURCES

Dealers in out-of-print books may call themselves out-of-print dealers or antiquarian or secondhand-book dealers. They may even call themselves bookstores, for many businesses deal in both in-print and out-of-print books. They are called out-of-print dealers here for that is the part of the stock and their work that is of concern to this discussion. In the United States and Great Britain there are four chief sources of out-of-print books. First, rare-book dealers work primarily with special libraries and special collections in large libraries and with private collectors. Frequently their catalogs are extremely informative and some of them include in their catalogs or their stocks items that are moderately priced and may be of interest to other than rare-book collectors. Second, there are general out-of-print dealers with large, diversified stocks. They also may deal in rare books and have specialties and issue special subject catalogs, but the bulk of their business is in general out-of-print books. Third, specialist dealers deal in subjects or geographic areas. Their offerings may be broad in scope, books in all of the social sciences, for example, or narrow, books on Alaska. Many of them do not maintain retail stores, working instead from their homes or from offices not open to the public, and do their business entirely by mail. There are also the junk shops, where old books from house sales mix with odd issues of old magazines and sometimes with other objects no longer in demand by our society. Searching for books for libraries in the junk shops is seldom rewarding. The fourth source is scouts. A scout is a bookdealer who keeps no stock; he buys from a shop or a private party and resells immediately, usually on a consignment. Scouts usually work for bookstores but some libraries have had good success with "our man in Paris" or his equivalent elsewhere. Libraries' chief sources are general out-of-print dealers and specialists.

In general, the out-of-print book trade is organized in Europe the same as in the United States, Canada, and Great Britain. Most dealers will accept and make good use of letters in English and they may reply in English or in their language. Bills that are not stated in U.S. dollars can be paid in dollars by getting the exchange rate through the local bank if not the business office. Many foreign dealers have U.S. bank addresses to which the library's checks may be sent. Many American and British dealers handle out-of-print books published on the Continent and elsewhere in the world; in general, those with offices abroad will be able to do a better job, but specialist dealers in the United States may have out-of-print foreign stocks in some depth.

Local used-book stores may be important sources for local history material and they may be useful for other out-of-print material as well. The United States Book Exchange has a stock of out-of-print books and issues lists of books. Librarians usually identify the USBE service with serials, but its book lists can be of value and not enough use of them is made by libraries.

Exchanges also can be sources of out-of-print books. Exchange lists published by institutions with collections similar to one's own may be valuable and some groups of libraries pool their duplicates for their mutual benefit.

Dealers in out-of-print books in the United States are listed in the *AB Bookman's Yearbook* (including some outside the United States), the *American Book Trade Directory* (Bowker, biennial), and the *Directory of American Book Specialists* (Continental Publishing Company). Outside the United States, the International League of Antiquarian Booksellers has published an international directory and *The Antiquarian Booktrade,* compiled by B. Donald Grose (Scarecrow, 1972) is useful. The Sheppard Press, London, issues directories for the British Isles and Europe and *Clique* magazine has a British directory. The best information about out-of-print dealers may be had from experienced acquisitions librarians.

MECHANICS

When a publisher's stock of a book is exhausted and the decision is made not to reprint, the book becomes the stock of the out-of-print business. Traditionally most out-of-print books came from the private collector. However, while the collector remains the chief source, the demise of the large private library in times of smaller homes, better public and academic libraries, and differing measures of affluence has affected the book trade. Dealers buy from other dealers largely by advertising, by visiting stores, or by employing scouts. Auctions are a more important source of books for dealers than they are for libraries. Sales of duplicates from public institutions is another source of books, although it does not produce as many items as other sources.

To librarians the pricing of out-of-print books is difficult to understand. One title can cost $4.00 in one store and, in the same condition, $17.50 in another. Both may be completely honest prices. The first consideration in comparing prices is condition. A modern first edition, unopened, with dust jacket—in mint condition—will be many times the price of the same title, second printing, no dust jacket, with backstrip faded. These are extremes in condition, but condition in more moderate forms governs prices also. The kind of dealer making an offer also affects the price of a book. A late Chicago book dealer was able to underbid anyone on a library's advertised list of general books. He worked from his home, did not receive customers, and consequently had low overhead. He sent out carbon copies of typed offers from time to time but never had even the most rudimentary catalog, and he must have done his own scouting. Clearly he could offer a copy of *Das Kapital* more cheaply than a dealer in the New York area who maintained the world's largest stock on Marx and Marxism, had a large shop on an expensive commercial street, employed a sales staff, and issued elaborate catalogs.

Out-of-print book dealers are professional people with professional skills for which they must charge if they are to make a reasonable living. Although there are wide variations, the out-of-print trade in general works on a markup of 100 percent. That is, if a dealer paid $7 for a book, he would have to charge a library $14 if he is to meet his overhead costs and make a profit. Dealers are extremely sensitive to discussion and criticism of book prices. They should recall that most libraries are publicly supported institutions and that librarians have an ethical and frequently a stated responsibility to spend public funds carefully. When librarians inquire about prices, take the lowest bid, and do other things that reflect this responsibility, dealers should not necessarily infer criticism. On the other hand, librarians should be aware that when they spend $10 in staff time to get a book for $5 that they could have obtained earlier for $15 they have not saved any money.

Determining how much a library should pay for an out-of-print book is not an easy task. The chief considerations are "how much is this book worth as a book and on the market" and "how important is this book for the library?" One rule-of-thumb that some libraries use for scholarly out-of-print books (not rare books or collector's editions) is: If the book costs more than a copy enlarged from film, it is too expensive. The copy is just as usable as the original edition and is probably on better paper and will last much longer.

In deciding value some librarians check recorded prices such as the annual auction records *American Book Prices Current* (Columbia Univ. Pr., annual), *Book Prices Current* (London, Dawsons, annual), *Book Auction Records* (London, Dawsons, annual), and the compilations from dealers' catalogs like *Bookman's Guide to Americana* (Scarecrow) and *Bookman's Price Index* (Gale). These prices can be helpful but they can also be very misleading; what was the provenance of the book, its condition, and was this an important sale at which all prices were high? These are among the questions that must be taken into consideration.

Many out-of-print dealers are one-man enterprises with very small capitalization. Bills from them should be paid as promptly as possible. Similarly, small dealers may find it difficult to cope with complex billing and order procedures, and the library's easing of them when it is possible may sustain a profitable relationship that might otherwise be lost. As in relations with dealers of in-print books, the establishment of a good relationship with an out-of-print dealer can be exceptionally beneficial to the library. Dealers have "preferred" customers who get the first offers and the best service.

DESIDERATA FILES

Most libraries build, in one way or another, desiderata files; that is, files of out-of-print books that the library wants. Characteristically, these files are in card form, frequently a part of the original set of order forms or the original order request form or a copy of it. Each card in the desiderata file should show what has happened to the book listed: when it was reported out of print; how and who reviewed it; whether it has been re-searched to determine if it has been reprinted; and what action has been taken to obtain it as an out-of-print book. By use of standard copying equipment, along with forms incorporating masks, these cards serve also as slips to be sent to dealers as desiderata lists. Most desiderata files are arranged by author entry to facilitate searching for items in it. Some files are arranged by language or country of origin if there are significant numbers of titles within these categories. Some libraries arrange desiderata files by broad subjects: social sciences, humanities, and sciences, or by special subjects for which the trade has specialist dealers or for which catalogs appear, such as: economics, German language and literature, and art history.

The desiderata file lends itself to marginal punched-card applications as well as to machine applications, for there is much information that can be coded with good purpose and that will permit the arrangement and, possibly, printing, of the file by subject, language, selecting unit or department ordering, dealer, length of time in the file or on order, and other information that may speed and ease the acquisition of out-of-print books. Most libraries keep this file in the acquisitions department and use acquisitions or selection subject specialists for searching for out-of-print books. Desiderata files should be reviewed periodically to be sure that the titles are still being sought actively, and they should be re-searched against *Books in Print* annually to discover if they have been reprinted. In a large library a desiderata file may contain tens of thousands of titles. At some point in the life of an item in the desiderata file, it should be considered for microforming or microform-enlarged printing if it does not have important illustrations and if permission to copy can be obtained. Some libraries have an automatic point at which this is done. This may be after lists have been circulated to three dealers, or advertised and then placed with a dealer for two years, or some combination of these or similar steps. Desiderata files become behemoths; they require continuing attention.

CATALOGS

One of the pleasantest types of mail coming to the desk of the acquisitions librarian is catalogs of out-of-print or secondhand books. They are in every shape, size, and condition and the acquaintance with them and the world of books they represent is one of the most rewarding aspects of acquisitions work. Their seasons are the same as those of the publishers of new books: spare summers, piles of new catalogs in the fall, a post-Christmas lull, and a renewal in the spring. Some of them are crowded, poorly mimeographed, and on bad paper. Some are handsome printings on good paper, and all may be useful to the library. Arrangements of entry can vary: geographically, by subject, by catchword titles, by no apparent classification, or by whatever else the dealer thinks will catch his customer's eye and sell books. The main entry may be somewhat informally established and not be the one a librarian would select, although some catalogs present excellent bibliographic entries. Careful preorder searching is required for most catalogs, and the searcher or searching supervisor will learn through experience which catalogs need thorough searching. The makers of catalogs often regard series information as inconsequential, and this omission can cause unwanted duplication in the library where the item offered is handled as part of a series, rather than as a monograph. Most dealers offer to accept returns if the items are not as described, but it is better for the acquisitions department to search thoroughly before ordering than to spend time and money returning duplicates.

It should be remembered that with few exceptions the out-of-print dealer's catalog refers to only one copy of each book listed. Consequently, these catalogs must be handled with great speed in the library. Although a catalog from a typical dealer has a life of as much as two months and some dealers include in their catalogs items that they usually carry in stock, the majority of the best items in a catalog will be gone within two weeks or in a few days for a particularly interesting catalog. The money invested in selection, searching, and ordering is wasted on an old catalog. Some libraries will not work on a catalog that has been in the library more than twenty-four hours, and when delays in mail handling and delivery that make most catalogs old when they are received are considered, this stricture may not be excessive. In the special handling given to catalogs they should be hand-carried to and from the person who is to read them. In some libraries where preorder searching and order writing cannot be completed within a day or two, telegrams, cablegrams, or air letters are sent to the dealer or he is contacted by telephone, and asked to reserve the items selected. Reserving before searching should be done only when the library is confident it will have few of them being held. Otherwise, the dealer may be put to excessive, unnecessary work and may lose other sales for the items.

Many libraries telephone, telegraph, or cable firm orders to try to get ahead of other customers for wanted books. The complexities of ordering and invoicing imposed upon some libraries force them to inquire of a dealer whether or not a wanted item is still available before they write a firm order. Most dealers are willing to undertake extra work to assist their customers. Another step in speeding action on catalogs is to work out means of moving them in the mail more quickly. A dealer may send catalogs first-class mail or airmail or he may send proof or even advance proof copies. Many dealers in Western Europe automatically send catalogs airmail at their own expense. Special arrangements of this nature are worked out individually between dealers and libraries, and librarians should be willing to pay for unusual service.

In colleges and universities, faculty members receive catalogs directly from dealers as well as from the library. Those who read and select for the library from the catalogs usually will cooperate in observing time limits when they understand that their work may be wasted if the catalog is old. If a faculty member submits an old catalog (on which he has invested several hours of his time), it is hardly politic to refuse to order the material. Sometimes the acquisitions librarian is surprised to discover that not everything in a catalog has been sold immediately.

Libraries use out-of-print catalogs in two ways: to check against their desiderata files in the search for specific titles already identified as needed and to read and select items for the library without reference to needs for specific titles, working with general collection development in mind. The latter use makes the same judgments as are made in the selection of newly published materials. Reading catalogs against a desiderata file is expensive in time used, but many libraries do it and are convinced of its efficacy in obtaining out-of-print titles. It is in this work that the arrangement of the desiderata file should match the arrangement of the catalog. This does not always occur. Despite the fact that very few catalogs are issued in one alphabet by main entry, the desiderata file should be kept in this order or in very broad subject or country/language arrangements.

When out-of-print catalogs are read for selection without reference to a desiderata file, the work usually is done by subject specialists whether in or out of the acquisitions department, faculty in colleges and universities, and the acquisitions librarian and the head librarian in smaller libraries. In other words, the same people who do other selection work for the library.

Some dealers are conscientious in reporting "sold" items for which a library's orders were too late. Others seem to throw away order slips for books they have already sold. Some dealers hold orders hoping to turn up another copy. In any case they would assist libraries greatly and save money for them in time spent on follow-up if they would consistently notify libraries when items are sold and when they are continuing to search. When firm orders are placed for catalog items with dealers most libraries file a copy of the order in the outstanding order file to prevent unwanted duplication. The claim system applied to the outstanding order file ultimately will remove out-of-print orders that are not going to be filled, but claim systems usually function less frequently than is desirable, especially for those items that can be known to be unavailable within a few weeks. Many libraries have special follow-up systems for catalog orders, keeping extra copies of orders together, arranged by date or by dealer and catalog, to facilitate follow-up on items offered by those dealers who do not report items sold, allowing them to reactivate these books as desiderata and disencumber funds.

LISTS

A frequently used technique for obtaining out-of-print books is to make lists of wanted books and send them to appropriate dealers. This is done in two ways: first, a list is sent to several or even many dealers asking them to quote on items they have; and second, a list is sent to one dealer at a time giving him an exclusive opportunity to quote or otherwise work on the list. In recent years dealer resistance has reduced the use of the former method. Many dealers believe that they waste time working on lists when other dealers are also working on them and that they are put into unfair competition with one another. Some dealers will not work on lists that are not exclusive. Distribution of a list to more than one dealer has a distinct advantage for libraries: it permits them access to more than one stock of books and they get more books in a shorter time than if they send out exclusive lists. They also may get books more cheaply, but if they are working with reputable dealers, as they should be, and place values on service and size of stock, price advantages may not be very great.

A modification of both types of lists is the list that is sent to a number of dealers in turn, asking them to quote on items they have in stock within a short time limit, not holding the list for search outside of stock. This allows the library to move a list to five or six dealers in as many months and this practice often is used to obtain books that are needed quickly. The most frequently used dealer listing technique is one in which the list is turned over to a dealer exclusively, for six, twelve, eighteen months or, perhaps indefinitely. With time and exclusive listing a dealer can proceed to look for an item for a library, using all of his acquisitions sources, confident that he will have a probable sale when he finds the book. Libraries having indefinite orders with established dealers continue to receive offers four, six, even ten years later. There is some evidence that most dealers quickly lose interest in a list and turn their talents and energies to newly received lists that will be more productive for them. Consequently, most libraries sending out lists set time limits, forwarding the lists to other dealers at the end of the time specified. When selecting the first dealer to whom a title is to be sent it is good practice to select the second and third and perhaps additional dealers in the event the book is not obtained from the first dealer or subsequent ones. Dealer selection is time-consuming, requiring the attention of an experienced staff member. Three dealers can be selected less expensively at one time than at three widely separated times. In the first case, the transfer of a book search from one dealer to another becomes automatic and can be done by a clerk. Lists that have been through one or two dealers should have new titles added to them, otherwise the later dealers may be working only on the most difficult-to-find titles, with the result that enthusiasm and consequent performance may decline.

Most libraries require quotations or offers before they can place a firm order for a book. Under a modification of the practice, which is coming into acceptance, a dealer is authorized to send anything on a library's list that costs under a specified amount per volume. For instance, a library may tell a dealer to ship and send a bill for any title on the list that will be priced at ten dollars or less per volume, twenty-five dollars from foreign dealers, and quote on items costing more. This saves paperwork for both the library and the dealer and gives the dealer even greater confidence of a guaranteed sale. Some libraries make a similar arrangement, agreeing to accept without quotation any book costing a set amount over the original list price. This has the advantage of keeping prices in proportion to value, but does not consider variations in scarcity and requires the library to search out the original list price, an extra step in many cases. Dealers like these kinds of arrangements and many of them perform very well on them.

Lists of desiderata should be in fields in which the dealer can do a good job. Subject or language specialties should dominate list-making, but astute acquisitions people can provoke dealer effort with subtler listings that they know speak directly to a dealer's interest, stock, and contacts.

If they are to make informed decisions when they select dealers, libraries must evaluate dealer performance and prices. A record should be kept for each list submitted to a dealer. It should show the percentage of titles offered, the time required before the offers were made, and the average price per volume. The result will be information such as "on music books Dealer A delivers more books in three months than Dealer B, but Dealer B's prices are lower." Such comparisons should be made fairly, and particular care should be taken that evaluations are not made on too small a sample of titles delivered. Critics of cold calculations of this nature should recall that such evaluations are superior to the subjective ones librarians tend to make.

ADVERTISING

Many librarians use advertising for all or part of their efforts in securing out-of-print books. Those who use it exclusively believe they reach the stocks of more dealers with advertisements and consequently get more books quickly than they would with other means. Advertised lists of books that are not highly specialized produce about a 50 percent return. The supporters of advertising also point out that library costs are lower because no time is spent checking catalogs against desiderata files or making up special lists, or corresponding with dealers. It is clear that advertising works well for some libraries; these appear to be small to medium-size libraries without large desiderata files or highly specialized needs; most of the books they want are in English. Critics of advertising say that the flood of quotes a library receives after each advertisement creates an in-house clerical burden that lessens the advantages of advertising. Larger libraries with large desiderata lists tend to use advertising only for books needed quickly or for titles they are unable to get elsewhere.

Two advertising media are available to librarians in the United States: *The Library Bookseller,* formerly called *TAAB,* and *AB Bookman's Weekly.* *The Library Bookseller* is exclusively an advertising service for libraries to which they must subscribe, as must the several hundred book dealers who quote on the library lists. Librarians pay for advertisements by the line in *AB Bookman's Weekly,* which is seen by more book dealers. Lists in *The Library Bookseller* cannot be very long or they are delayed for publication. It is often more productive to arrange lists by subject. In *The Library Bookseller* these special lists bring more quotations than miscellaneous lists, probably because the specialist dealer's attention is drawn to them.

Although libraries should wait to place orders after a reasonable number of dealers have had a chance to quote on an advertised list, they should not attempt to get the lowest possible price by waiting until all returns are in. If they wait too long many of the books on which there were early quotations will be gone. Quotes that should be accepted the day they are received include those from dealers known from experience to offer a good stock at reasonable prices, or from one who, as a result of his specialized stock and high turnover, may report uncommon titles as sold. The books not obtained from initial advertising may be held for readvertising at a later date, before going to a dealer or being considered for photocopying.

RARE BOOKS

The purchasing of rare books is outside the financial boundaries of many libraries, but even the smallest may seek out some rare items, especially materials on local history, local printings, or association items. They may also find it suitable and within selection policy and budget to buy early or fine printings, fine bindings, and illustrated editions for demonstration and exhibit to students and other library users. The special collection makes a library more visible to its potential users and to potential donors of gifts, and opens to both librarians and students the rich and stimulating world of rare book dealers and collectors.

Rare books are acquired by libraries in several ways other than direct purchase. Many rare acquisitions are identified by screening in the acquisitions department as purchases move through the receiving steps and gifts are sorted and considered for addition to the collections. It is here librarians find limited editions, important first editions, association copies, fine printing and binding and items that are rare by virtue of arbitrary publication date limits according to place of publication. The development of gifts is, of course, important in the acquisition of rare books. Collectors should be cultivated not only as potential donors of their collections but also with a view to purchasing their collections. The benefit gained from the work they have done in gathering their collections, probably when the items were easier to obtain, may be considerable.

Buying is done by selection from catalogs, at auction, through visits from dealers, and by visits to dealers by librarians. In contrast to general out-of-print buying, want lists are not often used because the percentage of positive responses from dealers would be very small. Books are usually ordered "on approval" to give the librarian an opportunity to confirm the dealer's description and to make sure there is no unintentional duplication of these, usually, expensive items. Items received "on approval" should either be paid for or returned promptly.

The bibliographic work done in acquiring rare books often must be in the hands of a skilled specialist because, in addition to a knowledge of the materials, the subject area, or languages, a knowledge of uncommon bibliographic tools is needed. In many cases, this work is done in the rare book or special collections department or in close coordination with members of that department.

The best way to learn about the fascinating world of rare books is through talking with dealers and collectors. Acquisitions librarians should seek every opportunity to know and work with good book dealers. Their knowledge of books and bibliography may be extensive and sound enough to be called scholarly.

AUCTIONS, BUYING TRIPS, AND COLLECTIONS

American libraries do not make extensive use of auctions for the acquisition of material. When they want to obtain books offered at auction they may appear at the auction and place their own bids, but most of the libraries who buy at auctions do so through book dealers. A dealer usually charges 10 percent for this service, a modest sum when it is understood that he puts just as much time and expertness into bidding on the books that the library does not obtain as he does on those on which it is high bidder. Determining the amount to be bid requires the assistance of a librarian or dealer who is thoroughly familiar with the material wanted. The auctioneer may be asked for his opinion on what a successful bid will be, but most librarians seek the advice of the book dealer and, together, they arrive at the top sum the library is willing to pay for a book or a lot of books.

The value of sending staff members on buying trips for obtaining out-of-print books is about the same as that of buying trips for books abroad. Negotiations to purchase out-of-print books can be made more successfully and cheaply by mail than in person. A buying trip can have the distinct advantage of bringing the librarian and book dealer to a closer understanding of each other's needs and methods of operation, resulting in the establishment of a mutually beneficial business relationship.

Purchases of collections of books have been an interesting and important feature of library acquisitions in the past fifteen years. Older libraries have been enriched and new libraries launched by the purchase of private libraries, collections of books brought together by book dealers, or complete bookstores. These are not, however, everyday functions of an acquisitions department. The initiative for these purchases may come from librarians, but it usually comes from the book dealer who seeks out the library for whom his collection may be appropriate.

A librarian concerned with out-of-print acquisitions will want to read at least the nonadvertising material in each issue of the *AB Bookman's Weekly* and the *AB Bookman's Yearbook*. He will also want to be aware of the activities of the Antiquarian Booksellers Association of America and the International League of Antiquarian Booksellers. One of the most important resources for acquisitions librarians is the exhaustive bibliography prepared by Felix Reichmann and appended to his article in *Library Trends* cited below.

REFERENCES

"The Antiquarian Book Trade in the Twentieth Century." In *AB Bookman's Yearbook,* 1969, pt. 2, p. 3–50. Newark: AB Bookman's Weekly, 1969.

Carter, John. "Book Auctions." *Library Trends* 9:471–82 (Apr. 1961).

Malkin, Sol M. "Organization and Structure of the American Antiquarian Book Trade." *Library Trends* 9:483–92 (Apr. 1961).

———. "Some ABCs of Antiquarian Book Trade." *AB Bookman's Weekly* 49:351–58 (Jan. 31, 1972).

Mitchell, Betty J. "A Systematic Approach to Performance Evaluation of Out-of-Print Book Dealers: The San Fernando Valley State College Experience." *Library Resources & Technical Services* 15:215–22 (Spring 1971).

Peckham, Howard H. "The Acquisition of Rare Materials." In *Rare Book Collections,* ed. by H. R. Archer. p. 26–34. Chicago: American Library Assn., 1965.

Perez, Ernest R. "Acquisitions of Out-of-Print Materials." *Library Resources & Technical Services* 17:42–59 (Winter 1973).

Piekarski, Helen. "Acquisition of Out-of-Print Books for a University Library." *Canadian Library Journal* 26:346–52 (Sept.-Oct. 1969).

Reichmann, Felix. "The Purchase of Out-of-Print Material in American University Libraries." *Library Trends* 18:328–53 (Jan. 1970).

Smith, Eldred R. "Out-of-Print Book Searching." *College & Research Libraries* 29:303–9 (July 1968).

Treyz, Joseph H. "O.P. Market." *Choice* 2:283–85 (July-Aug. 1965).

Wing, Donald G., and Vosper, Robert. "The Antiquarian Bookmarket and the Acquisition of Rare Books." *Library Trends* 3:385–92 (Apr. 1955).

9

REPRINTS AND MICROPUBLISHING

Because of advances in technology and the need for materials that are out of print or are otherwise difficult or impossible to obtain, reprinting and micropublishing have become major parts of the information industry. Publishers have often reprinted their older publications when they believed the publications and the market were suitable, an aspect of regular commercial publishing that may be called "reissuing" to differentiate it from the new commercial group whose primary function in publishing is republishing or reprinting rather than original publication. Every form of material is being reprinted or republished in microform, including government documents, periodicals, newspapers, and books. The primary market for these republications is college and university libraries, with public libraries standing somewhat behind them. The great surge in republication is a direct response to needs for more research and educational materials and the funding that has been made available to meet these needs, frequently government funds.

Reprints and microforms have far-reaching significance. Items have been brought into print that were nearly impossible to obtain. Without giant advances in republication, the advancements in library support of higher education demanded by new colleges, new universities, and new programs could not have been achieved.

THE REPRINT TRADE

Reprinting is a new phenomenon made possible by innovations in offset printing. Small runs are now economically feasible. A typical short-run edition for a scholarly title is between 400 and 1,000 copies for a book and 200 and 400 for an issue of a periodical. Few reprint runs are under 200 copies, but it is possible to achieve economical re-publication with far fewer copies using microform enlargement publication. With only a few exceptions, a reprint is a facsimile of the original book or periodical. Anyone can be a reprinter: a commercial publisher, a bookstore, a library or any other facility with the will and means. There are somewhere between 250 and 300 reprint publishers in the United States. Many of the earliest firms in the reprinting business were dealers in out-of-print books and periodicals, and many of the titles identified as appropriate for reprinting came from the desiderata lists of these firm's clients. Although most of the titles reprinted are no longer under copyright, some reprinters seek out and pay royalties to holders of expired or foreign copyrights. The major contact of reprint publishers with their customers is through direct-mail advertising. The reprint business is now so well established that reprinting is being done for those reprints that have gone out of print.

Acquiring Reprints

The criticism most often made of the reprint publishing industry is its practice of announcing publications that are not published, announcing prospective publication dates that are not observed, and announcing publications that are never published. Some reprint publishers have even announced titles as "available" when they were not yet published. These announcements can cause serious inconvenience or problems for libraries. A library will stop searching on the out-of-print market for titles, losing opportunities to secure them, while publication of the reprint may be delayed for years or abandoned altogether. Clerical costs involved in identifying for claims, asking for reports, and shifting encumbrances become excessive for the items in question. Encumbrances are held, sometimes for years, and with increases in the prices of library materials, holding funds for several years may seriously reduce the number of purchases that ultimately can be made. A more severe problem faces the library that must either spend all of its budget before the end of a fiscal year or lose it to institutional or state general funds. Such a library can ill afford to encumber money for reprints that will not be delivered. It is legitimate for a publisher to test the market for a title to determine not only whether or not he should publish it but also what the size of the printing should be. He should, however, indicate that he will publish the title only if enough interest is shown, and he should announce his decision quickly.

There are no uniform practices in arranging the formats of reprints and some practices are bibliographically chaotic. In some cases the original title page of the work being reprinted is omitted or there is no statement identifying the original edition. For other reprints the original title is offered, but with no title page for the reprint or any substitute making it clear when, where, and by whom the reprint was made. Frequently, original series information is omitted, new series are created, and sometimes the two are mixed. Problems in cataloging caused by these and similar practices increase library costs significantly.

Although librarians are usually satisfied with unaltered reprints, specialists often criticize reprints that offer no new critical apparatus. For example, a biography originally published forty years ago may be out-of-date in both method and material, and in need of at least a new preface to place it in proper perspective. Books are reprinted that are not really worth reprinting; they may have been superseded by newer information or better titles and, in some cases, they may never have been worth acquiring. The wholesale reprinting of titles on standard lists, such as *Books for College Libraries* edited by Melvin J. Voigt and Joseph T. Treyz (American Library Assn., 1967), without regard to the short life of some books is deplorable. Similarly, the rush to reprint everything in areas in which a library's holdings may be deficient, such as black studies, sweeps into print some titles that are of little value. Reprints sometimes have been made of books that are still easily obtainable on the out-of-print market. Publishers should be faulted for reprinting works that do not need reprinting, but part of the blame must go to librarians who insist upon buying them.

Prices of Reprints

A reprint copy of a book usually will be cheaper than an out-of-print copy of the original publication, although there are stunning exceptions to this axiom. The chief criticism of reprints is that they are expensive, and when the prices of reprints are compared to those of original trade, technical, or text publications, most reprints are much more expensive. It should be remembered that the press run for a reprint is much smaller than that for an original publication and that the costs of publication spread over a run of 500 copies, typical of a scholarly reprint, will be more per page than costs spread over 5,000 or 25,000 copies of an original publication. It is not possible for reprinters to reduce the cost per title by producing more copies because there is no market for the extra copies. Prices of reprints are based upon the number of pages, halftones, fold-outs, royalties, and other considerations similar to price basing of original publications. Reprints usually are issued in good library bindings and some reprinters are using long-life paper. In addition, most reprinters base the price of a book upon their expected sales within the first year or two after republication; they cannot wait many years to realize a reasonable return. Cost-per-page comparisons between reprinters show variations of 100 percent or more and indicate that some reprinters operate more efficiently than others or are satisfied with lower profits.

Serials

Reprint publishing of periodicals and journals grew from the business of dealing in backfiles of serials. One of the ways in which serial reprinting differs from other reprinting is that frequently only those parts of a serial that are difficult to obtain are reprinted; an offering of a serial title may be both in the original publication and in reprint. Most periodicals and journals are "out-of-print" as soon as the current issues are mailed. A few publishers print more copies than they need for current sale and continue to sell them until the supply is exhausted, and some publishers of scholarly journals keep their titles in print indefinitely.

Sources

The bibliographic control of reprints is chaotic; it is very difficult to determine what titles have been reprinted and where they are available as there is no comprehensive list of reprints in print. *Books in Print* includes many reprint publishers and reprints are listed in other bibliographies of current publications. Special publications for reprints are changing as more satisfactory bibliographic control emerges. *Guide to Reprints* (NCR Microcard Editions), edited by Albert James Diaz, is an annual, cumulative in-print listing of reprints excluding paperbacks. It is complemented by *Announced Reprints* (NCR Microcard Editions, quarterly) and *Subject Guide to Microforms in Print* (NCR Microcard Editions, annual). *Reprints in Print-Serials* (Oceana) is updated by listings in *The Reprint Bulletin—Book Reviews* (Glanville), whose introductory material is worth watching for new information about reprinting. *Catalog of Reprints in Series* (Scarecrow) is a long-established tool of use for American publications. *Bibliographia anastatica* (Amsterdam, P. Schippers, 1964–) is a bimonthly with annual cumulations and cumulative indexing that is helpful in locating reprints outside the United States, as is Renate Ostwald *Nachdruckverzeichnis von Einzelwerken, Serien und Zeitschriften* (Wiesbaden, Günter Nobis, 1965, 1968). The national bibliographies list many reprints. A set of the catalogs of the reprint publishers is an important source of information, although use is frequently complicated by the practice of listing each other's publications without naming the republisher.

MICROPUBLISHING

The technological capability for microfilming has existed for more than a century, but the business of publishing in microform for library use was developed only in the last thirty years. Most publishing in microform is republishing rather than original publishing. There is, however, a growing body of original micropublications, particularly dissertations and research and technical reports, that were originally produced in only a few copies. Microforms are inexpensive, and when they are properly manufactured, they last a long time. The major problem with microforms in libraries is lack of user acceptance. This may be alleviated by the development of improved reading equipment.

A microform may be on transparent or opaque stock in one of many reduction ratios. Usually the ratio is about 1:15 or 1:20, extending up to 1:150 for newer forms. The kinds of microforms in common use in libraries at the present are microfilms in 35mm and 16mm reels; microfiche, transparencies usually 3-by-5 or 4-by-6 inches; and microopaques, including microcards at 3-by-5 inches and other micro-opaques at 6-by-6, 5-by-8, and 4-by-6 inches. Ultramicrofiche or ultrafiche is the same size as microfiche but the reduction ratio is 1:50 or more. Libraries usually purchase positive microfilm or fiche because it produces an image of black print on white ground on most microreaders. This conventional image is easier to read and is more acceptable to users than white on black. Until recently most enlarger-copying machines turned positive microforms into negatives when enlarged copies were made, but recently machines have been introduced that successfully print a positive copy from positive film.

There are many library uses for microforms. Most libraries prefer to keep backfiles of newspapers in microform because there is a significant saving in space and because most newspapers are printed on paper that has a very short life. Backfiles of periodicals usually are much cheaper to acquire in microform than in the original or reprint, and they require less space. However, if the space they use requires special filing cabinets, this expense may negate the savings in space. Many periodicals are available only in microform and for some the paper deterioration problem is so severe that most libraries do not want them in the original. Similarly, deteriorating books are microfilmed by and for research libraries where these books must be preserved. Government documents, theses, and dissertations are common holdings in microform, especially in academic and research libraries. There are many microform projects in which difficult-to-obtain materials are gathered by period or subject and are issued in microform over a number of years. Such projects account for large parts of the microform holdings of many libraries. The U.S. Government Printing Office is investigating the possibility of making all U.S. documents available in microform. The latest development in micropublishing is ultramicrofiche projects that promise to bring thousands of titles into libraries. Perhaps in time large parts of a library's noncurrent book collection will be in this form.

Some micropublishers also publish hardcover books as enlargements from their stores of microforms. These publications may be called reprints and some of the micropublishers are reprint publishers. Most, however, do what is best termed "demand" publishing; that is, they enlarge one copy of a book when a purchaser orders it. The economics are not the same as for regular reprint publishing, but the economics may make no difference for libraries, for if a book is cheaper as a demand reprint than as a regular reprint or an out-of-print copy and the quality of the copy is at least as good, a library should buy the demand publication.

Acquiring Micropublications

Micropublications usually are ordered directly from their publishers. The number of commercial houses is relatively small; their chief customers are libraries; and much of their contact with their customers is personal and through direct mail. Subscriptions are one of the chief ways of ordering microforms. These orders cover subscriptions to periodicals as they are published in microform and subscriptions to the large projects issued over periods of years. It is usually necessary to have a current subscription to a periodical in its original format before a microform subscription will be honored, but some journals are being issued in both forms and subscriptions are accepted for either or both.

Apart from commercial publishers, libraries are the main source of microforms. They are not purveyors of micropublications, but are holders of negative films a library wants copied or, more often, holders of original materials that a purchaser wants copied. If the owning library has a copying laboratory, the purchaser may want to have the material copied there. Also, the owning library may require that it be copied there. The *Directory of Institutional Photocopying,* which was last published in 1969 and will be retitled *Directory of Library Reprographic*

Services with the next edition, may be used to discover the copying services available in major libraries. If a library borrows material to be copied, it may have the work done in its own laboratory or send it to a commercial firm. The different sources will have different prices, and these should be taken into consideration. Permission to copy must be obtained from the lending library, and it should be understood that in some instances a library owning a desired book will not permit it to be copied. This may be because copying would damage the book or because the library wishes to preserve the unique character of its holdings. Buying microforms from other libraries is so often an aspect of interlibrary lending that the two foms in common use, the Interlibrary Loan Request form and the Library Photoduplication Order form may, in fact, be the order forms used rather than a library's forms for conventional acquisitions.

A method of acquisition of microforms that is sometimes proposed to libraries is the exchange of backfiles of serial sets for microforms. These offers come from commercial firms who may expect to use the backfiles to make the microform or to sell the backfiles to purchasers who prefer them to microforms. Exchanges of this kind may be legitimate, but there is a history of malpractice in this business that should be a warning to librarians to examine offers thoroughly. In particular, they should be sure that value to be received is equal to or greater than value of the material to be released, that the firm is able to perform as promised, that the procedures for exchange are consistent with good business practices for the library, and that there is no aspect of secrecy about the transaction. The Bookdealer-Library Relations Committee, a part of the Resources Section of ALA's Resources and Technical Services Division, stands ready to give libraries assistance in evaluating offers of exchanges.

The bibliographic control of microforms is no less chaotic than that of reprints. No single source prevails for identifying and locating microforms. The most used item is *Guide to Microforms in Print* (NCR Microcard Editions, annual), which lists serials and books from about fifty U.S. publishers; it is accompanied by *Subject Guide to Microforms in Print*. The *Union List of Microfilms* (J. W. Edwards, 1951), compiled by the Union Library Catalog of the Philadelphia Metropolitan Area, and its supplement (1961) list microfilms and the location of masters through 1959. *The National Register of Microform Masters,* compiled by the Library of Congress, began in 1966. It lists microforms of serials and monographs from which libraries may acquire prints and avoid the unnecessary duplication of making another master. Master microforms are those that may not be used by a reader, but are retained for the sole purpose of making other copies. *Newspapers on Microfilm,* also compiled by the Library of Congress, is revised and published periodically; it lists and locates U.S. and foreign newspapers. The catalogs of publishers of microforms also are important sources. The pursuit of materials that have not been copied to micro-images involves locating original publications, using standard tools such as the *National Union Catalog.*

REFERENCES

Diaz, Albert. "Microreproduction Information Sources." *Library Resources & Technical Services* 11:211–14 (Spring 1967).

Gerboth, Walter. "Criteria for Quality in Reprint Publications." *Notes* 26:718–19 (June 1970).

Gregory, Roma S. "Acquisition of Microforms." *Library Trends* 18:373–84 (Jan. 1970).

Hawken, William R. *Copying Methods Manual.* Chicago: American Library Assn., 1966. 375p. (Library Technology Publication no. 11)

Malkin, Sol M. "The Specialist Reprint Trade." In *AB Bookman's Yearbook, 1969,* pt. 1, p. 3–5. Newark: AB Bookman's Weekly, 1969.

Nemeyer, Carol. *Scholarly Reprint Publishing in the United States.* New York: Bowker, 1972. 262p.

"New Microfilms for Old Books." *American Libraries* 1:137 (Feb. 1970).

Reichmann, Felix. "Bibliographical Control of Reprints." *Library Resources & Technical Services* 11:415–35 (Fall 1967).

"Reprinting: Problems, Directions, Challenges." Articles by Connie R. Dunlap, Carol A. Nemeyer, Fred Rappaport, Daniel C. Garrett, Robert F. Asleson, Howard A. Sullivan, and Eleanor Devlin. *Library Resources & Technical Services* 15:34–75 (Winter 1971).

Sullivan, Robert C. "Microform Developments Related to Acquisitions." *College & Research Libraries* 34:16–28 (Jan. 1973).

Taggart, William R. "Blanket Approval Ordering." *Canadian Library Journal* 27:286–89 (July 1970).

Veaner, Allen B. "Micropublication." In *Advances in Librarianship,* ed. by Melvin J. Voigt. 2: 165–86. New York: Seminar Pr., 1971.

Wiggin, Lewis M. "Aspects of Reprinting." *Scholarly Publishing* 2:149–61 (Jan. 1971).

10

BUYING SERIALS

It is estimated that several hundred thousand serial titles are published each year throughout the world. The number of titles increases annually and prices have been rising for thirty-five years, with percentage increases in recent years that are far greater than the increases in the general cost of living. The percentage of the budget spent upon serials in many libraries has grown and caused the amount available for other library materials to be diminished.

The *A.L.A. Glossary of Library Terms* (American Library Assn., 1943) defines a serial as "A publication issued in successive parts, usually at regular intervals, and, as a rule, intended to be continued indefinitely." The *Anglo American Cataloging Rules* (1967) modified this definition by changing "usually at regular intervals" to "bearing numerical or chronological designations." A commonly accepted interpretation of serial publication divides them into two parts; periodicals, issued regularly and more often than annually; and serials, all other serial publications including annuals, proceedings and transactions of societies, monographs in series, service publications such as those of investment and business services, and others. This differentiation arises from several points, including methods of acquisition, recording, display, cataloging and service, and varies between libraries as well as between the offerings of serial vendors. The terms magazine, periodical, and journal are, essentially, interchangeable; magazines in public libraries are periodicals in college and university libraries. Journals are professional or scholarly (or both) periodicals.

In a discussion of serials and libraries it is well to remember that most periodicals and other serials are not published for the benefit of libraries. Even if all of the libraries in the United States and Canada have subscriptions to one of the major newsweeklies, their combined number would be an insignificant part of the periodical's multimillion-copy distribution. Most industry and product magazines are meant for special markets, not for libraries and, as a result, many of them are moving to controlled free distribution to guarantee their advertisers the value of each copy in the market they are reaching. Even scholarly journals, for which libraries may represent a large block of the subscription list, cast their appeal to the specialists who write for them. It is unrealistic for librarians to think they can exert an important influence upon most periodical publishers.

ALLOCATIONS

Many libraries provide for serial payments in a fund that is separate from book funds. Frequently there will be separate allocations for periodicals (subscriptions) and for other serials (standing orders or continuation orders). Other libraries charge all serial payments to departmental or divisional allocations. In an attempt to encourage careful use of funds and to control excessively rapid expansion of serial lists, without giving up indefinitely the benefits in bookkeeping that are realized with a single fund, departments are often charged only for the first year or two of subscription costs. The provision of funds for the purchase of backfiles follows similar lines except that, since the purchase usually requires large expenditures, departmental or divisional funds are frequently supplemented from general funds or large purchases are made from general funds.

SUBSCRIPTION AGENTS

Subscriptions differ from other library purchasing in that payments are made in advance. Instead of paying for an item that has been received and noted as satisfactory, the library pays for a promised publication or series of publications. Most subscriptions are placed through an agent rather than directly because far fewer transactions are involved; even a small list of one hundred periodical titles is far more economically handled by one order and invoice than by one hundred orders and invoices. At one time, subscription agents were able to offer discounts to libraries because they received discounts from publishers based upon mass buying. A small library with a limited list of easy-to-obtain titles or a library system with multiple copies of standard titles still may be able to get a discount, but most libraries now receive little or no discount and, instead, may pay a service or handling charge on their subscription lists. American agents offer comprehensive services to their customers. Some concentrate on domestic publications but several have extensive offerings of foreign titles as well. Some agents also accept standing orders for nonperiodical serials and some are book dealers and backfile dealers offering a complete service in printed library materials, both domestic and foreign. In recent years there have been many changes in the business of subscription agencies. Agents have merged and many have been purchased by large firms. These changes have not always led to improved service and librarians should be sure an agent can perform as promised before giving him a subscription list.

BIDS

Until a few years ago many libraries sent their subscription lists for bids each year or two years and placed their orders with the lowest bidders. Some did this because they thought it was a good thing to do but most did it because the institutions or agencies of which they were a part (governments, schools, industries) required bids on all purchases from coal to paper clips. Some still require bids, but most have recognized that the bid system for subscriptions as well as for books is not the best way of obtaining periodicals and may be more expensive than a noncompetitive purchase order. At the same time, many subscription agents are refusing to make bids. Ironically, the best-informed bidder is usually the highest bidder, for in periods of increasing prices he quotes the latest price and is underbid by his less informed and possibly less competent competitors. Bids are rarely firm; they almost inevitably carry escalator clauses to enable them to pass on price increases to the customer.

Bids do not take service into consideration. Accuracy, attention to detail, prompt response to inquiries, financial responsibility, knowledge of the market, and other factors are the elements of service that cannot be incorporated in a bid. A poor agent may let subscriptions lapse and may be unable or unwilling to supply difficult-to-obtain titles, even after he has bid on them. When a library changes subscription agents, careful planning must be done well in advance of the subscription renewal dates to prevent or minimize duplicate or missing issues. Most often, missing issues can be recovered only on the back-issue market or by photocopy.

This involves an extraordinary expense in staff time. Perhaps the most serious criticism of the bid system is the annual or biennial change in agents which it almost inevitably provokes. Libraries should purchase periodicals by bids only where they are required to do so, and then only after they have made every effort to make the agency requiring bids aware of the inadequacy for this kind of purchasing.

No library should abdicate its responsibility to get the best possible price and service on its subscriptions. Some libraries have been able to move from the bid system to a system of periodically sending their subscription lists to several agents for quotations. If an agent understands that the list will not necessarily be given to the lowest quoter, he may be willing to go to the substantial effort that is required to make a quotation on a long, complex list. More practically, a library might ask its agents to quote terms, such as average discount or service charge, rather than itemize the price to be charged for each title or compute a total charge for the list, subject, of course, to price increases. Service is best judged either by past experience or by getting evaluations from other libraries who are using the agents in question. It is always necessary to remember that some agents have preferred customers, a status based, usually, upon longevity and size of contract. Some libraries with long lists divide their subscriptions between two or more agents, thus giving them their own comparative study.

SUBSCRIPTION ORDERS

In placing subscriptions or renewing them, a number of practices are followed by libraries to assure good service and economical operation. It is to the library's advantage to receive from its agency only one subscription renewal invoice (unless the library requires billing by fund), which the agent should be able to do. The invoice should be in a rational order, usually alphabetical by title, to facilitate checking it against the library's records and posting renewal dates and prices. A library should not have to send the agent a list of its journals for renewal each year; this should be a function of the agent, and it is usually done by submitting the renewal invoice. To advance this method of renewal, libraries should place "until forbidden" orders, which means that when a new subscription is placed the library intends to continue the subscription indefinitely until it notifies the agent to cancel. The library, then, sends the agent a list of the subscriptions that are not to be renewed for the next year, rather than a list of those that are to be continued. "Until forbidden" orders permit the agent to renew a library's subscription without waiting for confirmation, and some agents pay for subscription renewals before they receive payments from their established customers. Of course, the "until forbidden" arrangement dictates that notices of nonrenewal from the library should be made well in advance of the renewal date. Major agents send renewal invoices to libraries about six months before the subscriptions require renewal.

Libraries will place new subscriptions each year and these should be incorporated in the annual invoicing by the agent. Most libraries want all of their subscriptions with agents to have a common expiration date and, within limits, agents are able to do this. The usual subscription period is the calendar year beginning January 1, but some periodicals are sold only by the school year or some other period. The agent can adjust his operations to accept renewals and payment for these subscriptions on a calendar-year basis, although the library may be paying for a subscription in the summer of one year that is not to be renewed until September of the following year. These aspects of a large subscription list make changing agents an action to be approached only with good cause and careful preparation.

New orders, whether to agents or to publishers, should be placed well in advance of the date the library wants to begin receiving the periodicals; establishing a subscription with a publisher may take several months for either the agent or the library and if, as is common, the publisher waits for payment before entering a subscription, it may take still longer to get the first issue of a periodical into the library. Orders to an agent or a publisher should state whether they are new or renewal orders, and if they are renewals should indicate how the subscription was placed, naming the agent if one was used. Orders should also identify copy numbers if the order is for an additional copy, to prevent a dealer or publisher from rejecting the order as a duplicate. Libraries placing new subscriptions should indicate the volume and number they expect the subscription to begin with. Some publishers accept subscriptions only for full volumes, a practice that usually is in keeping with library customs.

Librarians should understand that the operations of most subscription agents and many large publishers are computerized. The moves to computerization have provoked many problems. The plaintive or indignant letter of complaint may produce no results and telephone calls to the president of the firm may be fruitless. The library must write to the computer and in so doing use whatever codes the agent has used.

Libraries should, on their subscription order forms, indicate that they want title pages, indexes, and supplements. The agent or other source should be asked to quote prices if there is a charge for them.

LONG-TERM SUBSCRIPTIONS

Long-term periodical subscriptions can be advantageous to libraries. Some publishers offer special, reduced rates for two- and three-year subscriptions. Others accept multiple-year subscriptions without reductions. These also can save money because the staff does not have to process renewals every year. The library will save money if the price of a journal increases as the library already will have paid for the subscription at the lower rate. More than 15,000 periodicals offer three-year rates with savings of approximately 20 percent. Scholarly and professional journals do not usually have multi-year rates. Most periodicals for which payment can be made for more than one year are identified in the lists issued by most of the subscription agents. If a library chooses to use long-term periodical subscriptions, it will want to divide the subscriptions into three parts, with one part, or one-third, coming up for renewal each year rather than having the abnormally high subscription invoice that would result from having them all renewed in one year.

Getting started on a long-term subscription plan is the greatest hindrance to the plan because of the extra money it requires. If a library discovers it can place three-year subscriptions for 300 periodical titles and decides to place 100 of them in the first year, the extra cost for that year, at an average price of $10 per year, would be $2,000, which may be a difficult sum to find in a limited budget. The second year would require $1,000 extra allocation and the third and ensuing years would not require extra money.

First year	200 subscriptions at $10	$2,000
	100 subscriptions at 30	3,000
		$5,000
Second year	100 subscriptions at $10	$1,000
	100 subscriptions at 30	3,000
		$4,000
Third and later years	100 subscriptions at $30	$3,000

A good subscription agent will be able to arrange all of the details of long-term subscriptions, including this multi-year phasing.

PRESORTING PERIODICALS

The bulk of the flood of mail arriving in a medium-size or large library consists of issues of periodicals. Some libraries achieve some degree of presorting of their periodical subscriptions by giving their agents and other sources coded addresses for their mailings. This code might be as simple as using the word "Periodicals." A library may use a code that appears on each mailing label to enable staff in the library's mail room to separate periodicals from other mail and send them directly to the periodicals recording file without opening them and without delay. Another library may use several codes to help its mail room send periodicals directly to divisional or departmental libraries. Sometimes local postal arrangements are such that mail is delivered directly from the post office to more than one library location; then coding may be used to get periodicals to their proper place without a library mail room sorting. Some large libraries have engaged post office boxes to achieve this presorting. This decision is made after an analysis establishes that rental of the boxes and mail pick-up by the library from the post office is less expensive than sorting in the library. Two notes of caution must be made: first, mass-volume mailers already may have so many codes on periodical mailing labels that the library's may not be distinctive, and, second, libraries should be careful not to use addresses that are long or they will find them abbreviated or condensed, with their coding lost or undecipherable.

PURCHASING FOREIGN SERIALS

Libraries with sizable lists of periodicals published outside the United States may wish to buy them abroad. There are many reliable agents in England and on the Continent, some of whom deal primarily in the subscriptions of their own country or languages. Others act as regional or international agents. They usually give excellent service. Foreign agents rarely offer discounts, so price comparisons must be made on the bases of the rate of exchange the agent uses and whether or not he charges for packing and shipping or mailing to the library. Outside

Europe there are only a few good agents, and libraries frequently rely on importers or regional agents who offer the publications of many countries. Larger libraries or those with area specialties probably will be most satisfied when they deal directly with agents supplying publications of their own countries. Most agents correspond in English and can prepare invoices in U.S. dollars. Working with agents is the same as working with domestic suppliers: they should receive complete bibliographic data along with ordering instructions, including the date a subscription is to begin, whether or not it is a renewal, whether it is a new subscription or a transfer from another vendor, and the subscription period. Agents can be located through *International Subscription Agents; an Annotated Directory* prepared by a joint committee of the Acquisitions and Serials sections of ALA's Resources and Technical Services Division. Many foreign periodicals are obtained by participating libraries through the several international cooperative acquisitions plans.

DIRECT SUBSCRIPTIONS

Even the smallest library will have subscriptions that cannot be obtained through an agent and must be ordered directly from the publisher. These may be the local newspaper and the journal of the local historical society. Many small publishers of magazines and some large ones do not accept subscriptions through agents and some agents are unable to obtain the publications of some publishers. Libraries sometimes prefer to deal directly with publishers when this appears to be to their advantage. Libraries often deal directly with firms that publish many journal titles, such as the University of Chicago Press; a dozen large publishers account for several hundred titles. Some libraries place orders directly with publishers to avoid the service charges of an agent, but before a library extends this practice very far it should be sure that the amount of money it is spending for staff on separate renewal orders and invoices is not greater than an agent's service charge. Some journals are available only on membership and many memberships are best handled directly rather than through an agent. Some publishers handle them only in this manner. "Little" magazines and the products of the underground press frequently must be obtained directly. Some libraries use specialist book stores for these materials.

Libraries have to keep special follow-up renewal files on direct subscriptions until they are sure the publisher will renew and bill. Publishers often treat libraries in the same way as they do private subscribers, that is, they insert renewal notices in issues of a magazine, where the periodicals recording clerk may not see them. The best practice with direct subscriptions to publishers is for the library to send a request for a renewal invoice well in advance of expiration. New orders placed directly should be accompanied by payment. Among the most difficult publishers for libraries to work with are the publishers of most daily newspapers. Not only do they not send renewal notices by they also do not send invoices when the library requests them. Libraries are such an insignificant part of their business it is necessary for the library to behave like a regular reader. That is, look up the price on the masthead and send a check along with a statement of the period to be covered.

STANDING ORDERS

Nonperiodical serials also differ from other library purchasing when they are purchased as series rather than as monographs. Libraries call these standing orders or continuations. Their acquisition differs from periodicals in that they usually are paid for issue by issue rather than by advance subscription, although there are important exceptions to this practice. Some subscription agents handle standing orders. They may also be purchased through the wholesalers or jobbers who handle books or ordered directly from the publisher. Purchasing is usually more satisfactory if it is done through firms that handle monographs rather than subscription agents. Success in obtaining parts of standing orders from these sources varies greatly and can only be known through trial or by recommendation of other libraries. The best chance of success will be found with agents who specialize in and invite standing orders. Publishers may maintain standing orders satisfactorily, but a library should not depend upon this and should be prepared to follow up with claims on publisher standing orders.

Because standing-order serials are almost always irregularly published, it is difficult to know when to claim them. Important promptings for claiming come from the appearance or notice of publication of a part of a series in bibliographies, journals, and catalogs. Standing orders for series published outside the United States may be placed with importers or with foreign firms. These are the same firms that handle books and subscriptions. Again, good results can be expected in Europe and less satisfactory results throughout most of the rest of the world.

MISSING AND BACK ISSUES

Claims

An important part of the acquisition of serials is claiming missing issues of periodicals. Checking or holding records must be set up in a way that will permit systematic claiming of periodicals. It is important to claim a missing issue while it is still available, but it is also important not to waste time in the library and the publishing office with claims sent before an issue is published. The library should know when to expect receipt of a periodical. This record is sometimes made by entering the date of receipt on the checking or holdings record, but this is a time-consuming practice. Nearly the same record can be kept by date-stamping issues of the journal, using the same stamp as is used for an ownership mark, and by noting on the checking record chronic irregularities or delays in receipt. In this way, the person reading the checking record for claiming can see that a periodical is usually late or can check the date of receipt on the last issue to determine whether or not an issue should be claimed. Periodicals sent from outside America come in batches by sea mail, and their receipt can be expected to be somewhat irregular.

Claiming should be done before issues go out of print and for many popular magazines this is almost immediately after publication. Many weeks or months elapse before these mass-market magazines appear on the shelves of the used-magazine or back-issue dealers. Claims are sent to publishers if the subscriptions are placed with them, and many subscription agents have their customers claim directly from publishers except in the case of foreign periodicals, which are almost always claimed through the agent. Agents frequently supply special forms for this purpose, but some libraries prefer to use their own forms, which are specially designed to relate to their records, their systems, and frequencies of claiming. Many libraries find a multiple-copy claim form useful: one copy for the publisher as a claim, another for the serials holdings or checking record to show the claim was made, and a third for a follow-up or second claim. The forms have a place for the agent or publisher to report and they are returned to the library.

Missing Issues

When claims have been ineffectual, or issues have been stolen from the library, or are lost or mutilated, the process of hunting for missing issues begins. If an issue is stolen or lost, the library may try first to purchase it from the publisher and this is sometimes successful. Publishers of scholarly and professional journals may attempt to keep many or all of their backfiles in print. Because a library cannot know whether or not a publisher has a copy of the needed issue, a letter of inquiry is sent. Some libraries have adopted the practice of asking permission to make a photocopy of the issue in question if the publisher does not have it in print. A library may then proceed to make the copy or have one made. It may wait until other sources have been exhausted, treating photocopying as a last resort.

Another major source for missing issues is dealers who work exclusively in this area or offer it as part of their service. They buy and stock issues of periodicals that they believe they will sell to libraries. The list of these vendors is *International Directory of Back Issue Vendors,* compiled by F. John Neverman (2d ed.; Special Libraries Assn., 1968). It lists sources for magazines, newspapers, and government documents in North America, Europe, Asia, and South America. The pursuit of missing issues can be very time-consuming and expensive. Rather than trying dealer after dealer for these issues, many libraries stop after several sources have been contacted and make a photocopy or micro-image. Some librarians are convinced that it is cheaper to do this immediately, and, in addition, they provide better service to patrons by having the item available quickly. Under any of these circumstances, the library should expect to pay a price for a replacement issue that is far above the cost of the original issue.

Backfiles

The acquisition of backfiles of serials is as closely related to the purchase of out-of-print books as it is to subscriptions and standing orders. The vendors may be out-of-print and reprint dealers, or general suppliers who include subscriptions along with backfiles and other library materials. In searching for backfiles for purchase the librarian should inquire of the publisher to see if he maintains a stock, especially in the case of scholarly and professional journals. Frequently, current issues of the journal in question will list stock and prices for its backfiles. Dealers may be able to supply these journals at a lower price than the publishers, primarily because these backfiles are not scarce. Librarians can work with dealers through their catalogs or through direct correspondence. Librarians usually send requests for quotations to several dealers, although some libraries place their wants with only one dealer at a time, expecting that he will work harder to obtain a difficult-to-find set if he is confident of an immediate sale. Catalogs were once the chief source of information for libraries but the great growth of collections in the sixties has made many titles so scarce that they never appear in catalogs. In recent years backfile catalogs have tended to concentrate on reprints.

Many backfiles have been reprinted; they are usually on good paper with better potential for long life than the originals. Many sets that are offered to libraries are a mixture of reprints and the original edition, with the reprints filling in the scarcer portions of the set. Librarians should be sure that the paper in the original edition is satisfactory for library use.

Libraries also purchase many backfiles in microform, either to replace deteriorated volumes or to extend the resources of the library. Microforms usually are much cheaper than reprints or the original edition, and they are especially satisfactory for backfiles of journals that are not often referred to but are, nevertheless, important parts of research and academic collections. Microforms of newspapers are especially popular since they require much less space than the originals and are easier to move and use. In addition, unless a newspaper was printed on rag paper, its paper will deteriorate beyond use within a few years.

USBE

An important source for missing issues and backfiles is the United States Book Exchange. The USBE, according to its by-laws, is established for "the promotion of the distribution and interchange of books, periodicals, and other scholarly materials among libraries and other educational and learned institutions of the United States, and between them and libraries and institutions of other countries." Libraries pay for annual memberships in the USBE, for which they receive periodic lists of magazines and books that are available from the vast USBE stock and can submit requests for specific issues or runs of periodicals. Librarians from member libraries also may visit the USBE stacks in the Washington, D.C., area to select items. Fees for these services are assessed according to the type of publication and the type of order. A major benefit of the USBE to all libraries is as a source for missing issues. New or newly developing libraries use it as a source for sets of periodicals. The USBE is also an excellent place to send the duplicates that meet the requirements it has established to ensure it will not be inundated by materials.

AIDS IN ACQUIRING SERIALS

The American National Standards Institute has approved Standard Serial Numbering (ANSI Z39.9-1971). The task of assigning numbers has been undertaken with the collaboration of ANSI's Z39 Committee on Library Work, Documentation, and Related Publishing Practices; representatives of the leading serial subscription agencies; the Library of Congress; and the R. R. Bowker Company. Standard Serial Numbers have been approved by the International Organization for Standardization as International Standard Serial Numbers (ISSN). The Bowker Company will publish these serial numbers in *Ulrich's International Periodicals Directory* and *Irregular Serials & Annuals*. Standard serial numbers provide unique identification for each serial and help eliminate the difficulties that arise when different forms of entries are used. Some libraries expect to include ISSN designations as part of their address to be used on labels to speed the recording of serials.

When serials die they usually do so quietly rather than with the fanfare of *Saturday Evening Post* or *Look*. Smaller journals rarely send notice of their cessations. Often these are discovered only after repeated claiming. Records of new, discontinued, and changed titles for periodicals are published in *New Serial Titles,* the *Bulletin of Bibliography and Magazine Notes* (F. W. Faxon, quarterly), and the *Stechert-Hafner News* (Stechert-Hafner). Cessations are noted in each edition of *Ulrich's*.

Libraries frequently wish to review sample copies of periodicals before they decide to begin new subscriptions. Many publishers send sample copies upon request, others require payment. Most agents ask publishers to send sample copies to libraries. Sample copies of many new periodicals are widely distributed to libraries and some libraries build files of these samples in anticipation of the day they will need one of them for review for selection. Rather than maintain sample files, it is probably less expensive to discard sample copies of titles the library does not want to subscribe to immediately and purchase samples when they are to be reconsidered for subscriptions.

The bibliography of serials begins with *The Union List of Serials in the United States and Canada* (3d ed.; Wilson, 1966), which lists 156,449 titles that began prior to January 1, 1950, and were held by 956 libraries. This is updated by another great set, *New Serial Titles,* published by the Library of Congress, which provides bibliographical control of 165,000 serials that began publication after January 1, 1950. It is published in eight monthly issues cumulating, ultimately, into ten-year sets. The R. R. Bowker Company is publishing a cumulation covering the years 1950–70. These are aids both for verification and for location of copies. There are, also, many national and regional union lists and library lists of serials that can be important, as well as the standard national and trade bibliographies.

Other tools are used for serials acquisition to find such information as price, publisher, frequency of publication, where a title is indexed or abstracted, and how large a circulation it has. The lists published by the subscription agencies are important sources for this data. Among the better-known and most-used tools is *Ulrich's International Periodicals Directory* (Bowker, biennial), which lists 50,000 domestic and foreign periodicals that are currently being published. Its companion publication is *Irregular Serials and Annuals: An International Directory* (2d ed., 1972), which lists nonperiodical serials. Both of these tools list titles in subject classifications. Another tool is the *Standard Periodical Directory* (Oxbridge), which has more than 50,000 titles; the third edition appeared in 1970 and its supplement in 1972. *The Ayer Directory; Newspapers, Magazines, and Trade Publications* (Ayer Pr., annual) lists publications from the United States and Canada, arranged by place. Its coverage of newspapers is important.

Subject bibliographies of serials are also valuable in acquisitions work. *The World List of Social Science Periodicals* (UNESCO), published with new editions at intervals of several years, is illustrative of these. There are special bibliographies of proceedings and international congresses, identified in the standard reference sources, which aid libraries in locating addresses and give other information needed for purchasing. Several special bibliographies are invaluable for finding information about little magazines and underground newspapers; among them are the *Directory of Little Magazines and Small Presses* (Dust Books) and R. H. Muller and Theodore Spahn's *From Radical Left to Extreme Right* (Campus Publishers), both issued in new editions every few years. Identifying new periodical titles may be difficult. One helpful source is Bill Katz's column on magazines, which appears regularly in the *Library Journal*.

REFERENCES

Allen, Walter C. *Serial Publications in Large Libraries.* Champaign, Ill.: University of Illinois Graduate School of Library Science, 1971. 194p. (Allerton Park Institute no. 16)

Barry, James W. "A Study on Long Term Periodical Subscriptions." *Library Resources & Technical Services* 3:50–54 (Winter 1959).

Brown, Clara D. *Serials: Acquisitions and Maintenance*. Birmingham, Ala.: EBSCO Industries, 1972. 201p.

Clasquin, Frank F. "The Jobber's Side of Acquiring Periodicals." *RQ* 10:328–30 (Summer 1971).

Hamann, Edmund G. "Out-of-Print Periodicals: the United States Book Exchange as a Source of Supply." *Library Resources & Technical Services* 16:19–25 (Winter 1972).

Huff, William H. "Acquisition of Serial Publications." *Library Trends* 18:294–317 (Jan. 1970).

———. "Periodicals." *Library Trends* 15:398–419 (Jan. 1967).

LaHood, Charles G. "Newspapers: Directories, Indexes, and Union Lists." *Library Trends* 15:420–29 (Jan. 1967).

Osborn, Andrew D. *Serial Publications: Their Place and Treatment in Libraries*. 2d ed. Chicago: American Library Assn., 1973. 454p.

Smith, Katherine R. "Serials Agents/Serials Librarians." *Library Resources & Technical Services* 14:5–18 (Winter 1970).

Welch, Helen, and Tauber, Maurice F., eds. "Current Trends in U.S. Periodical Publishing." *Library Trends* 10:289–446 (Jan. 1962).

11

ACQUIRING SPECIAL TYPES OF MATERIALS

All library materials are special in one way or another, but there are important groups which, in terms of acquisition, stand outside the mainstream of books and periodicals. They are sometimes called non-book materials or multimedia. They are grouped here because their form or sources or distribution systems differ from books and periodicals. For the most part, their bibliographic controls are not as well organized as those for other library materials and their best or only acquisitions tools may be selection tools. These materials are films, film-strips, videotapes, sound recordings, music, pictures, pamphlets, maps, technical reports and paperback books. These materials do not require different systems for purchasing and accounting, but forms and methods may have to be adapted in some instances.

The assignment of the responsibility for acquiring these materials in each library depends upon the size and organization of the library. Frequently the acquisitions department enters late in the ordering sequence. This is because the preorder searching and the securing of enough information to permit placing an order has been done by a competent and interested staff member in the reference department or by an expert in a departmental or divisional library. In some libraries a specialist in the acquisitions department may handle all of the ordering, receiving, and precataloging for one or several of these forms of library materials, and participate in the selection process as well. For example, a library with a large budget for materials may have a specialist in the acquisitions department who is responsible for order work on music books, scores, and sound recordings. This may be part or possibly all of his or her assignment. Careful coordination between acquisitions and service or special materials units is necessary under any acquisitions arrangement to assure that there is no duplication of work, that orders

130

move ahead without delay, and that all acquisitions regulations are met. Budgetary control usually is retained in the acquisitions department to guarantee that allocation or budgetary policies, such as rates of expenditure, are observed and that there is no overexpenditure. When acquisitions work is done outside the acquisitions department, it is good practice to have it done under the general supervision of the head of the acquisitions department to be sure that the work done is consistent with the library's policies and practices and to give the special unit the advantages of the head's expertise in acquiring materials and managing acquisitions procedures. He or she usually will delegate most of the responsibility to the special unit.

AUDIOVISUAL MATERIALS

Keeping up with technology and bibliography for films, filmstrips, videotapes, slides, sound recordings, and other audiovisual materials requires constant attention to the literature, including the specialized literature outside the standard library journals. A good list of this literature is "Periodicals in the Educational Media—A Selected List," which is one chapter in *Guides to Educational Media,* by Margaret I. Rufsvold and Carolyn Guss (3d ed.; American Library Assn., 1971). This book is the best single guide for the librarian for audiovisual materials. Its main section is comparable to an annotated bibliography of bibliographies, although the unpretentious title is "Educational Media Catalogs and Lists Generally Available."

For most audiovisual materials there are no lists comparable to *Books in Print* that show what is available, and general bibliographic record of what has been published is uneven if not chaotic. Most audiovisual materials are purchased directly from the publisher or producer/distributor, and for this purpose libraries collect and keep files of their catalogs. Together they form an "in-print" record. Identifying producer/distributors and their addresses is assisted greatly by the *Audio Visual Market Place* (Bowker, annual). It is an essential tool for all libraries which buy these materials.

Other important general guides are the *National Information Center for Educational Media* indexes (Bowker and NICEM). These indexes to films, filmstrips, transparencies, and other audiovisual materials are prepared by the Center at the University of Southern California. The *Library Journal* annual buying guides are available in almost all libraries and can be useful. The *Educational Media Index* (McGraw Hill, 1964),

in 14 volumes, was an ambitious venture of interest to all libraries because it indexed educational materials of all levels, kindergarten through
college and adult education. It has not been continued. A long-established standard source is the "Blue Book of Audiovisual Materials,"
published annually in the July-August issue of *Educational Screen AV
Guide*.

Many of the most up-to-date lists are made for schools but public and
academic libraries will find some of these guides very helpful. In this
context, the educational media selection centers that are being established in metropolitan areas especially for schools may be found useful
by other types of libraries. Guides to free and inexpensive materials are
important to libraries. Among the best known are the several guides to
free materials that are published annually by the Educators Progress
Service at Randolph, Wisconsin.

The librarian can expect that it will cost more to acquire audiovisual
than print materials; there will be fewer items per purchase order because there are not many wholesalers supplying them, and libraries
usually must pay transportation costs. Some nonprint materials are sold
as multimedia kits, and some of them include equipment. These pose
special acquisitions problems because materials and equipment are
usually purchased from separate budgets by separate agencies and different suppliers. Some audiovisual materials are sold through local
franchises.

Films, Filmstrips, and Videotapes

The relatively high cost of 16mm films has forced most libraries into
systems of cooperative ownership or rental. Although large libraries and
library systems purchase films, most libraries depend upon centralized
collections of 16mm films, such as those at state library agencies or state
universities or they have formed or joined film circuits. Sometimes a
library uses a combination of these sources. Film circuits are cooperative ventures to which groups of libraries contribute money to purchase
and circulate 16mm films. More libraries own 8mm films because they
cost little more than books. Super 8mm films are becoming standard
library materials also. They have larger frames than standard 8mm films
but their width remains the same. Unfortunately, not all 8mm equipment
is compatible. Videotapes are standard materials in most academic
institutions, although the collections are usually tailored to local situations and may be very impermanent because of changing needs and,
until recently, the high cost of the raw tape. On the horizon for libraries

are videotape cassettes or cartridges that are used with a converter and shown on any standard television receiver. These cassettes will be inexpensive and easily stored. Libraries probably will lend them as they now lend phonograph records or books. Unfortunately, the many systems now coming into being are not compatible; each requires its own equipment. Filmstrips are still photographs placed on a continuous perforated strip on either 35mm or 16mm film. They may be accompanied by a script or by a recording or tape.

Film evaluation guides are primarily selection tools, but they are also acquisitions tools of some significance. Among the most often cited for 16mm films are the *EFLA Evaluations* (Educational Film Library Assn.), a current card service, cumulated in *Film Evaluation Guide 1946–64* and its supplements, and *Landers Film Reviews.* (Landers Associates, monthly). For 8mm films the *8mm Film Directory* (EFLA), edited by Grace Ann Kone, is important. *Film Library Quarterly* (Film Library Information Council) is of interest to libraries.

Files of producers' catalogs are of first importance for films, filmstrips, and videotapes. The *Audio Visual Market Place* lists producers of these and gives addresses and information about their products. Catalogs of film loan and rental collections should also be collected. Excellent film catalogs come from many of the large universities. A new publication is the *American Film Institute Catalog of Motion Pictures Produced in the United States* (Bowker) to be in 19 volumes. Each volume will cover a decade of feature films, short films, or newsreels. Other approaches to these materials are listed in Rufsvold and Guss's *Guides to Educational Media* noted above. The chief bibliography is *The Library of Congress Catalog: Films and Other Materials for Projection* (the subtitle before 1973 was *Motion Pictures and Filmstrips),* which began publication in 1953 and is now published quarterly with annual and quinquennial cumulations. It lists all motion pictures and filmstrips of educational value released in the United States or Canada and cataloged by LC. It includes addresses of producers and distributors. It includes some television and theatrical film added to LC's collections.

Sound Recordings

Sound recordings include discs and tapes. It appears that disc recording eventually will be replaced by tapes, especially by cassettes. For the present, discs still dominate the commercial market, but 8-track cartridge tape and cassette tape appear as alternatives for many new releases.

A basic bibliography for the support of acquisitions of sound recordings is the *Schwann Record and Tape Guide* (Schwann, monthly with supplements). It is the "recordings-in-print," but it does not include educational materials, recordings sold directly by the artist or ·those sold only on a subscription basis. The *Harrison Tape Catalog* (M. and N. Harrison, bimonthly), available in most record stores, lists 8-track, cassettes, and open-reel tapes. The catalog of the National Center for Audio Tapes at the University of Colorado (1970, supplement 1971) lists tapes that are primarily educational or instructional. The *Educators Guide to Free Tapes, Scripts and Transcriptions* (Educators Progress Service, annual) includes videotapes and discs. Many libraries maintain files of producers' catalogs, building them by writing directly to the producers in response to advertisements and to listings in audiovisual directories. The Music Library Association *Notes,* published quarterly at the School of Music of the University of Michigan, is an important source for current music bibliography, offering reviews, lists, and new releases for recordings. Its many advertisements are a mine of information about recordings and music. The *Library of Congress Catalog: Music and Phonorecords,* which began publication in 1953, is published semiannually with annual cumulations and quinquennial cumulations. It lists both musical and nonmusical phonorecords received by the Library.

Most libraries purchase commercial sound recordings through one of the nationally known jobbers, seeking the optimum combination of discount and service. Discounts may range from none on educational recordings to as high as 38 percent on standard commercial releases from some jobbers. The usual discount range for commercial recordings is from 25 percent to 33⅓ percent. A local dealer probably will be unable to offer as much discount as a jobber, but, just as with book purchases at local bookstores, libraries use good judgment if they do at least some of their purchasing locally. A friendly relationship may be valuable when a recording is needed quickly or when it is important to listen to a recording before purchase. Some manufacturers have standing-order plans that offer libraries substantial discounts. Write them directly for information or watch for their advertisements.

Purchase orders should include the manufacturer's number and the price as well as the name of the author, composer, or performer and the brief title. Many libraries find that filing outstanding orders by label (manufacturer) and the manufacturer's number is better in avoiding duplication than filing by author, composer, performer, and/or title. The possibility of error through choosing the wrong entry is less with the label/number filing than with the more conventional name and/or title.

MUSIC

The acquisition of books about music is not different from the acquisition of other books, although they frequently have duplicate bibliographical listing with music, and dealers specializing in music usually also specialize in books about music. The material that requires special acquisitions knowledge and handling is music itself. General libraries usually do not have orchestra and choral parts for performance; these are the stock of the libraries of music attached to choirs, orchestras, or other performing groups. General libraries acquire study scores in place of scores in parts. They also acquire other music, usually solo or duo, which is published only in one form. Larger libraries and special libraries also have the collected sets of composers' works. Smaller libraries may have no music beyond folk and children's song books, but many find use for miniature or pocket scores.

Preorder searching for music and music recordings requires an expertness that is best supplied by or developed in a person who knows both music and languages. Titles of works slip from one language to another; parts of large works have separate titles; works have more than one title; or a popular title is used in place of opus and number. A well-built catalog to a music collection should lead the searcher to the correct entry, but few catalogs can provide for all possibilities. Searchers should know when to be suspicious of the information on an order they are searching. As with other special materials, an acquisitions department in a large library may have a music specialist, but more frequently the specialist is in the reference department or in the music or fine arts division or department.

There are three principal sources for the purchase of music: the publisher, local music dealers, and general dealers or jobbers who specialize in music. The advertising section of the Music Library Association *Notes* has names, addresses, and offerings of many dealers. Orders for current materials are usually concentrated with a few dealers. Most music published outside the United States is imported and is available quickly and conveniently from domestic dealers, but libraries with large-volume purchases may work directly with European dealers and publishers. Discounts to libraries for in-print music are customary. For out-of-print music there is a large trade with specialist dealers in the United States and abroad, most of whom publish catalogs. Most of these dealers also handle music literature. A significant amount of music has been reprinted in recent years by both specialists in music and by some of the general reprint houses. There is no "books-in-print" for music; the closest thing to it is the library's collection of publishers' and dealers' catalogs. Having the library placed on mailing lists for in-print and out-of-print catalogs may be done by writing to advertisers in *Notes* and in the standard music journals.

For music bibliography, all music published in the United States and in foreign countries that is deposited for copyright is listed in the U.S. Copyright Office *Catalog of Copyright Entries: Music.* The *Library of Congress Catalog: Music and Phonorecords* contains listings of music, musical and nonmusical sound recordings, librettos, and books about music and musicians. It covers material received by Library of Congress and by other American libraries participating in its cooperative cataloging program. The *British Catalogue of Music* (Council of the British National Bibliography, annual) is also a list of music received for copyright.

PAMPHLETS

Pamphlets usually are destined for vertical files in service units of libraries. They receive this treatment because most of them are ephemeral and full cataloging for them is excessively expensive when they can be handled well in the vertical file. Some pamphlets, ephemeral or not, move to the vertical file because that is the most appropriate place for them, the place where the staff member or patron would expect to find them. Unfortunately, acquisition costs for pamphlets cannot be bypassed as can cataloging costs, and in some cases free or inexpensive pamphlets cost more to obtain than expensive sets of books. This is because they are difficult to identify or their publishers or vendors are hard to locate. Many pamphlets are as valuable to library patrons as important and expensive reference books, even though their life spans are short, and these pamphlets deserve as much acquisitions time and expense as is necessary to obtain them. However, librarians should guard against spending more time on acquisitions than a pamphlet is worth. Preorder searching to avoid duplicating a dollar pamphlet may be better left undone; the duplication is cheaper than the time spent searching.

The sources for pamphlet selection are almost endless and there are many guides to them including library periodicals and indexes, *Library Journal, Wilson Library Bulletin, Booklist,* Public Affairs Information Service *Bulletin,* and the *Vertical File Index* (Wilson, monthly). The publications of the Educators Progress Service and other guides to free and inexpensive material, many of them devoted to special subjects, are important to many libraries.

Orders for pamphlets and requests for free materials are usually made directly to the publisher or distributor. Although some priced pamphlets cost as much as books, most are inexpensive. Payment should accompany the library's order because the process of invoicing will cost several times the price of the pamphlet. Pamphlet jobbers supply priced pamphlets and some of them obtain free pamphlets for libraries but most of them must charge for this service if they are not to lose money. A jobber offers the advantage of billing and permits the library to avoid writing checks for small sums. Libraries with small staff may find the services of a jobber valuable.

Most pamphlets are free and are obtained by sending a form letter or form postcard. Generally, the postcard is superior because it is cheaper to prepare and mail, but a letter is more likely to be forwarded if an out-of-date or incorrect address has been used. A personal letter, not a form, may be desirable when making a special request or when writing to an agency that does little distribution by mail. Having the library placed on the mailing list for some publications may require a personal letter signed by the library director. Form letters and postcards, in addition to requesting specific publications, may carry a note asking the publisher to place the library on the mailing list for future publications as they are issued. When it is uncertain whether or not there is a charge for the publication, the letter or card may contain a line asking that the library be notified if there is charge before the publication is sent or, if the library has the fiscal freedom to do so, it may ask the publisher to ship the item and send an invoice or otherwise notify the library of the cost of the pamphlet. In this fashion an extra step will be eliminated because a follow-up order need not be sent and the receipt of the item will not be delayed. Of course, the library will want to have some confidence that it has requested an inexpensive pamphlet and not a highly priced book. Letter forms requesting free pamphlets may be sent with return address mailing labels to assist the sender and expedite the shipment. The labels can also be coded to note the location of an order record.

Order records for priced pamphlets are maintained in the same way as other order records, but there is some question of whether or not it is useful to maintain order records for free materials. There are two reasons for maintaining a file on outstanding orders. First, if requests for free materials are centralized in a medium-size or large library, but more than one vertical file is maintained (business and economics, travel, etc.), it will be necessary for the acquisitions department to have a record that will permit the forwarding of pamphlets received to the proper library unit. Second, duplication of requests to a publisher may be small in number and inconsequential to both the library and the publisher, but occasionally a publisher keeps extensive distribution files or sends out very few publications. He may reply with wounded dignity that the library already has received the piece in question. Where it is decided that it is necessary to keep a file of free pamphlets that are on order, it is probably best to arrange the file by source, that is, the place from which shipment is to be received, and then by title, as many pamphlets do not have personal authors and establishing their corporate authors before receipt is difficult to do and usually impossible to verify.

The solicitation of free pamphlet materials is done by the service units that maintain the vertical files in many libraries, bypassing the acquisitions unit. In libraries where there is more than one vertical file the distribution problem is solved by having the pamphlets addressed directly to the service unit. If selection of pamphlets is done in the service unit, there is good reason to question whether the step of notifying the acquisitions department which titles to request is necessary, since the service unit could address its request directly to the publisher or distributor. As with all such arrangements, care should be taken that library policy concerning gifts is sustained and that coordination with the gift unit in the acquisitions department (or whatever other gift mechanism there is in the library) is assured. When a service unit sends for free materials, it is especially useful to include a self-addressed mailing label with the request or order so that the materials will get delivered to the service unit and not to the acquisitions unit, where they may not be recognized.

ART PRINTS AND PICTURES

There are several valuable guides for the use of libraries where art prints are collected either for loan or for use as study prints. Margaret Bartran's *Guide to Color Reproductions* (2d ed.; Scarecrow, 1971) lists fine art reproductions that are in publishers' catalogs. UNESCO's *Catalogue of Colour Reproductions of Paintings,* published in two parts, by period, with illustrations, and frequently revised, constitutes an important listing. *Fine Arts Reproductions: Old and Modern Masters* (New York Graphic Society), revised every few years, lists and illustrates reproductions that are for sale. Other sale catalogs that may be useful are those from the William Penn Publishing Company, New York, and the catalog of Fratelli Alinari, Florence. All of these give information about the reproductions, including source and price. Catalogs of study prints may be obtained from producers listed in the *Audio Visual Market Place*.

Pictures are often available free or inexpensively from commercial organizations, government agencies, tourist agencies, and other groups. Plans are underway for a revised edition of *Picture Sources* (Special Libraries Assn. Picture Division), the standard bibliography. Also useful are the publications on picture and poster sources from Bruce Miller Publications, Riverside, California. Purchases will almost always be direct from the publisher; when this is a museum or government agency or society, payment should accompany orders.

MAPS

Since the beginning of World War II there has been a great increase in the number of maps published. In the United States about three-fourths of the maps are published by federal, state, and local agencies, the balance by about fifty commercial publishers.

Acquistions work for maps that are government publications begins with gifts, since many libraries are depositories for maps of one agency or another. Among the agencies producing maps that may be important to and available to libraries are the U.S. Geological Survey, the Coast and Geodetic Survey, the Naval Oceanographic Office, the Army Topographic Command, and the Corps of Engineers Lake Survey. It is necessary to write directly to these agencies for information about their maps. The *Monthly Catalog of United States Government Publications* is useful for finding map catalogs rather than for listings of maps.

For current purchasing it is necessary to work with the catalogs and price lists of commercial and government publishers and with sources that are meant primarily for selection, such as reviews and lists in the geographical journals, accession lists from map libraries, the catalogs of out-of-print dealers in maps, and special subject or area bibliographies of maps. The *Bulletin* of the Special Libraries Association Geography and Map Division lists new maps and is an important source of information about maps and their handling. Maps are listed in or as supplements to many national bibliographies, but the chief international work is the comprehensive listing of the *Bibliographie cartographique international* (Paris, Colin, annual), prepared by the Comité Nationale Française de Géographie and the International Geographical Union. Maps are slow to appear in this bibliography as well as in the national bibliographies. The *Catalog of Copyright Entries Maps and Atlases* from the U.S. Copyright Office, Library of Congress, is an important source for identifying new maps. A useful bibliography of map listings is in the article "Cartography" by Roman Drazniowsky in *Library Trends,* (15: 710–17 [Apr. 1967]).

Maps are usually ordered directly from their publishers. While order writing, bookkeeping, and ultimate approval of payments rests with the acquisitions department in most libraries, selection, verification and, upon receipt, identification are done by a person who is knowledgeable in maps. This may be a bibliographer in the acquisitions department, but it will more likely be a member of the staff that organizes and gives reference service on maps.

TECHNICAL REPORTS

Technical reports are publications of government, commercial, and academic laboratories that report research, usually in science and technology. The research and the reports are often government sponsored. These reports represent a large field of publication and their acquisition is necessary for many academic and special libraries. Their importance often arises from the fact that they can be published faster as separate publications than as articles in journals, although many of them later appear in journals, usually edited and shortened. While there are many titles published as technical reports, there are usually few copies of each and acquiring them may be a complex and frustrating task. Their distribution is often limited. Many are available free and some are deposited in selected libraries. Those that are widely available are usually priced. Technical reports are not available from the usual book and periodical sources. They are seldom indexed in the conventional bibliographical tools used for acquisitions, and there is no union list of library holdings.

Several federal government sources of information are important in identifying and acquiring technical reports. Chief among these are *Government Reports Announcements* and the accompanying *Government Reports Index.* These are publications of the U.S. Department of Commerce National Technical Information Service (NTIS). They announce research and development reports and technical publications, and items listed may be ordered from NTIS unless another source is indicated. NTIS was formerly the U.S. Clearinghouse for Federal Scientific and Technical Information (CFSTI) and the publications have a history of changes in scope and names extending back to World War II. The National Aeronautics and Space Administration's *Scientific and*

Technical Aerospace Reports (STAR), the Atomic Energy Commission's *Nuclear Science Abstracts,* and the American Institute of Aeronautics and Astronautics' *International Aerospace Abstracts* are important sources of information about technical reports. Availability and source are given in these abstracting services. The U.S. Office of Education has a clearinghouse system called ERIC (Educational Resources Information Center), which disseminates information about educational research materials, including instructions for ordering, in the publication *Research in Education,* often referred to as ERIC. In these services many titles are kept in print indefinitely through reproduction in paper copy or microform.

Although many reports that are not government-generated are included in the titles listed above, others are not. These are usually obtained directly from the corporation or institution publishing them or from the author. The acquisitions librarian may have, at best, only the information from a footnote as a request for an order. If it is unverifiable and a source cannot be found, the best action is to write directly to the publisher or author, using standard reference sources to find addresses. The acquisitions librarian should not overlook the resources of other libraries, especially those with strong technical reports collections or those specializing in areas covering that of an elusive title to be obtained. These resources usually can be tapped through interlibrary loan photocopy.

PAPERBACK BOOKS

Paperback books are not usually identified as special types of materials as described in this chapter. Their form differs only slightly from that of other books and their bibliographic control is the same or nearly the same. They are special types of materials because the means of distribution for most of them differs greatly from that of hardbound books. These are called mass-market paperbacks to differentiate them from the so-called quality paperbacks. The latter tend to come from publishers of hardbound books or from specialty houses like Dover. They usually cost more than $1.25, they are printed on longer lasting paper than mass-market paperbacks, and they have inner or gutter margins that are wide enough to permit their being placed in sewn library bindings. Most library purchasing of paperback books is of quality items, but enough instances of a need for mass-market titles occur to make their acquisition a matter of serious concern. Some titles are published only as mass-market paperbacks. Many books are available only in this form when the hardbound editions are out of print, making it necessary to buy paperbacks as replacements or added copies. Some titles appear first as paperbacks because production can be faster than for hardbound books and these may be items of great topical interest for libraries. Some libraries buy quantities of paperbacks instead of hardbound books under programs that provide multiple copies for wide or intensive use.

Mass-market paperbacks are either not available or not easily available in the regular purchasing channels used by libraries. Jobbers or wholesalers do not supply them. Their distribution is approximately the same as that given other items at newsstands. Distributors have large stocks of relatively few titles, no stocks of back titles, and no provision for single copy orders or, in most cases, for orders for specific titles.

Most libraries order mass-market paperbacks from special jobbers or distributors who offer the service of supplying single copies and are willing to send invoices. They are listed in the *American Book Trade Directory* (Bowker, biennial), and some advertise in the library periodicals. In ordering, they may request or require a minimum number of copies for one order. Packing, mailing, and invoicing one-copy orders costs more than the distributor's markup; he must lose money on such an order. Most paperbacks are published with numbers and the distributor maintains his stock in numerical order; it is helpful if libraries cite the number of each title when ordering. Paperback distributors do not offer discounts. In developing good relationships with distributors, libraries often send all of their orders for paperbacks to them, including multiple-copy orders. Mass-market paperbacks also may be ordered from publishers. Some of them will not honor single-copy orders, especially if the library requires invoicing; consequently it is customary when ordering single copies directly to send a money order or a check and some libraries include a sum for handling and mailing. Local bookstores also may be good sources for mass-market paperbacks.

The standard acquisitions tool is *Paperbound Books in Print* (Bowker, semiannual).

REFERENCES

Horn, Andrew H. "Special Materials and Services." *Library Trends* 4:119–212 (Oct. 1955).

Kujoth, Jean S. *Readings in Nonbook Librarianship*. Metuchen, N.J.: Scarecrow, 1968. 463p.

Audiovisual Materials

Anderson, H. V. *Audio-Visual Services in the Small Public Library*. Chicago: American Library Assn., 1969. 21p. (Small Library Project Pamphlet no. 17)

Guidelines for Audiovisual Materials and Services for Public Libraries. Chicago: American Library Assn., 1970. 33p.

Hicks, Warren B., and Tillin, Alma M. *Developing Multi-Media Libraries*. New York: Bowker, 1970. 199p.

Pearson, Mary D. *Recordings in the Public Library*. Chicago: American Library Assn., 1963. 153p.

Stone, C. Walter. "Library Uses of the New Media of Communication." *Library Trends* 16:274–82 (Oct. 1967).

Wittich, Walter A., and Schuller, Charles F. *Audiovisual Materials: Their Nature and Use*. 4th ed. New York: Harper, 1967. 554p.

Music

Bradley, Carol June. *Manual of Music Librarianship*. Ann Arbor: Music Library Assn., 1966. 140p.

Duckles, Vincent. "Music Literature, Music, and Sound Recordings." *Library Trends* 15:494–521 (Jan. 1967).

Krummel, Donald W. "Observations on Library Acquisitions of Music." *Notes* 23:5–16 (Sept. 1966).

McColvin, Lionel R., and Reeves, Harold. *Music Libraries,* rev. by Jack Dove. London: A. Deutsch, 1965. 2v.

Pamphlets

Miller, Shirley. *The Vertical File and Its Satellites*. Littleton, Colo.: Libraries Unlimited, 1971. 220p.

Wells, Dorothy. "Vertical File Sources." *RQ* 10:150–55 (Winter 1970).

Maps

Freedman, Frederick. "Perspective—Music Reprint Industry." *Choice* 6:977–85 (Oct. 1969).

Miller, Shirley. "Maps." In *The Vertical File and Its Satellites,* p. 132–56. Littleton, Colo.: Libraries Unlimited, 1971.

Stephenson, Richard W. "Published Sources of Information about Maps and Atlases." *Special Libraries* 61:87–98, 110–12 (Feb. 1970).

Technical Reports

Boylan, Nancy. "Technical Reports; Identification and Acquisition." *RQ* 10:18–21 (Fall 1970).

Gillies, Thomas D. "Document Serials, Technical Reports, and the National Bibliography." In *Serial Publications in Large Libraries,* ed. by Walter C. Allen, p. 146–60. Champaign, Ill.: University of Illinois Graduate School of Library Science, 1970. (Allerton Park Institute no. 16)

Houghton, Bernard. *Technical Information Sources.* 2d ed. Hamden, Conn.: Linnet Books & Clive Bingley, 1972. 119p.

12

ACQUIRING GOVERNMENT PUBLICATIONS

The acquisition of the publications of government offices offers special problems for acquisitions or documents librarians. A large percentage of the material published throughout the world emanates from local, state or provincial, national and international agencies and governments. Issuing bodies may change or regroup with no notice and little record. Their publications vanish or reappear with new titles and frequencies, making acquisitions as much a matter of fortune as of the application of specialized training, experience, and diligence. The publications themselves may merge and change character or coverage, sometimes with excellent effect, but usually provoking confusion for the user or the librarian. For acquisitions purposes some government publications are never "in print," because the complete stock is distributed upon publication. The report of a city treasurer may be published and distributed in thousands of copies to residents or taxpayers, with no extra copies retained for selling or giving to libraries. Other government publications were never intended for distribution, never seen by their originators as of interest beyond narrow agency confines, but librarians or researchers have learned of them, listed them, and become determined to acquire them. Many government publications are mimeographed or otherwise ephemeral in nature, but they may contain information important to library collections and patrons. These characteristics are more common to government publications than to commercial publications.

Government publications are only rarely available through regular commercial channels. Their bibliographic control usually is different from other publications and is almost always less satisfactory. Catalog entries for government publications are time-consuming to use because of the low incidence of attribution to personal authors and the high proportion of titles without unique or even uncommon features; the corporate entry is the norm for government publications. Training acquisitions staff to do bibliographic searching for government publications is more difficult than training for other searching. The "U.S." drawers in any card catalog of size are testimony to the skill required to find a government document. Many libraries catalog and classify government publications in ways different from the cataloging and classification given to other publications. This is particularly true for United States and United Nations publications, which are collected in depth by many North American libraries and which have their own classification schemes and published indexes. Where separate bibliographic treatment is used, acquisitions staff requires special training for preorder searching, unless it is done by documents specialists. Clearly, government publications present more complex problems for libraries than regular commercial publications and consequently are more expensive to acquire.

Those libraries with separate documents collections have staff members with expert knowledge. They may be part of the service staff or they may constitute a separate documents staff. Frequently in such libraries these specialized staff members do all or most of the work in acquiring government publications. They may send orders for the purchase of government publications to the acquisitions department, completely searched, with all of the information needed to place an order. In these cases the acquisitions department is required only to type and mail the order. They may work in a similar way with a gift and exchange unit, or they may bypass such a unit and work directly with gift sources. It sometimes is good practice to use the skills already held in a documents staff rather than duplicating them in the acquisitions department. On the other hand, where documents acquisitions is a large enterprise and especially where there is no separate documents service staff, the best use of staff may be in the provision of a documents specialist in the acquisitions department. Such a position requires, of course, careful coordination with other work being done with documents in the library.

U.S. GOVERNMENT PUBLICATIONS

The United States Government Printing Office (GPO) is the world's largest publisher, and approximately as much material is published by the United States government outside the GPO as in it. Acquiring a few or all of these publications is an important and usually demanding task for all libraries. More than one thousand United States libraries are depositories for U.S. government publications. Except for a limited number of regional depository libraries, all depository libraries select those publications they wish to receive rather than accept all of the publications from the GPO. Selections are made by series and groups of publications in advance of printing rather than title-by-title as they are published. In general, there may be two depository libraries in each congressional district, designated by the representative from the district, and two depositories designated by each senator. State libraries, the libraries of land-grant colleges and universities, the libraries of the independent agencies of the United States government, and of the major bureaus and divisions of departments and agencies of the government are depositories. Some congressional districts have more than two depository libraries because of redistricting, which occurs decennially. Once a depository library is designated it cannot lose its privilege unless it so chooses or goes out of existence. It can, however, be discontinued if it does not abide by the laws governing the depository program.

Libraries that are not depositories and depository libraries requiring more than one copy of a government publication may place orders through the Government Printing Office. The GPO does not ship and bill; payment in the form of a check or a money order must accompany orders for publications. Libraries may also purchase coupons in denominations of five cents from the GPO and send the correct total coupons equivalent to the price of the document they wish to purchase. They may establish a deposit account by sending money against which their purchases are charged. The minimum deposit is twenty-five dollars. Either method is especially suitable for libraries that have difficulties with payment-in-advance orders, and either works well for inexpensive publications when the business office is unable or unwilling to write checks for small sums, especially those under one dollar. Some government publications are sold by the issuing agency only. Selections made from the Superintendent of Documents biweekly *Selected United States Government Publications* and from the price lists give instructions on ordering. The chief source of information is the *Monthly Catalog of United States Government Publications,* published by the GPO, which gives symbols after entries noting the source for purchase, as well as giving complete instructions for purchasing documents. Orders that utilize the printed GPO order forms or order blanks in the *Monthly Catalog* or use the biweekly *Selected United States Government Publications* order form are processed more quickly than other orders. Libraries should use GPO catalog numbers with the complete title and price of each item. Orders for periodicals or subscription services should be submitted separately from orders for individual publications. Renewal notices are sent ninety days ahead of expiration, and prompt return of subscription payments is required if periodical receipt is to continue uninterrupted. Claims for missing issues should be made promptly since the GPO has a limited supply of back issues.

Documents also may be purchased from commercial services such as Bernan Associates. They accept standing orders, a service not available from the GPO, and their location in the Washington area, coupled with their special services for regular customers, makes them popular with many nondepository libraries as well as by depositories requiring duplicates.

Many free mailings of government publications are available to libraries, some from the GPO and others from departments and branches. There are some publications of general interest and value that come to libraries on special mailing lists but are not available as depository items. Some libraries obtain priced and unpriced publications through their congressmen. They would save time by corresponding directly with the issuing agency on free publications. Some priced publications are available from the agency without cost, because they have a special supply for free distribution. It may be less expensive in terms of library staff time to purchase all documents, rather than solicit them from several possible sources and end by having to purchase some of them, perhaps after their season of greatest demand has ended.

Problems in Larger Libraries

For larger libraries, the special problems relating to United States government publications concern the extent or completeness of their acquisitions. Most larger libraries are depositories but, as noted above, the Superintendent of Documents controls and distributes to depositories only a portion, perhaps half, of the publications of the United States government. The balance are outside his control; larger and specialized libraries must secure them outside the depository privilege. The 1962 revision of the depository law directed that non-GPO publications were to be included in depository distribution. Several steps have been made to meet this directive, but funding has not been adequate so that it stands essentially without implementation. The Documents Expediting Project, begun after World War II to secure foreign documents, has been working for subscribing libraries to secure nondepository publications that are also difficult or impossible to obtain from the issuing agencies. The project is now a part of the Federal Documents Section at the Library of Congress. Some federal agencies have created specialized depository systems outside that of the Superintendent of Documents, including the National Aeronautics and Space Administration and the Census Bureau.

The Readex Microprint Corporation offers microprint sets, by sub-scription, of all publications listed in the *Monthly Catalog*. These are offered in two series, depository and nondepository publications. The latter provides excellent coverage for libraries that must have most non-depository publications and the former permits libraries to discard little-used original publications in favor of the space-saving microform. The publications of many agencies are available on separate subscription, to meet the needs of special library collections that do not need all publications.

Not all government publications appear in the *Monthly Catalog*. The Library of Congress is designated to receive all government publications, and it now publishes *Non-GPO Imprints Received in the Library of Congress,* which lists many of the government publications that are printed outside the GPO and are not listed in the *Monthly Catalog*. Coverage of *Non-GPO Imprints* begins with 1967.

The GPO plans to make U.S. government documents available in microform for distribution to depository libraries. It is expected this will include all of the printed publications that are available to de-pository libraries.

Catalogs and Guides

There is no "books-in-print" for United States government publica-tions, but the GPO has in the planning stage a computer-based Publica-tions Availability File, which will serve inventory control functions at the GPO and will be for sale to libraries to assist them in determining what is available and to simplify ordering government publications.

The basic tool for current acquisitions purposes is the *Monthly Catalog of United States Government Publications* (GPO, monthly). It attempts to include all publications for sale by the Superintendent of Documents or available from the issuing agencies. It has monthly and annual indexes and decennial indexes for 1941–50 and 1951–60. There is a *Decennial Cumulative Personal Author Index to the Monthly Cata-log* for the years 1941–50 and 1951–60, supplemented by the *Quin-quennial Cumulative Personal Author Index* for 1961–65 and 1966–70 (Pierian Press).

Price lists are published and kept up-to-date by the GPO. They are arranged by subject and at any one time there are between fifty and eighty current ones. They are extremely useful in determining what is available but, taken together, they do not constitute a significant list of government publications in print. Price list number 36 is the useful "Government Periodicals and Subscription Services."

Several guides are very helpful in selecting and learning about U.S. documents and may be of assistance in establishing acquisitions information. Chief among these is John L. Andriot's *Guide to U.S. Government Serials and Periodicals* (Documents Index, annual with supplements). ·

A useful handbook is the *United States Government Organization Manual* (GPO, annual), which may be used in identifying agencies, changes in name and organization, and in finding addresses. Frequently, the best way to solve difficult acquisitions problems is to send a letter of inquiry to the Superintendent of Documents or the issuing agency. The answer will probably be cryptic, on a form letter, but this course will possibly be far easier and more successful than laboring through the labyrinth that can present itself when an elusive item must be identified and acquired.

Backfiles

Many important United States publications of the past have been reprinted or made available in microform. In some instances, more than one reprint or microform is available. The GPO reprints some documents but most reprinting is done by commercial publishers, especially reprint publishers. Where a title is available from more than one publisher or in more than one form, the acquisitions librarian should compare prices and other features such as paper and binding, ease of storage, convenience to the user. Some publishers announce reprint government publications under popular title or without reference to the original issuing body. One must assume this is done unintentionally but the effect for many librarians has been that they have purchased expensive sets that were already in the documents collections. Antiquarian and out-of-print book dealers also are an important source of backfiles and out-of-print titles.

STATE AND LOCAL DOCUMENTS

There are almost as many methods of issuing the publications of states as there are states. Obtaining information about these publications is difficult. The chief interest of most libraries is in the publications of their own state, and transferring this interest to actual acquisitions may require some skill and some trial and error. Many states issue checklists of their documents and many have a central agency for the distribution of some and occasionally all state publications. Most state publications are available free to the libraries in the state and frequently to libraries outside the state as well. When prices are given in the checklists, acquisitions librarians should send checks or money orders with their orders rather than expect shipment and invoicing. Once a library has been placed on a publications mailing list, it should maintain a special procedure for claiming them as lists may be considered temporary by some agencies or be subject to changes in budget support. The *Book of the States* (Council of State Governments, biennial) lists state officers and officials and is a good source for addresses. Manuals or bluebooks are published for most states and these are useful in identifying agencies that have publications and securing their addresses, as well as for basic information about the states themselves. *State Bluebooks and Reference Publications: A Selected Bibliography* (Council of State Governments, 1972) is a useful guide.

The principal bibliography is the Library of Congress' *Monthly Checklist of State Publications.* Important as this is and although its coverage increases each year, it is not complete. When the Library of Congress is recognized by all states as a depository for all of their publications, we may expect the *Monthly Checklist of State Publications* to be complete. Librarians also use the *National Union Catalog,* the Public Affairs Information Service *Bulletin,* and the *Legislative Research Checklist* (Council of State Governments, quarterly) for identification of state documents. The checklists from the states must be used if acquisitions are to be comprehensive. Some of them are inclusive bibliographies and others are incomplete or selective lists, while some states issue no lists. An extensive compilation of the activities of states relating to their publications is in the paper by James B. Childs cited in the references to this chapter. A useful current bibliographic guide is Peter Hernon's, also cited in the references.

The acquisition of local documents generally costs more in library staff time than the documents cost. Most of them are free, but to obtain them requires constant vigilance in discovering which city and county agencies have publications and in getting on and remaining on their mailing lists. Watching local newspapers is one of the best ways of learning of new local publications. Bibliographical coverage is extremely poor. Some of the best information has come from the lists published by the municipal reference libraries of some of the larger cities. *Notes,* published by the New York (City) Municipal Reference Library until 1971, was a useful tool. References in the Public Affairs Information Service *Bulletin,* and notices, reviews, and news notes in journals concerned with local government are also useful. *Index to Current Urban Documents* (Greenwood, quarterly with annual cumulations) attempts to index the publications of the larger cities and counties in the United States and offers for sale microfiche copies of the documents indexed.

FOREIGN DOCUMENTS

The acquisition of documents from outside the United States may require resourcefulness, skill, and determination. As with other documents, they may be ephemeral, go out of print quickly if not immediately upon publication, and be very difficult to identify bibliographically.

Many countries do not have the highly centralized control of document publication that the United States has. In some countries it is necessary to work directly with issuing offices which may be scattered throughout the government. Correspondence with these offices usually must be in the language of the country. Other countries have central government publishing offices. The documents of many countries may be obtained through commercial channels and the best course of action for most libraries is to seek to obtain documents through exporters and importers for trade books in the country in question. Most British documents, for instance, can be obtained through book and periodical exporters. In some cases, arrangements may be made to receive foreign documents on exchange.

The acquisition of foreign documents is generally a continuing action of large research and academic libraries and the people doing the work in these libraries are the best source of information about techniques of ordering.

UN DOCUMENTS

Acquisition of the publications of the United Nations and its related agencies each year ranges from the dozen or so titles from UN and UNESCO that will be in almost every library to the thousands that will be acquired by a research library with a special interest in international intergovernmental publications. The UN and its special agencies (UNESCO, ILO, WHO, FAO, and others) are independent of one another and they publish independently. A useful guide is *Publications of the United Nations System,* edited by Harry N. M. Winton (Bowker, 1972).

For material coming from the United Nations, "publications" are for public consumption and are offered for sale and "documents" are not intended for public use. The most popular UN publications are listed in the annual *United Nations Publications.* The United Nations also publishes, periodically, a reference catalog or books-in-print, which contains a more detailed listing of publications available as well as periodic checklists of newly issued publications. The bibliography of UN publications and documents is the *United Nations Documents Index,* issued eleven times a year with two annual cumulations, the *Cumulative Checklist,* and the *Cumulative Index.* This set, prepared at the United Nations Headquarters Library in New York, lists and indexes all publications and documents of the United Nations (except for restricted materials and internal papers) and all printed publications of the International Court of Justice. Until 1963 the *United Nations Documents Index* listed publications of the specialized agencies, FAO, WHO, IAEA, GATT, WMO, and the others. This listing was not complete. UN publications may be obtained from distributors around the world or from United Nations Publications, at the United Nations in New York. The tools listed above give instructions for placing orders.

UNESCO and the other specialized agencies have their own publications services or deal through distributors whose addresses may be obtained by writing to the agencies. Several agencies offer comprehensive lists of their publications and almost all agencies issue sales catalogs periodically. In 1973 the R. R. Bowker Company announced the introduction of *International Bibliography, Information, Documentation (IBID),* a quarterly that contains a bibliographic record for all priced publications of agencies within the UN system.

REFERENCES

Federal, State, and Local Documents

Boyd, Anne M. *United States Government Publications.* 3d ed. Revised by Rae Elizabeth Rips. Bronx, N.Y.: Wilson, 1949. 627p.

Brewster, John W. "To Catch a Government Document: Doc Ex." *Wilson Library Bulletin* 44:941, 943–46 (May 1970).

Childs, James B. "Bibliographic Control of Federal, State and Local Documents." *Library Trends* 15:6–26 (July 1966).

Darling, Rowland E. "The Government Bookstore." *Special Libraries* 62:8, 10–11 (Jan. 1971).

Free, Opal M. "Commercial Reprints of Federal Documents." *Special Libraries* 60:126–31 (Mar. 1969).

Gillies, Thomas D. "Document Serials, Technical Reports, and the National Bibliography." In *Serial Publications in Large Libraries,* ed. by Walter C. Allen, p. 146–60. Champaign, Ill.: University of Illinois Graduate School of Library Science, 1970. (Allerton Park Institute no. 16)

Hernon, Peter. "State Publications." *Library Journal* 97:1393–98 (Apr. 15, 1972).

Jackson, Ellen P. *A Manual for the Administration of the Federal Documents Collection in Libraries.* Chicago: American Library Assn., 1955. 108p.

Kling, Robert E. *The Government Printing Office.* New York: Praeger, 1970. 242p.

Locker, Bernard. "Expediting Acquisition of Government Documents." *Special Libraries* 62:9, 12–16 (Jan. 1971).

Paulson, Peter J. "Government Documents and Other Non-Trade Publications." *Library Trends* 18:363–72 (Jan. 1970).

Schmeckebier, Lawrence F., and Eastin, Roy B. *Government Publications and Their Use.* 2d rev. ed. Washington, D.C.: Brookings Institution, 1969. 502p.

Shaw, Thomas Shuler, ed. "Federal, State and Local Government Publications." *Library Trends* 15:3–194 (July 1966).

United States. Congress. Joint Committee on Printing. *Government Depository Libraries: the Present Law Governing Designated Depository Libraries.* Revised Apr. 1970. Washington, D.C.: Gov. Printing Office, 1970. 41p.

Welsh, William J. "The Processing Department of the Library of Congress in 1970." *Library Resources & Technical Services* 15:191–214 (Spring 1971).

Wilcox, Jerome. *Manual on the Use of State Publications.* Chicago: American Library Assn., 1940. 342p.

Foreign Documents

Paulson, Peter J. "Government Publications and Other Non-trade Publications." *Library Trends* 18:363–72 (Jan. 1970).

Pemberton, John E. *British Official Publications.* Elmsford, N.Y.: Pergamon, 1971. 315p.

UN Documents

Brimmer, Brenda, and others. *A Guide to the Use of United Nations Documents.* Dobbs Ferry, N.Y.: Oceana, 1962. 272p.

Childs, James B. "Current Bibliographical Control of International Intergovernmental Documents." *Library Resources & Technical Services* 10:319–31 (Summer 1966).

Groesbeck, Joseph. "United Nations Documents and Their Accessibility." *Library Resources & Technical Services* 10:313–18 (Summer 1966).

13

GIFTS AND EXCHANGES

Acquiring materials for a library includes the selection, solicitation, and evaluation of gifts, and may include the establishment and maintenance of exchange agreements with other institutions.

GIFTS

The receipt and initial handling of gifts and the management of gift funds are seen as acquisitions operations in most libraries. Other units participate in gift selection and solicitation, and the arrangements for large and important gifts may be handled by the head of the library or its governing board or, in some cases, by someone outside the library such as a member of the faculty. For smooth functioning in a frequently sensitive area, policies for solicitation must be stated and understood and careful methods for the coordination of operations should be designed and observed. Solicitation may be done by service units or by the acquisitions unit; in either case each should inform the other of its action.

In smaller libraries, work with gifts is only one part of one position. In larger libraries it is a separate unit in acquisitions or closely related to it. Gift work is usually combined with exchange work to make a gift and exchange unit. The accounting for gift funds is normally done as part of the total acquisitions bookkeeping operations, but the gift unit may be responsible for the selection of materials to be purchased on gift funds. More frequently it is responsible for the maintenance of records showing what items have been purchased from each fund, to demonstrate that the fund is being used according to the wishes of its donor.

Selection

Basically, two kinds of materials are given to libraries: those solicited as specific titles and those offered as unsolicited items or collections. Work on the first kind, specific titles, is similar to work done for purchased acquisitions after selection. Searching is done to prevent unwanted duplication, to gather enough information to do the soliciting, and to establish the main entry where that is necessary. Many free items are destined for pamphlet collections and need not be given the full handling in the acquisitions department that is given to titles going into the cataloged collections. In many libraries the solicitation of pamphlet materials is done by the service unit where they will be housed, or the gift unit acts as a forwarder of requests submitted by the service unit, without searching and record-keeping. The acquisition of free pamphlet materials is discussed more fully in chapter 11, "Acquiring Special Types of Materials."

Libraries may gain greatly from gift collections, but several tests should be applied before a gift is accepted: Is the gift collection appropriate to the library collection; can the library handle it and, if necessary, keep it up-to-date; and can the library meet any special limitations that may be placed upon the processing, housing, or use of the collection? The question of what is appropriate does not have easy answers for any but the smallest libraries. Clearly, a library is unlikely to turn down the gift of a valuable rarity, even if it will only be used for exhibition and advancement of the prestige of the library. In some instances, a collection may not fall within the selection policy statement of a library but nevertheless should be accepted. For instance, a collection of specialized Victorian literature may not be within the collecting interests or curriculum of an academic institution, but it might be wise to accept it, with a view toward the future when it could be an important resource. It is possible that a good collection may generate an area for research that will be of value to an academic institution. On the other hand, libraries always should be alert to the possibility of redirecting gift offers to libraries where the materials could be more appropriately housed. For example, if a collection of materials on furniture design is offered to a library located within twenty miles of one of the best furniture design collections in the country, the offer should be redirected to the strong collection.

In considering the acceptance of a gift collection it should be decided whether or not the library can afford to catalog the collection in addition to its regular work load and give it shelf space. Most collections are not static and must grow with new materials as they are published or become available on the out-of-print market. Can the library allocate the money for this without sacrificing regular acquisitions? Sometimes the nature of gift materials requires special housing, and some gifts are made with special requirements for handling, including where or how they may be used. Every gift offer should be examined with great care to be sure that the library can manage it and that the investment in it will be commensurate with the value to be received from it.

Solicitation

A large percentage of most gift collections received in libraries are not used because they duplicate items already owned, are inappropriate to the collection, or are in poor condition. A library should accept gifts with the understanding that they will be used to the best advantage of the library, with the library exchanging, selling, or discarding unwanted material. The donor should be informed of this so there will be no mis-understandings, and it is good practice to have a printed statement that tactfully describes the conditions of gift acceptance to give prospective donors. There will, of course, be offers of rare or unusual items or important collections that should be accepted in toto, without qualifications.

The skills of gift solicitation are highly developed in many larger libraries and in certain special libraries. In these cases, knowledgeable staffs work continually to discover and acquire valuable collections and to maintain contact with prospective donors. In libraries with smaller potentials for large giving, the work with gifts and donors should nevertheless be done thoroughly and tactfully. Gift collections are very important in building library collections. Many great collections owe their greatness to their benefactors. Hence, the importance of nurturing the interests of collectors in a library should not be underestimated.

Gifts should always be acknowledged. A form letter or postcard is sufficient for most acknowledgments, especially to publishers of material offered for free distribution. Gifts of special value, including most donations from individuals, should be acknowledged with a personal letter signed by the head librarian. Most librarians working with gifts are aware that one small and possibly unimportant gift may mark the beginning of a relationship beneficial to the library collections, and at the same time aid the donor in finding a suitable repository for his collection or an object for his benevolence.

"Friends of the library" groups have been successful in many libraries in adding collections and funds. Friends groups require substantial investments of staff time if they are to be successful. The chief responsibility for the organization of these groups usually lies with the director of libraries or the head of the rare books or special collections unit.

Appraisals

Many donors of books and other library materials want to use their gifts as tax deductions. The library should not make appraisals, both because it is an interested party in the transaction and because it may not be able to provide the expert book price knowledge that is required. The Rare Books and Manuscripts Section of the Association of College and Research Libraries has prepared a statement of recommended library policy regarding appraisals. Included as Appendix A in this book, this statement reminds librarians that the best practice is to engage an independent appraiser and points out that the appraisal of a gift is the responsibility of the donor. The donor usually pays for the appraisal as it, too, is tax deductible.

In many instances appraisals are not practical, and the advice given to libraries and donors is a burden that may mean not getting a wanted gift collection. For example, for a standard collection of books that are unexceptional in monetary value but important to a library, the cost of the appraisal may be greater than the donor or the library can afford and in some cases may be greater than the value of the books. The usual practice is for libraries to assist the donor in finding prices for materials by using the standard bibliographies and dealers' catalogs. Donors may be referred to sources of prices, such as *American Book-Prices Current* (Columbia Univ. Pr., annual), *Bookman's Price Index* (Gale), *Bookman's Guide to Americana* (Scarecrow), and similar titles. The evaluation of many collections of materials that are not unusual can be assisted by reference to the original list price, using the *Cumulative Book Index, Books in Print,* and the other standard bibliographies that contain price information. Many colleges and universities have institution-wide policies on gift evaluations that the librarian must observe.

Librarians have sometimes found it useful to prepare and print a statement drawing attention to some of the facts of book values. A book is not valuable just because it is old. Condition, binding, edition, illustrations, and other details must be taken into consideration. Such a statement is offered to some prospective donors as well as to people who ask for assistance in evaluating their old books. The Antiquarian Booksellers Association of America has a useful leaflet entitled "Books and Values."

Records and Procedures

The library's outstanding-order/in-process file is one of the key instruments in record-keeping for gifts. When specific titles are solicited, records should be added to this file to avoid duplicating requests and to assist in moving materials to their proper destination when they are received. As noted earlier, some libraries handle pamphlets outside the regular acquisitions process, but others consider that centralization reduces handling and the possibilities of confusion and error. Those items from gift collections that are to be added to the library should be "carded" and filed in the outstanding-order/in-process file as quickly as possible after receipt to eliminate the possibility of purchasing an item that is already owned by the library. Gifts are processed after their receipt in much the same way as purchases, including searching to establish the main entry; ordering Library of Congress cards, if this is done; and precataloging, if this, too, is done in acquisitions. Some libraries "card" gift collections using their regular order forms and noting the titles as gifts; others have special forms for gift processing, similar to order forms. The use of multiple-copy forms can be as desirable for gifts as it is for purchases.

Periodicals should join purchased items in the serial check-in files and be handled in the same manner as other titles except that they may require different procedures for claiming missing issues. The claim form will be worded differently and the gift unit may wish to have claims routed through them or may establish special conditions for claiming some gifts where a routine claim might be inappropriate.

Donor records, arranged by donor name on cards or sheets, are used in gift operations to record what has been received from each donor. In the receipt of gift collections it is usually important to record each title and its disposal, that is, whether added to the library, sent for exchange or sale, or discarded.

EXCHANGES

The responsibility for the exchange of library materials is usually assigned to the acquisitions department as part of the same unit that handles gifts. In libraries where acquisitions and serials are in separate departments, exchanges may be a part of the serials department because most items of exchange received in larger libraries are serials. An exchange unit solicits exchanges with other institutions, obtains material to offer on exchange, and maintains appropriate records of exchanges, including claiming. The staff usually participates in the selection of items that the library wishes to receive on exchange, does the bibliographic searching necessary for the identification of exchange materials, and plans and organizes the work of exchange.

Even the smallest libraries may exchange materials, but the principal agents of exchange are university and special libraries, large public libraries, and scholarly societies. International exchanges dominate the literature of librarianship and comprise the bulk of the work in exchanges in large libraries. Domestic exchanges of scientific and technical publications and of duplicates are, however, of continuing importance. Many libraries have given up or substantially reduced their exchange programs because analyses of costs indicate that it is usually less expensive to buy books and serials than to obtain them on exchange. The costs in library staff time in correspondence, record keeping, and special handling may exceed regular acquisitions costs. At one time libraries, especially those in universities, were able to obtain without charge many of the university press or bureau or institute publications needed for exchanges. Now the trend is to charge the library for these publications. There remain, nevertheless, many materials published outside the United States that are available only by exchange. These are materials that never appear in the regular book trade or that appear in countries for which there is no book trade that is usable by American libraries. It is also desirable to exchange materials with institutions in countries from which, for monetary or political reasons, it is difficult to do importing.

Establishing Exchanges

The management of exchanges in most libraries must proceed from the needs of the institution, rather than from an altruistic desire to support the distribution of scholarly materials. The promotion of internationl understanding that might be a feature of the exchange of materials must depend largely upon work done through the national libraries and international exchange bureaus.

The selection of materials wanted on exchange is a simple extension of the selection policies and practices of a library; only titles that are appropriate to the collection should be obtained. While some of the items solicited on exchange may have originated with the faculty or librarians doing selection without regard to their source or means of acquisition, the practical reality is that exchange lists offered from other libraries are used for selection. That is, selection decisions are based upon availability. Great care must be taken that materials are not selected because they are free and that the selector remembers that it is probably cheaper and faster to buy the item in question than to ask for it on exchange.

Exchanges are usually made directly between individual institutions, but international exchange may be conducted indirectly through national exchange centers. Direct exchanges offer speed; indirect offer economy in negotiation and transportation. The majority of American libraries with international exchange operations conduct them directly.

The first step after selection in establishing exchanges is the identification of potential exchange partners. The UNESCO *Handbook on the International Exchange of Publications* (3d ed., 1964) is an important source. It is supplemented by the *UNESCO Bulletin for Libraries*. The *World of Learning* (London, Europa, annual), *Yearbook of International Organizations* (Brussels, Union of International Associations), *International Library Directory* (London, A. P. Wales), *World Guide to Libraries* (2d ed., 1968; distributed in the U.S. by Bowker), and other directories are important sources of identification of issuing bodies and their addresses. The UNESCO *Handbook* also contains extensive explanations and discussions of international exchanges. The usual procedure is to send an exploratory letter with a proposal and sample copies of items offered. The Committee on the Exchange of Publications of the International Federation of Library Associations has developed a standard multiple-copy form for the request for exchange publications. It provides space for response and copies for both the requestor and the responding agency.

Sources of Exchange Materials

American libraries may have three types of materials to offer for exchange: their own publications and publications of the institutions of which they are a part, surplus duplicates, and books specially purchased to give to the exchange partner. They may have a great variety of their own and institutional publications, extending from the library's bulletin, through university press publications, agricultural experiment station bulletins, and the reports of institutes and other units. Most university presses are now required to operate at a profit or, at least, without subsidization. Consequently, libraries usually buy press publications when they are used for exchanges. Sometimes special discounts or remainder offers are available from university presses. Libraries may also have to pay for publications from units other than the university press. Surplus duplicates are usually the parts of gift collections that are not added to the library but are appropriate for the holdings of other libraries. Offering them on exchange is one means of disposing of them with benefit to the libraries involved. Some libraries purchase books at the request of their exchange partners and forward them on exchange. They may do this because they do not have enough materials or appropriate materials to offer on exchange and they cannot get the materials they in turn want except through exchange.

Records

Libraries maintain records to determine that material is being received from an exchange partner and to see that value of the material being received is the same as the value of that sent. The simplest form of exchange is of journal titles on a one-for-one basis, a page-by-page basis, or price. Some foreign libraries require price equivalency in exchanges and some American libraries prefer to keep their records in this way, but piece-by-piece exchange is more common because it is less time-consuming. Of course, it is necessary to be sure that the pieces are roughly equivalent in size and importance, but elaborate record keeping is expensive and it is unlikely that exchanges can be exactly equivalent. Records are usually kept on file cards or in loose-leaf notebooks and should be free of excessive detail.

Duplicates Exchange

One way of disposing of duplicates is to offer them on exchange to other libraries. There are several national duplicates exchange groups to which libraries belong. They usually operate with lists of periodicals and books offered by participating libraries, with provisions to allow all participants a fair opportunity to secure the materials for the price of postage. The oldest of these is the one run by the Medical Library Association. There are several others operated cooperatively and successfully by special libraries. A general group is the Duplicates Exchange Union administered through a committee of the Serials Section of ALA's Resources and Technical Services Division. It is geared to the small college and public library that is trying to build up its collection, primarily, of domestic books and periodicals. The costs of listing, record keeping and searching offers against holdings for lacunae may be more than the cost of paying a dealer to search for items, especially for medium-size and large libraries. From time to time, libraries with similar collection needs have arranged for the exchange of duplicates on a regional basis, usually by metropolitan area or by state. In some of these there has been no preparation and exchange of lists; instead, a central deposit area is established where members can send appropriate duplicates and visit to select materials for their collections.

USBE

The United States Book Exchange is not an exchange organization but a membership group having as its primary function the supplying of back issues of periodicals, at cost, to member libraries. In addition, it is an excellent place for a library to send duplicates with the knowledge they will be available to other libraries at reasonable cost. The price of this reassurance is the USBE membership fee and shipping charges from the library to the USBE headquarters in the Washington, D.C., area.

REFERENCES

Archer, H. Richard. "Special Collections." *Library Trends* 18:354–62 (Jan. 1970).

Blake, Fay M. "Expanding Exchange Services." *College & Research Libraries* 24:53–56 (Jan. 1963).

Briggs, Donald R. "Gift Appraisal Policy in Large Research Libraries." *College & Research Libraries* 29:505–7 (Nov. 1968).

Edelstein, Jerome M. "On Disposal of Duplicates." In *AB Bookman's Yearbook 1968*, pt. 2, p. 6–7. Newark: AB Bookman's Weekly, 1968.

Lane, Alfred H. "Gifts and Exchanges: Practicalities and Problems." *Library Resources & Technical Services* 14:92–97 (Winter 1970).

Novak, Victor. "Let's Exchange Profitably." *Library Resources & Technical Services* 9:345–51 (Summer 1965).

Shinn, Isabella E. "Toward Uniformity in Exchange Communication." *Library Resources & Technical Services* 16:502–10 (Fall 1972).

Thompson, Donald E. "Exchanges." In *State of the Library Art*, ed. by Ralph R. Shaw, v.1, pt. 5, p. 545–92. New Brunswick, N.J.: Graduate School of Library Service, Rutgers—The State University, 1961.

―――. "Gifts." In *The State of the Library Art*, ed. by Ralph R. Shaw, v. 1, pt. 4, p. 529–44. New Brunswick, N.J.: Graduate School of Library Service, Rutgers—The State University, 1961.

UNESCO. *Handbook on the International Exchange of Publications*. 3d ed. Ed. and rev. by Gisela von Busse. New York: UNESCO, 1964. 767p.

14

ORDER ROUTINES

After the completion of preorder searching, including revision of the searcher's work if necessary, orders move through a series of steps that are similar in all libraries. Most variations arise from differences in size and type of library and from demands caused by extra-library factors, such as institutional purchasing requirements or computer capabilities. Some variations occur because there is no single best way to perform some tasks.

STEPS IN PLACING AND RECEIVING ORDERS

1. Designate the fund to which the order is to be charged and determine that there is sufficient money to permit placing the order. Fund designation is frequently done at the time the book is selected and the determination of the availability of money may precede book selection.

2. Select the vendor to whom the order will be sent.

3. Prepare the purchase order. Type multiple-copy order forms or make copies by Xerox or other copying methods, supplying all of the information necessary for good vendor performance as well as for effective library use. The typist works from the order request card or list that was used by the preorder searcher. In some libraries order typing is revised, although this can be defended usually only when a new typist is being trained or when a typist is preparing orders in a language with which he or she is unfamiliar.

4. Type the purchase requisition. Some institutional business procedures require the use of a purchase requisition that is used by all institutional units. It may be necessary to list each item being ordered

164

or it may be possible to attach copies of the multiple-copy order slips with a statement on the purchase requisition to the effect that the library is ordering the titles as listed and described on the attached order slips. Frequently, the defense for the use of the purchase requisition is that it states the conditions of order, including directions for delivery and billing. These conditions can be printed on the back or the front of multiple-copy order forms or a duplicated form letter or slip citing the conditions can be included with the order forms in each envelope mailed. Most libraries are now able to use a copy of the multiple-copy order form as an official purchase requisition, eliminating the duplicate typing and handling caused by the preparation of purchase requisitions.

5. Distribute copies of the multiple-copy order form.

6. Address, stuff, and mail envelopes to vendors. If it is necessary to use a purchase requisition, it is usually possible to design the form to make use of the typing of the vendor's name and address with a window envelope to avoid a second typing on the envelope. Labels or envelopes may be duplicated in quantity for vendors to whom a library sends many orders.

7. File copies of multiple-copy order forms. This is done in the file of outstanding orders, which usually is also a file of books in process of addition to the library. Copies may be put in other files in accordance with the needs of each library, usually including a copy for encumbering funds and often a copy for ordering printed catalog cards. Some libraries file copies of outstanding orders in the library's catalog with a clear notation that items are on order.

8. Encumber funds.

9. Receive materials. In many libraries, the acquisitions department receives all of the mail and shipments for the library; in others, the receiver may be the serials department, if there is one, since the largest part of any library's daily mail is issues of serials. The first step in receiving materials is sorting mail and shipments before opening. Many items can be sorted and sent to their destinations before opening, including most maps, audiovisual materials, United States government publications, many periodicals, and other items easily identified from their covers. Acquisitions items are opened and contents of packages are verified with their invoices or packing slips to be sure they are complete. If there is no invoice or packing slip with the shipment, it is common practice to save with the shipment the mailing label or envelope to assist in identifying the materials. It is usually helpful to arrange large shipments in the order of the invoice to facilitate checking in.

10. Check in materials at the outstanding-order/in-process file. The outstanding-order card is dated to show receipt or removed if the file

is exclusively for outstanding orders. The book and invoice are checked against the order to determine that the correct title was sent 'and that the conditions of sale were met, including price, discount if there is one, condition of the volume, library binding, and other details that may be appropriate. If there are obvious imperfections in a book, it should be noted for return to the vendor, but most libraries have discontinued the time-consuming practice of collating each volume. The price paid is recorded, usually on the order slip or another copy of the multiple-copy order to form a "permanent" record or to send instructions to such a record. During the checking-in process it may be discovered that the preorder searcher had incomplete or inaccurate information about a title and it may be necessary to re-search the title in the library's catalog to be sure it is not already in the collection.

11. Place ownership marks on the book. Most libraries do not stamp or otherwise mark books until they have passed through the outstanding-order file and it has been determined that the vendor has sent the correct book or, in some cases, that the library has ordered the right book. Books with ownership marks may not be returnable under some arrangements and their resale value is lessened.

12. Accession the book. Accession records have passed from use in most libraries and the shelflist or a file of copies of the multiple-copy order form are accepted as substitutes. Many libraries use the equivalent of an accession number by assigning unique order numbers to each title and copy purchased. This number is then recorded in each volume and in the shelflist or another permanent record. This unique number can be helpful when the collection is inventoried, in circulation when differentiation between books is a problem, and in leading auditors or others to the original order. Other libraries view the call number, including the copy number, as an adequate substitute for the accession number.

13. Forward the book for cataloging. Most processing procedures now include sending at least a copy of the multiple-copy order form with the book to the catalog department and many order departments forward an in-process slip showing where a title was searched and where it was verified before it was ordered.

14. Forward the invoice for payment. Either in the library or in the institution's business office or treasurer's office, invoices listing more than one item are checked to be sure additions and applications of discounts are done correctly. Approving invoices is easily done with a rubber stamp that has a place for the date of approval and signature of the library staff member who is responsible. If invoices are changed in any way, the changes should be perfectly clear to the vendor. Requesting a new invoice is sometimes done, but it delays payment and causes extra

work for the library; changing invoices should be done only if the vendor is to receive a copy of the invoice showing the changes along with the check. Some wholesalers issue blank credit memos to libraries, which the order librarian attaches to the appropriate invoices when changes are made.

15. Disencumber funds and enter price paid in the bookkeeping records.

16. Remove the order slip from the outstanding-order/in-process file upon notification from the catalog department that catalog cards have been filed in the library's catalog. This may be done by returning the copy of the multiple-copy order form or the in-process slip that was sent to the catalog department.

17. Notify the selector that the book he selected has been received and is ready for use. Notification of the selector is often the responsibility of a unit other than acquisitions, one further along in the line of processing.

18. Claim orders not received. This step should be necessary for only a few titles ordered. It may be done through routine review of the outstanding-order/in-process file or through maintenance and review of a separate file, arranged by dealer and/or by date of order.

PRINTED CATALOG CARDS

In many libraries the acquisitions department is responsible for identifying and acquiring printed catalog cards from the Library of Congress and the H. W. Wilson Company. The chief reason for this assignment is that information on card availability is frequently determined during the selection and preorder searching process, and, in the interests of having books available for use as quickly as possible after they are received, cards are ordered at the time books are ordered. Wilson cards are published for more than 3,000 titles of general interest to libraries each year. They are used by school libraries and many smaller public libraries. Cards are sold in sets and libraries determine their availability through lists sent to customers by the Wilson Company. Library of Congress cards are available for all titles cataloged by the Library. Card numbers appear in many standard selection tools used by libraries, in advertisements, in national and trade bibliographies, and in most trade books published in the United States. LC cards must be ordered on LC forms. They may be ordered citing the author and title of the book if the card number is not available, although cards ordered in this manner are more expensive. Full information should be sought from the Library of Congress Card Division.

Cataloging in Publication (CIP), an experimental program in co-operation with publishers begun in late 1971, provides LC cataloging information printed in the book in an attempt to reduce library process-ing costs and speed books to users. Libraries can make their own cards from this information or use it for temporary bibliographic controls while waiting for the arrival of printed cards. Some libraries subscribe to Library of Congress proof slips. They are distributed well ahead of issues of the *National Union Catalog*. They may be used for book selec-tion, in which case each slip may follow through the order process, pro-viding excellent information for preorder searching as well as the LC card number. They also may be filed in the processing department and copied for use in preparing catalog cards.

RECEIVING FOREIGN FREIGHT SHIPMENTS

Large shipments from foreign countries may be sent by sea freight rather than by sea mail. When this is done the dealer usually notifies the library, including the name of the ship, the port of arrival, and the date of arrival. The library then engages a customhouse broker to move the material through customs. Many institutions of which libraries are a part have established broker relationships for other kinds of shipments and these brokers can be used. Failing this, the "Yellow Pages" of the tele-phone directory in the port city will yield the names and addresses of brokers. Unless the broker is engaged well ahead of the time the ship-ment is due, the library will pay storage charges for each day the shipment is held.

RECORDS AND FILES

Order Records for Auditing

The library's parent body—whether a government, corporation, col-lege, or other institution—will have some provision for auditing opera-tions that are responsible for the expenditure or receipt of money. It is the responsibility of the comptroller or his counterpart in the parent body to approve library procedures that may be audited, including proper record keeping. A common audit procedure is to work from institutional payment records through invoices to purchase orders. This procedure requires the retention of library purchase orders well beyond the time they are directly useful in acquisitions. A less common, but more penetrating, audit works from payment or approved invoice records to the material. In this case the auditor requires the library to demonstrate that it has the materials paid for. Under this audit the shelflist and circulation records become important as a permanent file of orders. Special problems are posed by books that have been lost or stolen, or worn out and discarded, or are ephemeral in nature and do not have a useful life of more than a year or two. It may be necessary to keep special records on withdrawals, but libraries should not be expected to provide records indefinitely, and only for very short periods for ephemeral items like pamphlets, some technical reports, or books bought for reserve or other special use. In some cases, materials are just as expendable as pencils and paper. In the matter of audit the library should be expected to exercise reasonable guardianship without excessive record keeping.

File Organization and Management

The files maintained in the acquisitions department should be constantly reviewed to be sure they are needed. Before establishing files for special purposes librarians should view them critically to be sure that they are necessary and that their purpose could not be served as well by modifying existing files. Before beginning a new file its cost of maintenance should be determined and its worth to acquisitions operations should be weighed.

The mechanics of claiming may present an interesting exercise in cost comparisons. Some libraries arrange copies of their multiple-copy order forms in a separate file to facilitate claiming materials that are overdue. This file is basically arranged by date of order and may be refined in a variety of ways. It may be arranged by domestic and foreign orders or by dealer, and it may be expected to serve other purposes as well as claiming. Other libraries depend upon periodic routine reading of the outstanding-order file to identify orders that need claiming. The costs of maintaining the separate file can be calculated as can be the costs of reading the order file. The two should be compared and a decision made on costs alone if no other factors enter into the picture.

The order number file may be used as an example of difficult decision making, because its value cannot be weighed entirely in dollars and cents. Vendors sometimes write, "We have cancelled your order number

403121 because the book is out of print" or otherwise refer to an order number without referring to the author and title of the book (despite the library's admonition printed on the order to report only by author and title). When this problem occurs more than once, the reasonable reaction of the acquisitions staff is to begin a file of copies of the multiple-copy order form arranged by order number or by vendor and order number. Of course, a letter can be sent to the vendor asking for more information and it is probable that such letters would be far less expensive to prepare, send, and receive replies to than the maintenance of an order number file. Unfortunately, in most cases the vendor will not have kept a record of the order and will be unable to answer. The title in question will remain in the outstanding-order file until it is turned up in routine review for claiming, at which time it may be recognized or it may be claimed, a claim that is almost sure to bring the response that the vendor has no record of the library's order. The question, then, is whether or not the library can and should support a separate file or whether it might take the risk of not performing properly on needed items and not letting the selector know an item he may be expecting will not be arriving. The cost of maintaining the file is weighed against service. Most acquisitions librarians will choose the risk; perfect performance rarely lies within their grasp even under the best of circumstances.

In establishing files, skills required to maintain them should be taken into consideration. For example, a file arranged numerically rather than by author and title is less expensive to maintain because numerical filing can be done by unskilled staff while training is required for author-title filing. The only files that should be established and maintained are those that function, not those that are essentially defensive. Simple systems using minimum files and records are the most accurate and easiest to use.

Outstanding-Order/In-Process File

An acquisitions department may have files recording materials on order, materials received but not yet cataloged, and printed catalog cards waiting for books still on order. These can be combined into one file arranged alphabetically by author with a measurable reduction in the time required to maintain the files, as well as a reduction in time spent in preorder searching and in receiving materials. The searcher who is required to check both an on-order and an in-process file will spend more time and have more opportunity for error than if he searches a single in-process file, even though the combined file is larger and somewhat more complex than either of the separate files. Similarly, materials waiting for the receipt of the book can be kept in the in-process file if they are the right size or can be folded to the right size, obviating checking in two or more places during the receiving process. In some large libraries the outstanding-order/in-process file is arranged by title rather than by author because the experience of the order librarians is that it is easier to train nonprofessional assistants to search by title rather than by author and that author entries established before receipt of the item or cataloging are less apt to be accurate than titles.

Unwanted duplication will result unless the in-process file contains cards for out-of-print books for which a firm commitment has been made. This file includes books that have been ordered from dealers' catalogs and books on exclusive want lists for which the dealer may send titles without quoting the price. Cards for books on exclusive lists that require quotes probably should be filed in the in-process file in fairness to the dealer who is searching for them, but they should be marked to alert the preorder searcher to the circumstances so he will not pass over an item listed in an antiquarian catalog or offered by another dealer.

It is sometimes desirable to have separate in-process files for special types of materials. These include orders for nonbook materials like maps, which do not interfile easily with orders for books. They also include orders for pamphlets and similar ephemeral materials for which an acceptable main entry is impossible to establish before the piece is in hand. Caution must be maintained to be sure supplementary files are limited to only the necessary and most useful. Duplication of work as well as of materials is the inevitable result of proliferation of files.

Received-Order File

The maintenance of a file of orders received after the material has been fully cataloged is difficult to justify, especially as a holdings record. If the cataloging records, including the shelflist and the serial record, do not serve the purpose that is claimed for the file of received orders, either the records should be modified or the claim investigated. When for auditing or other purposes a library must keep a record of its orders, the most efficient way is to use a copy of the multiple-copy order form, possibly one that has also been used for another purpose, and arrange it by purchase order number. If the file cannot be discarded after a few years, it should be microfilmed to reduce the expense of storage.

Serials

Serial records also may be combined to effect economy of searching, filing, and receiving. One file can show current holdings, in the form of a current checking record for periodicals; backfiles; records of orders, payments, renewal dates, and other order information; and binding information. It may be possible to try to make a serial record do too many things, but the tendency is to proliferate rather than overload.

Invoices

A file of invoices that have been paid is usually maintained. The invoices show the institution's check number or other confirmation of payment and they are arranged by vendor. This file serves the purpose of determining whether invoices have been paid when claims are made by vendors and usually serves demands made for auditing. Whether or not this file is in the library is immaterial as long as the library has access to it. The usual practice is for the file to be under the care of the parent institution's business office or treasurer. The maintenance of duplicate invoice files in more than one place in an institution could only be defended by unusual circumstances.

Publishers' Catalogs

Acquisitions departments usually keep files of publishers' catalogs arranged by publisher. The *Publishers Trade List Annual* (Bowker, annual)'is used in place of most catalogs, but new catalogs appear after it is published. Furthermore, a few publishers are not represented there; some who are represented have lists of special materials, such as texts, that are not in their *PTLA* catalogs; some publishers' catalogs give more information; and foreign publishers are not included. Determining which of the many catalogs coming to the library should be saved and filed after they are reviewed by selection staff is a matter requiring some experience in preorder searching.

FORMS

Of the many forms in use in libraries, a large share are for acquisitions purposes. Their use is an important feature in saving time in repetitive, routine operations and in assuring that work is done accurately and as completely as necessary. Proper acquisitions management requires that forms be available for the operations where they are useful, as well as that forms continue to serve the purpose for which they were designed. It is a common occurrence that a form eventually assumes a life of its own after it is no longer needed. Conversely, a good form may not be used because the people doing the work do not understand what it was meant to accomplish or how it was meant to be used. The question of the introduction of new forms or the analysis of existing forms is greatly aided by flow charts showing what the forms do and where they go.

The design of forms can be handled by a perceptive acquisitions librarian who makes the effort to review the subject and its application to his or her situation. He can be aided greatly by representatives of the manufacturers of forms, not only for costing but also for design. Many small and medium-size libraries are served well by forms available from the library supply houses. Needs may be satisfied by standard forms or by the "custom" service some of them offer on forms. The major drawback of the forms offered by these suppliers is that they are designed to be acceptable to all potential buyers, with the result that they do not completely satisfy any. Typically, they provide spaces and names for far more information than any single library would or should want. Many libraries are well advised to use them with modifications because of the higher cost of specially designed forms ordered in small quantities. It is always important, however, to consider that staff cost in using an unsuitable standard form may be greater than the savings made by its use.

Whenever it is possible, a form should be made to serve more than one function. A form should ask only for information that is needed. Forms should be standard sizes to adapt to standard filing equipment (3-by-5, 4-by-6 inches, etc., or sizes that can be quickly folded to these sizes) and, as far as possible, make use of standard paper sizes for reasons of economy. The popularity of the 3-by-5-inch size in acquisitions work is due primarily to the close working relationship between acquisitions and cataloging, and the card catalog is almost universally made up of 3-by-5-inch cards. Forms that are to be typed should have spacing, both vertical and horizontal, that is, compatible with the spacing of the typewriters that will be used by those completing the form. Vertical alignment should be arranged so that a minimum number of settings of the tab stop are required. A typist should be able to use the form with his or her eyes on what is being copied, not on the form. Forms that are to be handwritten should provide enough space for normal writing. Forms should be arranged for easy use; if, for instance, information about a book is to be entered on a form, the information should be requested in the common bibliographical sequence of author, title, publisher, date, etc. This will be the sequence the person completing the form will probably have at hand and will be the sequence used by the preorder searcher and the order typist. There should be correlation between forms. A purchase order and request form should list information in the same order, information that is to be used by a dealer should be separated from information which is intended for internal use.

The appearance of a form is important not only in making it easy to use but in encouraging its proper use. It should be possible for the user to know immediately the purpose of a form: if a form is a purchase order this should be boldly stated, so that a book dealer will know immediately what he has in hand. If it is an order-request slip to be used by faculty it should say that it is a library order-request slip, not to be confused with textbook orders, and it should indicate clearly what is expected of the faculty member and its proper completion should not depend entirely upon reference to a faculty manual. Visual confusion is a frequently observed fault of forms, particularly small ones. A purchase order form available from one library supplier has 21 holes to fill, requiring the use of at least 8 tab stops on the typewriter. Forms should give prominence to what is being ordered, how many, and the name of the library doing the ordering. For library use forms should be designed so that prominence is given to the first filing word. The use of a complex form can be aided by using different type sizes and faces, different colored types, and lightly colored or shaded blocks.

The quality of paper used for each form should be commensurate with its intended use and life expectancy. Forms with several carbon copies will require the use of light-weight paper to assist in attaining a good typed image on the last copies. Whenever forms are to be mailed, consideration should be given to the design of the forms and the envelopes. All forms should be numbered to give them easy and unique identification, and it is desirable to date forms as part of their identification, especially where a new form is replacing an older form that should not be used.

Among the forms that are used in acquisitions are order requests, occasionally with different ones for use by library staff and nonstaff; processing slips, with separate designs for purchases, gifts and exchanges, or books, and continuations and other serials; purchase orders, sometimes with different ones for serials and audiovisual materials; forms for claiming unfilled orders, frequently a part of the multiple-copy order form or photocopied from one of the multiple-copy order slips; forms for bookkeeping, often a part of the multiple-copy order form; recording forms for standing orders, subscriptions, gifts and exchanges; forms for soliciting and acknowledging gifts and exchanges; statistical recording forms; forms for special instructions for handling materials, such as "rush processing" flyers to accompany books through processing; bookplates; and form letters for communicating with vendors, donors, patrons, and other people with whom the acquisitions unit works.

Order-Request Forms

The order-request form is filled out by the person selecting and requesting the purchase of a book or other material for the library. If it is to be used by members of the library staff, it can be a fairly simple form since the users can be expected to provide all of the information they have that will be useful in preorder searching and placing an order. Patrons, faculty members, students, and others using a request form usually need to be reminded of this information, and it is customary to provide titled spaces on the form for author, title, place, publisher, date of publication, price, series, and edition. Space for the name of the recommender should be included if he or she is to be notified of the status of the order request. It may be necessary to give the recommender instructions on how to use the form and how to route it to acquisitions and to inform him or her of what to expect from the acquisitions department or the library. This may be done by printing on the back of the order-request slip.

Many libraries provide a two-part order-request slip that permits the selector or recommender to keep a copy of his request, and some libraries provide a third copy for the use of departmental or divisional libraries. Space on the order-request slip is also needed for acquisitions department use. This includes space for assignment of the vendor, the order number, and special instructions to the typist. It also includes space for reports to the selector on the status of his request, such as whether or not the item is already in the library or on order, and out-of-print status or other reports on publication from the vendor. Since the order-request slip in acquisitions in many libraries ends its circuit as a notification to the selector that the item has been received, space is sometimes made for the classification number. The date the order request was received and the date the order was placed may be important information for management and space will be required for them.

Space for recording the steps taken in searching and information found and not found is usually provided on order-request slips. This ranges from a blank where the preorder searcher can write in his own information to comprehensive lists of symbols for library tools and bibliographies that the searcher checks to record his handling of the request slip. In some large libraries the order-request form serves also as a processing or precataloging slip that records information gathered throughout the acquisitions process to prevent duplication of effort in cataloging and speed books through processing. Clearly, no 3-by-5-inch slip or card, even when printed on both sides, can provide for all of this information. The first consideration should be given to deciding which information is needed and which may be left off the form. It should also be determined whether files and operations could be changed to accept a form larger than 3-by-5 inches, or whether order-request forms 5-by-6 or 3-by-10 inches that fold to fit 3-by-5-inch drawers could be used. Libraries using automated acquisitions systems have found that order-request forms printed on IBM cards can be used for filing in data-processing equipment, and the form, larger than the conventional 3-by-5 inches, provides the additional space that is often needed.

Multiple-Copy Order Forms

The order form most often used for purchasing library materials is the multiple-copy order form, which permits a single typing of order information to produce several or many copies for a variety of uses. Multiple-copy order forms may be carbon interleaved or use chemically treated carbonless paper. Each set of forms may be separate or may be held together in blocks of two or three or six, with perforations between the sets. Arranging them in blocks reduces handling during typing. Forms in continuous rolls are also available and these are especially desirable where a large amount of order typing is done as they further reduce handling during typing. To prevent slipping of the copies and unacceptable registration of typing on them, continuous forms are made with perforations for use with a pin-feeding mechanism that is attached to a typewriter. Although pin-feeding devices usually can be removed to permit use of the typewriter for other than multiple-copy order typing, removal tends to be time-consuming and libraries using continuous forms usually reserve one typewriter for this kind of typing. Order forms may be 3⅛-inches tall to assure they will be visible and not lost when placed in permanent files of 3-by-5-inch cards.

A multiple-copy order form may have as few as three parts: one for the vendor, one for the outstanding-order/in-process file, and one to use as a temporary slip in the library's catalog, or in a fund accounting file, or as a claim to the vendor. It is rumored that there are or have been multiple-copy order forms with as many as sixteen copies. A five- or six-part form seems to serve the needs of most libraries that find three copies insufficient. In a typical form in use in libraries, copy one is the purchase order to the vendor, copy two is for the vendor to return in the shipment or use as a report, copy three is for the outstanding-order/in-process file, copy four is for the fund accounting file, and copy five is a processing slip accompanying the book through cataloging. Copy five returns to clear the outstanding-order/in-process file and moves on to the selector to notify him the item has been cataloged. A sixth copy often used is the order slip for Library of Congress catalog cards described below. Other copies may be used for files arranged by order number or by vendor, for temporary records for the library's catalog or shelflist, or other uses in cataloging, and for notifying the selector that a book has been received but has not yet been cataloged.

Format. The format of the multiple-copy purchase order can be relatively simple because it is prepared by an acquisitions department typist who does not require the reminders necessary on forms being used by people outside of acquisitions. The chief feature will be as large a space as possible to permit typing the description of what is being ordered, including author, title, publisher, place (if important), date of publication, edition, series, translator, illustrator, and other details important in identifying a book or other library item and differentiating it from other editions. The name of the library should have a prominent place on the form. Its address should be prominent if the forms are to be sent to vendors without covering letters or purchase requisitions. The conditions of the order should be included if there is no covering document; they are frequently printed on the back of the slip that is sent to the vendor. Libraries are moving to simplification of instructions so that a slip sent to the vendor may need only the name and address of the library, identification as a purchase order, and a billing instruction, such as "invoice in duplicate." The form should give prominent attention to the number of copies being ordered.

Other spaces provided on the form are for the name of the vendor, the library's order number, the list or catalog price, and other data relevant to the order system. The latter might include the International Standard Book Number, the Library of Congress card number, the name of the requestor, and the fund to be charged. Space for use after the item is received may also be needed, including places for the price paid, the date received, and the classification number if slips are to be used for temporary records in cataloging or for notifying selectors of availability and location of items. To avoid confusion, information that is to be used for internal library use should be kept separate from information that is for the vendor. Information for internal use need not appear on the vendor's copy of a purchase order if partial carbons are used.

Each form in a multiple-copy order form set may have different printing to reflect its different purpose. For instance, on the slip that is returned to the selector might be printed "This title is ready for use and can be obtained from the library under the call number listed above." Special instructions or titling may be printed in differently colored inks. All such special printing adds to the cost of a form and may be an unsupportable extravagance for the smaller library, but the library using many thousands of copies of a form each year may find that the cost adds only a small fraction of a penny to each set and may be well worth the cost.

LC Cards. Until 1968, Library of Congress catalog card order slips were included in most multiple-copy order form sets. At that time the Library began using optical character-recognition equipment to mechanize the card-ordering procedure, and it now requires that orders for cards be on forms that meet its optical-scanning specifications. Single-part card order forms are provided free of charge. To obviate separate typings for book orders and card orders, it is possible to incorporate card order forms that meet LC's requirements into a multiple-copy order form. The arrangement of information on the LC card order form severely limits the ability to design an order form that meets the tests of good form design, but forms with acceptable solutions are offered in the catalogs of the library supply houses and can be made by the manufacturers of multiple-copy forms. The acquisitions librarian should be sure the form meets LC's requirements before placing a definite purchase order. Approval may be had by submitting samples to the Card Division of the Library of Congress.

STATISTICS OF HOLDINGS

Records of the holdings of a library's collections are often made at the time material arrives in the library and a decision is made that it will be added to the library. The acquisitions department often carries this responsibility although it may be delegated to those units acquiring materials that may not pass through the acquisitions department, such as government documents and maps. In many libraries statistics of holdings are recorded in the catalog department after materials are cataloged. As statistics of holdings reach national and international standardization, three forms emerge: physical piece, bibliographic volume, and title. Libraries are keeping statistics by volume for books and bound periodicals; by piece for microforms, films, sound recordings, and similar materials; by bibliographic volume for unbound periodicals and for periodicals, newspapers, and other serials in microform; and by title for books (including book titles in microform), government documents, audiovisual materials, periodicals, and other materials in the library collections.

A simple standard form is kept at each station where materials are added to the library. This form provides space for recording each addition by day, week, or month, depending upon the rate at which material is added. Statistics of holdings are usually reported for the same fiscal year as that for expenditure reporting.

BOOKKEEPING

Bookkeeping or fund accounting is done, primarily, to assure that funds will not be overspent or overencumbered unintentionally. In addition, the information provided is valuable in recording and evaluating the library's growth and use of resources and in budgeting for future years. In some libraries, fund accounting records are kept to be sure money is spent and does not sit unused when there is need for it elsewhere or when it will revert to control outside the library if it is not spent within a fixed time.

Maintaining records of the amount of money used for library materials and the amount of money remaining for use is one of the responsibilities of most acquisitions departments. Writing checks and maintaining final records of expenditure are usually done by the city treasurer, comptroller, university business office, or other fiscal agent of the institution or unit of government of which the library is a part. Some public libraries receive and hold their own funds and act as ultimate fiscal agents subject to audit; they usually establish internal business departments separate from the acquisitions department since the funds are for personnel, equipment, and maintenance as well as for library materials. The fund accounting or bookkeeping done in the acquisitions department may represent a responsibility delegated by higher authority. In some cases the maintenance of encumbrances is assigned to the library acquisitions department; in others, one or two large funds are assigned to the library where they are further divided in budgeting, with the acquisitions department responsible for keeping records of both encumbrance and expenditure.

The design of systems for bookkeeping should be coordinated with the institution's business office or treasurer to prevent duplication of work and files and to determine how the work of the units can mesh to keep operating costs as low as possible without unreasonable sacrifice of service. Bookkeeping or accounting is a clerical chore. When the size of a budget or institutional requirements so dictate, an acquisitions unit should have a bookkeeper.

Bookkeeping is done in a great variety of ways, and no single scheme or selection of schemes can be presented as ideal. Few acquisitions departments are free to decide the most efficient means of keeping their fund records because local fiscal control and procedures vary and because the libraries' needs also vary. A library might have a single fund or account for all library materials but the minimum number would more probably be two accounts, one for books and other materials for which encumbrance and expenditure is a "one-time" transaction, and the other for subscriptions for which orders are not completed but continue from one budget year to the next. More commonly, a library will have several funds, such as adult books, children's books, reference books, subscriptions, binding, and audiovisual materials; or it may have funds for general books, reference books, bibliographies, serials, and replacements. Larger libraries and academic libraries may have several dozen funds, including departmental and divisional allocations and trust and other gift funds, and the largest research libraries may have scores of funds.

Multiple-Copy Order Forms

In one simple scheme that is used in many libraries, a copy of the multiple-copy order form is filed as an encumbrance against the appropriate fund. As the slip (or, more usually, groups of slips) is filed or removed, the estimated price may be added to or removed from an adding machine tape or a card at the beginning of the file to update the encumbrance. If there are not too many of them, all of the slips in the file may be added weekly or monthly. If the record of expenditures against funds is kept in the institution's business office and reported periodically (usually monthly) to the acquisitions department, the condition of each fund can be discovered by combining the encumbrance total with the expenditure total. In this scheme it is necessary to coordinate the cut-off date for the payment of invoices.

For example, if the business office closes its books on the last working day of the month and observation indicates that invoices received there from the library five working days before the last working day of the month will be paid and included in the month's computation of expenditures, the library's tally of encumbrances on the fifth working day before the end of the month can be combined with the business office reports of expenditures to make a statement of the total condition of each fund. Anticipating the irregularity caused by absences, vacant positions, and other problems that may make it uncertain that invoices will be paid exactly on schedule, the library can stamp invoices as they are approved for payment with a legend, such as "September business," signaling the business office that the library needs to have such invoices returned for recalculation of encumbrances if they are not, indeed, paid in September.

Frequently a library is required to keep the record of expenditures for each fund as well as for the encumbrances. This may be because the library further allocates funds after allocation from its parent or because the library requires a title record of the expenditures against each fund. The latter circumstance may occur where the library is viewed only as the guardian of the allocation and wishes to or is required to provide complete accountability to the person or agency making selections against the fund. Maintenance of expenditures by fund accounts is done by moving the order slip from the encumbrance file to an expenditure file and confirming or correcting the price on the slip. When funds are nearing depletion it is usually necessary to keep a daily balance to prevent overspending. A daily balance is maintained by posting encumbrance and expenditure changes to a ledger every day as orders are placed and invoices are paid, batching them by day or by vendor rather than listing each title.

Standing and Blanket Orders

Standing orders for series and subscriptions must be taken into consideration and funds encumbered for them. This may be done by carrying in the encumbrance file a card for each standing order and subscription, with an estimate of the amount of money that will be required during the year to pay for new volumes or renewals. Cards are updated or removed as expenditures are made. As a substitute some libraries estimate the total amount that will be required for new volumes in series or renewals by calculating the amounts spent for these categories in the previous year. They adjust the amounts for price increases, carrying only these summary figures as encumbrances and subtracting from them as payments are made. To simplify bookkeeping and to protect and preserve funds for the purchase of monographs, many libraries do not charge subscriptions to each fund account but have a separate fund account that embraces all subscriptions without regard to subject matter, audience, or form.

Blanket orders also require encumbrance and the same method as used for serials can be applied. One of the special problems that blanket orders cause is that while the total amount the library may expect to spend with one dealer on an approval plan may be known and negotiated, the amount that will be spent from each of many fund accounts will be difficult if not impossible to estimate. This problem is one of the reasons that libraries are moving from allocations. Another problem is posed by blanket orders for all of the publications of a press, or for certain categories or subjects from a press, when it is impossible to know what the output of the press will be during a year. The best that can be done is to make an estimate and carry an agreement that the blanket order can be cancelled during the year if the library can no longer afford it.

Ledger Bookkeeping

Because slips and cards may be misfiled or lost, some libraries believe that using these records for bookkeeping is open to error when multiple accounts and large budgets are involved. In their place a ledger is maintained for each account. A typical ledger sheet provides for the entry of each transaction under date, vendor, order number, encumbrances, and expenditures. Each order or group of orders to one vendor is listed by order number or numbers, with the estimated price. As orders are filled, the estimated price is removed from the encumbrance section and the actual price paid is entered in the expenditures column, again citing vendors and order numbers. Most ledgers provide columns for running balances for encumbrances and expenditures. Cancelled orders, credits, and additional appropriations to the account may be provided for by showing them as credits in encumbrances or expenditures, as appropriate, or by having separate ledger columns for credits. Encumbrances for standing orders and subscriptions usually are entered, en bloc, as estimates at the beginning of each fiscal year. Deductions are made from the encumbrance as bills are paid and entries are made as expenditures.

Discounts

Discounts that a library will receive may be taken into consideration when encumbering funds, but it is often impossible to anticipate at the time of order what the discount on a book will be. Libraries whose primary ordering is standard trade books usually forecast the actual price they will pay for each title. Those that order a greater variety of books may calculate the average discount they received on all books in the recent past and subtract that discount from the list price of each encumbrance. They may modify this procedure by making more exact estimates of discounts on multiple-copy orders of long-discount trade books, for in this group each percentage point may mean a difference of many dollars in encumbrances. Many academic libraries make no provision for discounts in their encumbrances because such a high proportion of the items they order have short discounts, have no discounts, or have service charges added. In these libraries the amount of money freed between encumbrance and expenditure is seen as a buffer that permits them to send out want lists for out-of-print books without encumbering funds but with some assurance that funds will be available when dealers make offers.

Binding

Binding or rebinding is sometimes charged to a separate binding fund and other times charged to book funds. When binding is charged to several fund accounts, the practice is to use an average cost for encumbrance purposes, rather than try to calculate the exact price that will be charged for each volume.

Contingency Fund

Acquisitions librarians may be required to give a large amount of attention and time to bookkeeping matters such as daily balances, estimates of discount, and estimates of the costs of standing orders and subscriptions. They may be caught up in meticulous bookkeeping that is inexact at best. It is questionable whether such efforts serve the best interests of a library. In the library that has many fund accounts a contingency fund should be available that will free acquisitions personnel from the necessity of giving excessive attention to overdrafts of fund accounts.

REFERENCES

Order Routines

Dougherty, Richard M., and Boone, Samuel M. "An Ordering Procedure Utilizing the Xerox 914 Electrostatic Process." *Library Resources & Technical Services* 10:43–45 (Winter 1966).

————, and Heinritz, Fred J. *Scientific Management of Library Operations.* Metuchen, N.J.: Scarecrow, 1966. 258p.

————, and others. *Policies and Programs Designed to Improve Cooperation and Coordination Among Technical Service Operating Units.* Champaign, Ill.: University of Illinois Graduate School of Library Science, 1967. 45p. (Occasional Papers no. 86)

Ladenson, Alex. "Budget Control of Book Purchases and Binding Expenditures in Large Public Libraries." *Library Resources & Technical Services* 4:47–58 (Winter 1960).

Lyle, Guy R. "Business and Financial Affairs." In *The Administration of the College Library.* 3d ed. p. 320–49. Bronx, N.Y.: Wilson, 1961.

Melcher, Daniel. *Melcher on Acquisition.* Chicago: American Library Assn., 1971. 169p.

Wulfekoetter, Gertrude. *Acquisition Work: Processes Involved in Building Library Collections.* Seattle: Univ. of Washington Pr., 1961. 268p.

Statistics of Holdings

American Library Association. Statistics Coordinating Project. *Library Statistics: A Handbook of Concepts, Definitions, and Terminology.* Chicago: The Association, 1966. 160p.

Schick, Frank. "International Library Statistics Programs." *American Libraries* 3:73–75 (Jan. 1972).

————. "Library Statistics: A Century Plus." *American Libraries* 2:727–31 (July-Aug. 1971).

USA Standard for Library Statistics, New York: United States of America Standards Institute, 1969. Z39.7-1968.

15

AUTOMATION OF ORDER ROUTINES

Automation here refers to the application of computer-based machine methods and mechanization to methods that are not computer based. Libraries apply machine methods to their operations to do a job better, or less expensively, or to do something that cannot or would not be done by manual methods. Doing something better may mean doing it more accurately or more quickly or both. Some tasks cannot be done manually and others are too large or complex for manual systems. Evidence of these are circulation systems that are collapsing from overload and processing systems that are hopelessly behind in work completion. Projections for future needs and workloads also bear upon considerations of automation and mechanization. Complete systems analysis must be done before automation is begun. The automation of a poor manual system will produce a poor automated system and probably cost much more.

The tasks best suited for machine methods are those that are repetitive, require few intellectual decisions, and represent a high volume of work. Files that are extensive and require substantial maintenance and updating operations are prime targets for automation. Files that are too large, however, can be excessively expensive to add to and maintain.

Acquisitions operations have frequently been the first to receive machine applications, not only because they are the first in the chain of processing that leads through cataloging to circulation, but also because many of the operations are repetitive and require few intellectual decisions and the files are large and dynamic. In addition, machine applications for business operations in commerce and industry are well established and there is a transferability, at least in understanding, to the business operations that are a part of acquisitions in libraries. The chief acquisitions routines that are automated or mechanized are the preparation of purchase orders, fund accounting, and the maintenance

185

and updating of outstanding-order/in-process files. In addition, machine routines are used to assist in the management of acquisitions, especially in scheduling workloads, anticipating overloads, and reporting performance. The chief advantage that libraries have reported is in automatic fund accounting, followed by claiming and bibliographic control of each item while in process through technical services.

COSTS

The experience of many libraries is that it is unrealistic to expect large savings to result from the introduction of machine methods to acquisitions. Usually these methods cost more than manual ones and inevitably they cost more in their initial periods of operation. Development costs in planning and implementing a new system push costs up even when they are amortized over the first few years of operation. Most libraries enter mechanized and automated systems to do a better job in acquisitions rather than to save money. In this context, it is important to consider the total resources of an institution. It may be decided that a particular job does not need to be done better or does not need to done at all.

The largest costs in automation in acquisitions are for storage of machine-readable information and for printing. It appears that these costs will go down, especially the costs for storage. In estimating costs, librarians should look askance at computer time offered free or at unrealistically low rates. These usually will be computers in educational institutions that are under-utilized and can be expected to be realistically priced within a few years.

There is need for standard methodology for cost analysis in machine applications and for reporting costs. Reliable estimates of costs of conversion are extremely difficult and usually impossible to find.

An important aspect of costs lies in transferability. Libraries should investigate the possibility of buying existing software packages (that is, programs or systems) rather than design new ones to fit their unique and seemingly important local situations. Transferring a program or a system requires that the equipment and the operating system be the same and that libraries change their own requirements and procedures and those of the governmental bodies or institutions of which they are a part to adapt to existing programs. Acquisitions programs should be based upon acceptance of the Library of Congress MARC tapes whether or not they can be introduced into a system as it is initiated.

STEPS IN AUTOMATION

It is important to understand and analyze a library's existing manual acquisitions system before planning any automation. The existing system should be given as complete a cost analysis as possible. A total system for a library should be developed before any single system is planned or put into operation. Subsystems for parts of the acquisitions process should be part of the acquisitions subsystem, which is a part of the processing subsystem, in itself part of the library's system. To avoid high and unnecessary costs for redesigning systems, each part should fit into the whole as it comes into existence.

The principle of recording information only once should be applied wherever possible, a principle that has as much relevance for a manual system as for an automated one, but becomes possible more often in an automated system. Steps that could be automated but need not be, should not be, especially where cost is a consideration. Equipment that can be used in subsystems other than the one under consideration should be chosen.

In place of locally produced and developed programs, most libraries should seek out or participate in the establishment of regional processing centers if they cannot continue with manual methods or use the simpler noncomputer mechanical procedures.

AUTOMATED ORDER ROUTINES

A Typical Off-Line System

The sample computer-based, off-line acquisitions system outlined here is typical of systems in operation in some libraries, but is not descriptive of any one of them. In an automated system the functions remain the same as those outlined in the previous chapter, "Order Routines," including placing orders, maintaining appropriate records of orders, receiving orders, claiming them when they are not received in a suitable period, processing invoices for payment, and maintaining records of encumbrances and payments. An automated system may be able to perform additional tasks that may be highly desirable but are not essential to the acquisition of materials. In automated systems the steps in acquisitions through searching and dealer selection remain the same as in unautomated systems, although the outstanding-order/in-process file usually is in a form other than cards.

The order-request slip used by the person selecting material and by the preorder searcher is similar to others except that it has fixed locations for coding. The searcher and the person who does vendor selection assign numerical codes for the vendor, the fund, the time at which an item should be claimed, the number of copies, and such other aspects of ordering as the departmental or divisional library to which the item is to be sent, the form of the material, whether serial or monograph, bound or unbound. A unique order number also is assigned. In this sample or theoretical system the completed, coded order-request slip is sent to a keypunch operator, who punches a set of cards for each title. The cards include complete bibliographical information plus the coded information. The columns available on a punched card are limited and this dictates that multiple cards will be required to accommodate the length of author-title entries. The punched cards for titles to be ordered are gathered and sent to the computer center twice a week, where a packet of purchase-order forms, an outstanding-order/in-process file, and a fund file are printed and returned to the library.

The purchase-order packet contains a purchase order to be sent to the dealer, along with a return slip for him to send with the material, a slip for filing by vendor and order number, and a slip to be used for notification of the selector after the item has been received and cataloged. Purchase orders have been automatically arranged by vendor and include the vendor's name and address for mailing in a window envelope. With the purchase-order packet are three prepunched update cards, which were prepared by the computer and contain enough information to identify an item. This identification is a brief author-title entry (in some systems it may be only the unique order number). These cards are used to update information about the order in the files. When the item is received, one of them is sent to the computer center with the date of receipt punched into it. Another has the actual price paid punched into it after the invoice is approved and is sent to the computer center. The third is used for deleting the item from the order records after it has been cataloged. Additional punched cards may be prepared in the library for other updating information, such as a vendor report, like "not yet published." After the purchase order and vendor return slip are mailed, the rest of the slips, the prepunched update cards, and the original order-request slip are filed by vendor and order number to await receipt of the material.

The computer center prepares a printout that records, alphabetically by main entry, all items on order or in process, including complete data about the status of the item. For instance, if an item is in process, it records the date it was received in the library and the price paid, as well as all of the other bibliographic and coded business information outlined above; or, if an item has been claimed it shows the date of claim, and if a report was received from the vendor it shows the substance of the report. Ideally there would be a new computer printout every time punched cards were sent to the computed center, but practically, cost being a consideration, there is a new printout once a month with weekly printouts of additions and changes cumulating during the period between monthly printouts. Multiple copies are made of all of the printouts so that each preorder searcher will have easy access to one and to provide a sufficient number for reasonable use by other library units.

The computer center produces a weekly listing of all purchases arranged by fund. This listing is sent to the selector or department responsible for the fund to confirm that orders have been placed and to permit a review to be sure charges to the fund are legitimate. The fund file represents the accounting subsystem that also produces monthly statements of balances in each fund. The prepunched update cards function to inform the computer of changes in encumbrances and expenditures.

Receipt of materials is the same as in a system that is not automated, except that the prepunched update cards are used to inform the computer to update the outstanding-order/in-process and fund files with receipt and actual price paid data. The order-request slip, selector-notification slip, and prepunched update card for deletion are forwarded for cataloging. After cataloging, the deletion card is sent to the computer center for removal of records of the order.

The coding punched at the time of the order notes the schedule on which claims should be made. The claim is computer generated by the fund file. The computer prints and addresses claim letters and they are sent to the library for auditing and mailing. The claim cycle can be adjusted or bypassed to suit the needs of the library.

At the time a library enters acquisitions automation a file of vendors is set up on punched cards with vendor codes assigned and printed out. It is updated as necessary and is used to print vendor names and addresses for purchase orders and claims. A file of funds is also set up each year, showing the allocation for the year. This is used to create the fund file and the monthly statements.

This sample automated order system differs from a conventional order system in several significant ways. The outstanding-order/in-process file is printed rather than prepared on cards, and as such it may be made available in more locations, it may be easier to use, and it requires less space. The acquisitions department is relieved of the tasks of bookkeeping, except where they are necessary to check system performance. Claiming is done automatically.

This sample system is moderately complicated and has in it features that could be eliminated to reduce costs. A vendor file, for instance, is far from necessary and may be only marginally desirable.

Variations on the Off-Line System

Within the framework of an off-line system there is room for many variations on the scheme outlined above. Some library systems maintain and print out a computer file arranged by dealer and invoice number, including order numbers and prices paid. It is used to confirm payments and replaces the invoice file kept in some institutions. Many systems provide for the creation of statistics of holdings by coding material type and retrieving it as items are received or cataloged. The possibilities of obtaining useful management data are great, including information about vendor performance, time between receipt and payment, time between receipt and cataloging, work loads, anticipated work loads, and backlogs. It is also possible to correlate acquisitions, expenditures, curriculum, enrollment, declared majors by department, faculty by department, and similar data. To be cost-effective, such data should be by-products, not separate autonomous projects.

The sample system refers to keypunching in the library. Other systems use "slave" keypunches, attached to electric typewriters. The multiple-copy purchase order is typed in the library and at the same time cards are keypunched to be sent to the computer center for updating files. It is also possible to punch paper tape rather than cards on a slave device.

Computer-output microfilm can be used in place of printouts. A library with a large outstanding-order/in-process file may find even monthly printouts very expensive and microform available much more cheaply.

On-Line Systems

Up to this point, the computer operations described have been in the "batch" or "off-line" mode. Input has been typically punched card or paper tape oriented, data have been processed in periodic batches, and the results returned to the user in large lumps. The advantages of having a computer automatically perform a routine and repetitive set of operations are obvious, but the turnaround time between input and final output is an equally obvious disadvantage, particularly as budget deadlines are approached.

With an on-line system the user is able to make additions and changes to data files and to initiate processing and file manipulation directly from a remote terminal, without appreciable turnaround time. For this reason, on-line systems are sometimes described as "real-time" systems, indicating that the computer operations are immediate rather than being held as a batch for later processing. An on-line system can accommodate from one to several hundred or even thousand users, each of whom seems to have exclusive use of the computer: the users take turns, but so rapidly that there is no discernible delay. On-line systems available to libraries usually have traffic of fewer than fifty or one hundred concurrent users. The size and design of the equipment, the sophistication of the time-sharing programs, and the nature of the work being processed all influence the effective maximum traffic level at which efficient processing can be maintained.

User input with an on-line terminal is normally with a typewriter-like keyboard. Large data files transferred from other sources can be used as input by other means, including punched cards and magnetic tapes. Display, one means of output, may be either "typewritten" or presented on a cathode ray tube (CRT). Connection between the terminal and the computer may be one of several grades of telephone line or some form of coaxial cable. Distance between terminal and computer is often the single greatest cost factor and needs to be carefully calculated in addition to the other computer and computer-related expenses.

Time is foreshortened with an on-line system. While a simple program change in a batch system may require two weeks, with an on-line system that same change can easily be accomplished in five minutes. Specific automated acquisitions operations may be similarly speeded up with an on-line system.

Although relatively few libraries have significant experience with automated systems, only a very few of these have any working experience with on-line systems. The design and development of an on-line system is vastly more complex than for a batch system, requires much more time, and therefore demands more consistent budgetary commitment. However, once implemented, the on-line system may prove to be less expensive to operate than either batch or manual systems, providing the same quality of controls and array of outputs. Certainly, it is a false assumption that blindly asserts that on-line means more expensive.

For some acquisitions operations an immediate response is highly desirable if not mandatory. Searching the on-order/in-process file on-line can be highly rewarding, because the search results are available for immediate use and decision. However, producing a monthly new acquisitions list is just as well accomplished in the form of a batch job. Thus, in creating an on-line acquisition system, the intelligent systems analyst and librarian will design some parts to be on-line and other parts, which are less subject to time constraints, to be batch. The more economical and effective mode for each set of operations can be selected.

One of the hallmarks of batch systems is the mountain of paper printouts. Going to an on-line system can eliminate the need for much of this paper, but care should be taken to ensure that a permanent, paper record is provided; budget changes accomplished through a CRT terminal may be correct, but there is no subsequent documentation to prove that correctness to an auditor. In designing an on-line system, it is necessary to think in terms of networks of two or more libraries sharing files and computer services and working more closely together than would otherwise be possible.

Although both batch and on-line systems can employ indexing to the same degree, the sheer volume of paper tends to discourage such efforts unless the indexes are accessible on-line. An out-of-date paper printout is not much use except as waste paper. Each time an index is updated, all previous printouts are superseded, but with on-line access, the superseded index ceases to be a problem since it has been replaced by the new index in the storage area of the computer.

Given the present level of computer technology, an idealized library automation program would be conceived as a "total on-line system" affecting, directly or indirectly, essentially all aspects of the library. Acquisitions would be one module, probably the first, since it is a logical point at which to begin to capture bibliographic and fiscal data that can be carried forward to be used without re-input at each successive use point. The on-order/in-process file, the serial record, the catalog, the fund account, and the circulation control can be conceptualized as forming one central file, accessible to and used by each unit according to its needs. Not only can the repetitious recopying of data be eliminated, but duplication of files (and the problem of simultaneous maintenance) can similarly be eliminated.

In implementing a batch system it is imperative that the previous manual system be maintained in parallel until confidence in the new system has been firmly established. In this way the performance of both the old and the new can be observed side-by-side. The implementation of an on-line system requires the same methodical parallel operation until confidence has been established. The period of parallel operation may need to be longer due to the greater complexity of the programs.

Of course, it is essential that constant testing and trial runs be performed prior to implementation.

MARC DATA

MARC, MAchine Readable Cataloging, is the Library of Congress project for preparing and distributing cataloging data in magnetic-tape form. Many automated acquisitions systems use or plan to use MARC tapes as a source of bibliographic data. The system standardizes the format of machine-readable bibliographic records and makes possible their interchange between libraries. Stated in the simplest terms, MARC tapes are obtained and stored by libraries (or groups of libraries); order requests are automatically searched against this data base for verification; and orders and the on-order/in-process file are created from it without the need for keypunching. Ultimately the information obtained is used for cataloging. Tapes issued before July 1973 are for English-language titles only, and most of them are titles published in the United States, cataloged since the beginning of 1969.

FUND ACCOUNTING

The computer may be of special importance in fund accounting. Some libraries have made this their only acquisitions application. Some libraries begin their automation projects in fund accounting because of the relative ease of doing so and because, under most circumstances, the advantages are clear. In many organizations and institutions accounting is partly automated and it is relatively easy to adapt or broaden the system for library use. Encumbrances and expenditures are recorded automatically and quickly, and up-to-the-minute fund balances can be produced easily.

The University of Hawaii system described by Ralph Shaw (see References) is the simplest reported. Punched cards were prepared in the library on a keypunch shared with other library operations. Each card showed the order number, fund, and estimated price for each item. These were fed into the computer for updating funds and returned to the library, where the actual price paid was punched into them when invoices were processed. The cards were returned to the computer and periodic printouts were obtained showing fund balances. The system was less expensive than the manual system previously in use.

Many modifications of this basic computer system are possible. Some libraries obtain punched cards or tapes for fund accounting by a punch attached to a typewriter that is used for typing orders. Others have made author and title entries as well as entries for accounting data and have used this information for lists of new accessions. Generally, libraries will want to design computerized accounting systems as subsystems of computerized acquisitions systems, which in turn are part of the total library system.

MECHANIZED ORDER PROCEDURES

Many libraries have good mechanized systems that are not related to computers. They use what is called "unit-record equipment," which includes a keypunch, collator, sorter, and accounting machine. The collator matches or merges two sequences of punched cards, the sorter sorts cards alphabetically or numerically, and the accounting machine prints. As with computer-based systems, the order-request form provides for coding that is copied by the keypunch operator, along with bibliographic information. Cards are sorted and re-sorted to print purchase orders, order lists, and fund balances. Updating is done by interfiling. Sorting and interfiling are done by machine (occasionally by hand) rather than by computer. Mechanical systems are slower and less flexible than computer-based systems. They are also much less expensive in machine time. Medium-size libraries may find them functional and economic. Some libraries have used mechanized routines as the first step toward automation. Careful planning is necessary to assure that the one can lead to the other.

REFERENCES

Auld, Larry, and Baker, Robert. "LOLITA: An On-Line Book Order and Fund Accounting System." A paper presented at the 1972 Clinic on Library Applications of Data Processing, University of Illinois Graduate School of Library Science.

Baker, Robert S., and others. "LOLITA: An On-Line Demonstration." In *Communication for Decision-Makers*, p. 311–19. American Society for Information Science. *Proceedings,* v.8. Westport, Conn.: Greenwood, 1971.

Bishop, Gwynneth H. "Computers and Acquisitions: The Experiences of the Library at the State University of New York at Binghamton." *Library Resources & Technical Services* 14:407–20 (Summer 1970).

Boss, Richard W. "Automation and Approval Plans." In International Seminar on Approval and Gathering Plans in Large and Medium Size Academic Libraries, 1969. *Advances in Understanding Approval and Gathering Plans in Academic Libraries,* p.19–34. Kalamazoo: Western Michigan University, 1970.

Burgess, Thomas K. "Criteria for Design of an On-line Acquisitions System at Washington State University Library." In Clinic on Library Applications of Data Processing. *Proceedings,* 1969, p. 50–66. Champaign, Ill.: University of Illinois Graduate School of Library Science, 1970.

Chapman, Edward A., and others. *Library Systems Analysis Guidelines.* New York: Wiley-Interscience, 1970, 226p.

Dunlap, Connie R. "Automated Acquisition Procedures at the University of Michigan Library." *Library Resources & Technical Services* 11:192–202 (Spring 1967).

————. "Mechanization of Acquisitions Processes." In *Advances in Librarianship* 1:37–57. New York: Academic Pr., 1970.

Hayes, Robert M., and Becker, Joseph. *Handbook of Data Processing for Libraries.* New York: Wiley, 1970. 912p.

Heiliger, Edward M., and Henderson, Paul B. *Library Automation: Experience Methodology, and Technology of the Library as an Information System.* New York: McGraw-Hill, 1971. 333p.

Kennedy, James H., and Sokoloski, James S. "Man-Machine Considerations of an Operational On-line University Library Acquisitions System." In *The Information Conscious Society,* p.65–67. American Society for Information Science. *Proceedings,* v. 7. Washington, D.C.: ASIS, 1970.

Marshall, Patricia. "Mechanized Library Accounting System: Another Example." *APLA Bulletin* 32:90–98 (Dec. 1968).

Morrissey, Eleanor F. "Mechanized Book Order and Accounting Routine." *Southeastern Librarian* 15:143–48 (Fall 1965).

Parker, Ralph H. "Automatic Records System at the University of Missouri Library." *College & Research Libraries* 23:231–32, 264–65 (May 1962).

————. "Development of Automatic Systems at the University of Missouri Library." In Clinic on Library Applications of Data Processing, University of Illinois. *Proceedings,* 1963, p.43–54. Champaign, Ill.: Illini Union Bookstore, 1964.

Shaw, Ralph R. "Control of Book Funds at the University of Hawaii Library." *Library Resources & Technical Services* 11:380–82 (Summer 1967).

Spigai, Frances G., and Mahan, Thomas. "On-line Acquisitions by LOLITA." *Journal of Library Automation* 3:276–94 (Dec. 1970).

Taylor, Gerry M., and others. "Cut to Fit; Computer Procedures Applied to an Emerging University's Book Purchasing Program." *Library Resources & Technical Services* 14:31–55 (Winter 1970).

Thomson, James W., and Muller, Robert H. "The Computer-Based Book Order System at the University of Michigan Library: A Review and Evaluation." In Clinic on Library Applications of Data Processing. *Proceedings,* 1968, p.54–78. Champaign, Ill.: University of Illinois Graduate School of Library Science, 1969.

Veaner, Allen B. "Application of Computers to Library Technical Processing." *College & Research Libraries* 31:36–42 (Jan. 1970).

———. "Major Decision Points in Library Automation." *College & Research Libraries* 31:5, 299–312 (Sept. 1970).

Wedgeworth, Robert. "Brown University Library Fund Accounting System." *Journal of Library Automation* 1:51–65 (Mar. 1968).

16

CENTRALIZED PROCESSING

Cooperative centralized processing began to be an important feature of the library scene in the late 1950s, but its antecedents may be observed in many forms in metropolitan area library service of the last several generations. The support of the idea of centralized processing lies principally in the premise that large organizations provide benefits that cannot be had from small organizations, or that in acquiring, cataloging, and preparing library materials increased volume decreases unit costs. Also, it is clear that there is a significant duplication of processing effort in libraries. If fifty libraries order the same book at one time using one method, it should be less expensive than if they order them at fifty times and in fifty ways. In acquisitions work it is assumed that large-volume purchasing will produce better service and discounts from vendors than small-volume purchasing; the large unit will get more attention and benefits because it is a more valuable customer. For smaller libraries, centralized processing relieves the local library staff of work that is often largely clerical in nature, and frees them to extend and refine public services. Most small and medium-size libraries are unable to afford to use new technology, especially that involving automation, but if they combine their money and efforts, they may be able to gain the benefits promised by automation at prices they can afford.

PROCESSING CENTERS

Most processing centers purchase, catalog, and fully prepare books for libraries, including spine labels, book pockets and cards, plastic jackets, and other features that are required to put a book into use.

The libraries usually do their own book selection, but some centers offer book selection as a service or provide special book selection aids,, such as centralized display of books received on blanket-order plans with publishers or wholesalers, and evaluation. Some centers provide no acquisitions service and concentrate on cataloging, either with the book in hand or by providing sets of catalog cards ready for filing. Some centers confine their activities to monographic books, leaving standing orders, periodicals, and other types of orders to the individual library. Others may offer a complete acquisitions service, including library binding, the securing of free materials, searching for out-of-print materials, and the acquisition and processing of nonbook materials.

Centers take one of several forms. They may be the processing unit of an autonomous library—either large public, university, or research— that has divisions, departments, branches, and other service units. Although calling processing units of large libraries processing centers may be questioned, they are similar in their offerings to disparate service units. Other processing centers serve a cluster of autonomous libraries that are similar in the materials they acquire and the services they offer, such as public or academic libraries of similar size. Systems of libraries based upon regions, districts, and counties usually have centralized processing and may extend their processing services to other libraries or systems. Some states have assumed responsibility for processing and give service to libraries within and sometimes outside the state. Centers also may serve more than one kind of library, although this is not common. Centers may be located in quarters apart from any library and operate independently of any single library. They may also be located in a library where they may be operated as a service of that library or may be only occupants of space that is available in that library. In many instances states serve as sources of funds for centers and as planning agents for bringing centers into being.

Procedures

The organization and management of acquisitions procedures in processing centers is a topic apart from this book and is viewed here only at those points where it relates to participating libraries. In establishing a center or entering the circle of an already established center, it is important that careful planning be done to avoid expensive and unnecessary duplication of effort at the center or at the library. Occasionally libraries continue to maintain files and do other acquisitions tasks that are no longer necessary, thereby passing over the savings they might achieve with centralized processing and, in some instances, effecting increased acquisitions costs because work is done twice.

Most procedures between libraries and processing centers utilize multiple-copy order forms. A copy or copies are kept in the library; others are for the vendor and for the center. Usually the library controls unwanted duplication by maintaining a file of outstanding orders arranged by author or title against which new selections are searched before they are sent to the center for order. In some cases the center maintains this record and searches to prevent unwanted duplication. The library may be billed for the cost of the materials and the cost of processing, or it may turn its funds over to the center to permit direct charges to funds, in which case periodic reports of fund charges and balances are made to the library.

An important effort of centers serving public libraries is to order all copies of a title at one time. This effort is made to achieve obvious economies in operation and possible savings through greater discount. In an attempt to pool orders, centers may place a limit on the amount of time a library may take to make a decision on a new title. The penalty for passing the limit may be a higher charge for processing or slower processing. Another important effort of centers is the maintenance of a continuous flow of orders from libraries, to avoid the backlogs that are caused by peak loads. Some public and school libraries may have established patterns in which books are ordered only a few times each year. If these times are the same or nearly the same for several of the center's customers, processing peaks and valleys will occur. Academic libraries may be required to spend all of their money before the end of the fiscal year or to encumber it several months before the end of the year. This demand also causes peak loads and backlogs. In these cases efforts must be made by the center and participating libraries to change methods of funding, allow libraries to carry over balances, or anticipate allocations.

Centers may deal with jobbers or publishers and participate in special standing-order or blanket-order plans, just as would an autonomous library. They will usually use more than one jobber in an attempt to avoid overloading any one of the them. Book contracts customarily guarantee a continuous flow of orders and require shipments once or twice a week.

Most libraries using processing centers keep a local processing capability to handle specialized materials. These may include serials, gifts and exchanges, archives, and other forms of materials that the center is not equipped to handle or are more efficaciously ordered locally. If a library does not contract to purchase all of its books from a center, the two units should agree on the percentage of the library's materials budget that is to be spent through the center. The staff of the center must know levels of work that can be expected if they are to plan and work effectively.

Librarians experienced in the use of processing centers emphasize the importance of allowing ample time for the center to function well. It may take several years before full benefits can be realized or justification can be found for abandoning centralization.

Costs

It is difficult to get cost data about centralized processing that would permit easy comparisons with processing done locally. Some centers clearly demonstrate cost savings, while the existence of others, if not in peril, can only be justified by superior service. Many centers were begun with subsidies from state and federal bodies, and some continue with this funding, making it difficult to get cost data that can be used for comparative purposes.

One interesting dimension of costs and centers is the matter of discounts. Although several centers have realized greater discounts than would have been received by local libraries, most reports indicate that there is little or no advantage in combining to achieve greater discounts. Large libraries will not get much better discounts at processing centers.

ADVANTAGES

In addition to the advantages of centralized processing already noted in this chapter, several others should be noted. The space saved when most of the processing is moved out of a library can be significant: the cost of new library building and continuing maintenance and operating costs are high. Another advantage that should appear in cost analyses is the lower costs of supplies when they are purchased in the bulk used by a center rather than at the lower level of local library use.

The use of specialists, especially subject and language specialists, may be an important asset of centralization, especially for academic libraries, which may be unable to afford individual specialists. A center often can afford to own, use, and make available to participating libraries bibliographic and other tools that libraries alone could not have. These two assets could make possible for an academic library, for instance, the support of area studies programs that would otherwise be a serious burden upon the library's staff and its resources.

Small libraries may have no facilities for specialized or exceptional ordering, such as on-approval and other blanket-order plans or out-of-print books. A processing center can be large enough to offer services of these kinds at reasonable cost.

PROBLEMS

There are acquisitions problems in centralized processing that must be taken into consideration when decisions are to be made. The chief problem is that centralized processing imposes an intermediate step in the order process. Libraries concerned with getting materials quickly will not be as well served, unless they put into use alternate order systems that bypass centralization, a step that may contribute to high costs and ultimate disenchantment with and abandonment of centralized processing. Evaluations of the performance of centers almost always cite delays in deliveries as serious problems. Librarians are perhaps more critical of the delays in processing centers than they would be of those in their own libraries. They may not remember accurately the speed at which materials were acquired and processed under their own direction. Nevertheless, books are not acquired as quickly through centers chiefly because a middleman has been introduced to the process.

With any group of libraries there are problems of satisfying each of them when standardization and concomitant conformity must be used to achieve effective centralized processing. Libraries must be prepared to sacrifice some of their local practices if they move to the use of centers. As noted earlier in this section, an even work flow is necessary to the efficient and successful functioning of a center. Achieving this may require some extraordinary efforts from participating libraries.

Finances may pose problems. Libraries may be funded differently from one another and it may be necessary to change the entire funding structure of a library if it is to participate in a center. Also, centers require capitalization to finance their beginning, including money for equipment, space, and staff. This initial capital outlay may require special allocations from participating libraries, outside funding, or other special arrangements that are not within the regular budget structures of the libraries involved.

Communications over long distances may be a problem for libraries. Although the telephone or teletypewriter (TWX) may be easily accessible, the ability to visit the acquisitions department and personally pursue a title in its files with its staff is more satisfactory.

Mixing Libraries

Most processing centers serve only one type of library. It is not generally considered satisfactory to do otherwise, although there have not been enough centers serving a variety of libraries to permit good conclusions. It appears that very large processing centers may be able to serve more than one type of library successfully, probably because they can develop specialized services to satisfy their customers.

School, public, and academic libraries usually are funded differently, a point that may cause conflict or at least difficult-to-solve problems in processing centers. The duplication of titles among these types of libraries is relatively small, hence one of the chief advantages of a center is lost. Most of the other problems relating to combining types of libraries in centers relate to cataloging and classification.

CONCLUSION

A discussion of processing centers and acquisitions must recognize that centers are established primarily for the advantages to be gained from centralized cataloging. Acquisitions becomes a part of centralization because it is rational that books and other library materials be purchased by and delivered directly to the center rather than forwarded to local libraries. It is apparent there can be some important advantages to centralized purchasing, but it is difficult to develop a thesis supporting centralization for purchases for all materials for all libraries. In considering the centralization of acquisitions, it is important to investigate carefully both delivery time and costs to be sure they have the potential for being as good as or better than existing arrangements. Commercial processing centers are also an important aspect in the consideration of centralized processing. They may be able to serve a library better at less cost, and some government agencies that might be vehicles for centralized processing are unwilling to compete with private enterprise.

REFERENCES

Dougherty, Richard M., and Maier, Joan M. *Centralized Processing for Academic Libraries: The Final Report (Phase III, Jan. 1-June 30, 1969) of the*

Colorado Academic Libraries Book Processing Center: The First Six Months of Operation. Metuchen, N.J.: Scarecrow, 1971. 254p.

Hendricks, Donald D. *Centralized Processing and Regional Library Development: The Midwestern Regional Library System, Kitchener, Ontario.* Kitchener: The System, 1970. 85p.

———. "Cooperative Growing Pains." *Library Journal* 90:4699–703 (Nov. 1, 1965).

———. "Organization for Processing at the Book Processing Center, Oak Park, Illinois." *Library Resources & Technical Services* 10:479–89 (Fall 1966).

Kurtz, Helen G. "Centralized Processing, Diversified." *Library Journal* 95: 1807–12 (May 15, 1970).

Leonard, Lawrence E., and others. *Centralized Book Processing; a Feasibility Study Based on Colorado Academic Libraries.* Metuchen, N.J.: Scarecrow, 1969. 401p.

Nelson Associates. *Public Library Systems in the United States.* Chicago: American Library Assn., 1969.

Renfro, Kathryn R. "Nebraska Centralized Processing." *Mountain-Plains Library Quarterly* 13:4–6+ (Winter 1969).

Schmidt, C. James, and others. "Library Services to University Branch Campuses: the Ohio State Experience." *Library Resources & Technical Services* 14:562–73 (Fall 1970).

Stenstrom, Ralph H. *Cooperation between Types of Libraries, 1940–1968: An Annotated Bibliography.* Chicago: American Library Assn., 1970. 159p.

Summers, F. William. "State Libraries and Centralized Processing." *Library Resources & Technical Services* 14:269–78 (Spring 1970).

Vann, Sarah K. "Cooperation between Different Types of Libraries in Technical Services." In *Cooperation between Types of Libraries,* ed. by Cora E. Thomassen, p.12–35. Champaign, Ill.: University of Illinois Graduate School of Library Science, 1969. (Allerton Park Institute no. 15)

A NOTE ON
BIBLIOGRAPHY AND
REFERENCES

The inclusion of references at the end of each chapter of this book is intended to guide the reader to additional information about the topics discussed. Taken together, these references do not form a bibliography on acquisitions work although they should represent a distillation or selection of recent useful material on the subject. On some acquisitions problems there is a plethora of writings, on others very little has been done. The references reflect this imbalance: good articles or books may not be included while some of limited usefulness are cited because there is nothing else.

There are books and series essential or important to understanding acquisitions work that are not included in the references or are referred to only in part. A basic source of information is Maurice Tauber's *Technical Services in Libraries* (Columbia Univ. Pr., 1954), which surveys cataloging, preservation, and other aspects of processing as well as acquisitions. The issue of *Library Trends* for January 1970, "Problems of Acquisitions for Research Libraries" edited by Rolland E. Stevens, is of first importance, as is Evelyn Hensel and Peter Veillette's *Purchasing Library Materials in Public and School Libraries* (American Library Assn., 1969). Mary Duncan Carter and Wallace Bonk's *Building Library Collections* (3d ed.; Scarecrow, 1969), which emphasizes selection, contains valuable acquisitions information especially in its description of national and trade bibliographies, and Mary Gaver's *Background Readings in Building Library Collections* (Scarecrow, 1969), also concerned primarily with selection, contains some useful readings on acquisitions. *Melcher on Acquisition,* by Daniel Melcher (American Library Assn., 1971), is a highly personal but valuable discussion of acquisitions problems, especially as they relate to producers and vendors. Gertrude Wulfekoetter *Acquisitions Work* (Univ. of Washington Pr., 1961) remains useful. For bibliography, *Library Acquisitions* by Bohdan Wynar (2d ed., Libraries Unlimited, 1971) is helpful and *Library Literature* (Wilson, quarterly) is irreplaceable. The *Encyclopedia of Library and Information Science* (Marcel Dekker, 1968–) contains articles and bibliographies on acquisitions and acquisitions-related topics.

Books about types of libraries may contain sections on acquisitions. For public libraries, Joseph Wheeler and Herbert Goldhor *Practical Administration of Public Libraries* (Harper & Row, 1962), Dorothy Sinclair *Administration of the Small Public Library* (American Library Assn., 1965) and Nelson Associates *Public Library Systems in the United States* (American Library Assn., 1969) have helpful information. For college and university libraries, sections on acquisitions are included in Guy R. Lyle *Administration of the College Library* (Wilson, 1961) and Rutherford Rogers and David Weber *University Library Administration* (Wilson, 1971). Special libraries acquisitions are represented in Edward Strable *Special Libraries* (Special Libraries Assn., 1966) and the Joint Reference Library *Administration of a Public Affairs Library* (Public Administration Service, 1971).

In addition to the standard library journals, continuing publications that may contain material of interest for acquisitions librarians include *Proceedings* of the American Society for Information Science (Greenwood, annual), the Society's *Annual Review of Information Science and Technology* (Encyclopaedia Britannica), *Advances in Librarianship* edited by Melvin Voigt (Seminar Pr., annual), and the *Proceedings* of the Clinics on Library Applications of Data Processing (University of Illinois Graduate School of Library Science). *The Bowker Annual of Library & Book Trade Information* is a good source of acquisitions-related information. The "year's work" articles on acquisitions and serials that have appeared in *Library Resources & Technical Services* have been useful compilations and the journal is, of course, the single most important serial for acquisitions librarians.

A Statement on Appraisal of Gifts

Developed by the Committee on Manuscripts Collections of
the Rare Books and Manuscripts Section of the Association
of College and Research Libraries, 1973

1. The appraisal of a gift to a library for tax purposes generally is the responsibility of the donor since it is the donor who benefits from the tax deduction. Generally, the cost of the appraisal should be borne by the donor.
2. The library should at all times protect the interests of its donors as best it can and should suggest the desirability of appraisals whenever such a suggestion would be in order.
3. To protect both its donors and itself, the library, as an interested party, ordinarily should not appraise gifts made to it. It is recognized, however, that on occasion the library may wish to appraise small gifts, since many of them are not worth the time and expense an outside appraisal requires. Generally, however, the library will limit its assistance to the donor to:
   (a) providing him with information such as auction records and dealers' catalogs;
   (b) suggestions of appropriate professional appraisers who might be consulted;
   (c) administrative and processing services which would assist the appraiser in making an accurate evaluation.
4. The acceptance of a gift which has been appraised by a third, and disinterested party, does not in any way imply an endorsement of the appraisal by the library.
5. An archivist, curator, or librarian, if he is conscious that as an expert he may have to prove his competence in court, may properly act as an independent appraiser of library materials. He should not in any way suggest that his appraisal is endorsed by his library (such as by the use of the library's letterhead), nor should he ordinarily act in this fashion (except when handling small gifts) if his institution is to receive the donation.

Guidelines for Handling Library Orders for In-print Monographic Publications

Prepared by the Bookdealer–Library Relations Committee of the Resources Section, Resources and Technical Services Division of the American Library Association

BOOKDEALER–LIBRARY RELATIONS COMMITTEE

ABIGAIL DAHL-HANSEN (TO 1971)
PHILIP R. DANKERT (TO 1971)
W. STUART DEBENHAM, JR.
ASHBY J. FRISTOE (TO 1971)
M. ANN HEIDBREDER
JOHN M. BRUER
EDNA LAUGHREY
MURRAY S. MARTIN (CHAIRMAN)
NANCY PARKER
HARRIET K. REBULDELA (FROM 1972)
LEO R. RIFT (SERIALS SECTION REPRESENTATIVE)

The Committee also thanks all the individual librarians and dealers whose suggestions have helped to improve these guidelines. Particular thanks are given to Norman Dudley, Roma S. Gregory, and Ronald Hagler for their careful attention to detail.

INTRODUCTION

These guidelines are issued by the Bookdealer–Library Relations Committee of the Resources Section, Resources and Technical Services Division, American Library Association, for the advice of librarians and dealers.

Their purpose is to set forth basic recommendations concerning the relationships between librarians and bookdealers in handling orders for in-print monographic material. Included in the scope of these guidelines are books, pamphlets, and most monographs as defined in the glossary of *Library Statistics: A Handbook of Concepts, Definitions, and Terminology* (Chicago: ALA, 1966). These definitions are:

> *Book.* A unit of publication, either bibliographically independent or a volume in a series published under the same title, consisting of leaves, sheets, or signatures sewn or otherwise bound together, covered or uncovered. Bound volumes of periodicals and newspapers are not considered books. [*Note:* For the purpose of these guidelines such bound volumes may be considered subject to the same ordering procedures when ordered separately from a dealer and not by subscription.]
>
> *Monograph.* A treatise on a particular subject, usually detailed in treatment but not extensive in scope. It is generally a book or pamphlet, but need not be bibliographically independent. [*Note:* Only bibliographically independent publications are considered in these guidelines.]
>
> *Pamphlet.* An independent publication consisting of a few leaves of printed matter fastened together but not bound; usually enclosed in paper covers. . . .

Monographs in series are covered here but not serials or periodicals. The greatest attention is paid to U.S. publishers and dealers. The guidelines have been considered at meetings of the Bookdealer–Library Relations Committee and of the Resources Section and have been circulated widely among librarians, bookdealers, and publishers.

BASIS OF RELATIONSHIP

Librarians and bookdealers conduct their business on a contractual basis, whether formal or informal. The object of the relationship is to provide the best possible service to the library for a reasonable cost.

The guidelines are concerned principally with the service elements of the contract. The efficiency of a dealer's service to a library will undoubtedly be reflected in the cost of that service but it must be realized that the hidden costs to a library of an inefficient dealer may outweigh the apparent savings achieved by low-cost service.

Librarians should realize that their own contribution to efficiency is of paramount importance. Responsibilities, routines, and procedures within the library must be under continuous scrutiny to ensure that they achieve the best results. A procedures manual which is kept up-to-date is of great value. Selection of materials and of their source of purchase is not within the scope of these guidelines; however, sound decisions, based on informed professional judgment, will contribute to efficiency and cost effectiveness.

All successful relationships depend on the goodwill and cooperation of both parties. Continuing discussion of goals, needs, and problems is an integral part of every relationship between librarian and bookdealer.

LIBRARY GUIDELINES

Library Orders

I. Purchase-order forms

Libraries are responsible for the design and preparation of purchase-order forms. Because the needs of individual institutions vary greatly, one standard form does not seem feasible. Nevertheless certain basic information is essential and its location on the forms used should be consistent. Forms should meet the needs of both library and dealer. Libraries should, therefore, consult with their major dealers when designing new forms.

A. Layout and design

Two types of purchase-order forms are in general use: individual forms for each title ordered, and list forms. Both are acceptable but call for different design approaches. Identify all forms, however, as purchase orders, name the purchasing institution and name the dealer to whom they are addressed, and keep them as clear and simple as possible.

1. Individual forms

   (a) Use a separate form for each title.
   (b) Label each element on the form clearly; e.g. "author," "title," "no. of copies," etc. Unidentified data, especially figures, are confusing.
   (c) Group the elements so as to separate, as far as possible, library- and dealer-oriented information. This step is extremely important; failure to include it is the source of much confusion to librarian and dealer alike.

(d) Do not crowd areas where the content is of variable length; e.g. author, title, series.

(e) Do not place together elements which look alike; e.g. International Standard Book Number and Library of Congress card number.

(f) Designate clearly the purpose of each copy of multiple-copy forms. If a copy is to be returned with the book, incorporate this statement on the appropriate copy.

2. List forms

(a) Place orders for books from each publisher on a separate list form. If this is not feasible, group titles by publisher.

(b) Use a separate purchase-order number for each list and identify each item separately. The preference would be for a number-letter combination such as: Purchase Order Number 99, Item A, B, C, etc.

Include on all purchase-order forms clear instructions about where to send invoices, correspondence, and the items ordered. It is also helpful to have space on the form for dealers to record their own actions. If the library will cancel unsupplied orders on the expiration of a given period, this must be stated on the form sent to the dealer. (See also Cancellations, IV, below.)

Incorporate only those elements relating to ordering. Library notes such as "put on reserve for J. Jones" or "for Physics Library" confuse dealers.

Abbreviations have their place but they should not be used where they may cause confusion. "Gt. Brit." or "U.S." is acceptable in corporate entries in manual systems but may cause filing or identification problems in a machine system. Include in full in the title statement such phrases as "Introduction to" or "Concise history of" since these may serve to identify specific books more quickly. Above all, avoid ambiguous initials; e.g. "O.U.P.," which may mean the university press of Oxford, Oregon, or Oklahoma.

B. Basic data elements

1. Items that identify the title ordered

(a) *Author*. Be as complete as practicable. For personal authors cite surname first. Corporate entries require particular care. A publication by the Air Environment Center of the Pennsylvania State University should not be entered simply as

Pennsylvania State University, nor should machine-produced entries cut off such an entry before completion.

(b) *Title*. Give the complete title. Include the subtitle if possible, particularly if the main title statement is general; e.g. Sir George Grey: Pioneer of Empire.

(c) *Format*. State the particular format required. "Pbk" for paperback may be used. State special requirements such as "Library ed.," "Text ed.," "French ed."

(d) *Publisher*. Give the name in full. For a society or institution give complete details of name and address. If these are not known, it will help to say so on the order form; e.g.: Penn State University has at least twenty publishing bodies on the main campus, each with a different mailing address, and not specifying the proper one may delay an order by several weeks.

(e) *Place*. Give the name of the city. If there is need to distinguish between cities, add state or country; e.g. London (ONT) for the Canadian city.

(f) *Date*. Give the date of publication of the edition required. A copyright date is best.

(g) *Editor*. Give the editor if not part of the main entry.

(h) *Edition*. Give the number or other descriptor of the edition; e.g. 2d, 2d rev. ed. Be specific.

(i) *Series*. Cite a series note if it will help identify an item. It should be complete and include the number of the item required; e.g. California publications in classics, no.1.

(j) *Price*. Cite the publisher's list price. Be sure to quote the correct price of the edition being ordered. Do not, for example, request a paperback edition and quote the price for the hard-bound edition.

(k) *International Standard Book Number*. Cite this number when known. While not now universally available, it precisely identifies publisher, title, and edition. Do not confuse the numbers applied to paperback and hardcover issues of the same title.

(l) *Number of volumes*. Cite number of volumes, if known. If only one volume of a set is required, say so; e.g. Vol. 2 only. See 2-b, below.

2. Items relating to the purchase transaction

These elements identify the transaction and activities connected with it rather than the item concerned, and they should be grouped together on the form.

(a) *Library purchase-order number and date of order.*

(b) *Number of copies required.* This should be stated clearly; e.g. one of each volume, or one each, vols. 1 thru 6 only, or 6 copies.

(c) *"Rush" requests.* These should be noted prominently, and, as indicated below, made only when necessary.

(d) *Unique instructions.* These refer only to the specific item; e.g.: Quote price before supplying; Bill separately.

(e) *General instructions.* These refer to all orders, including such facts as addresses for the dispatch of books and invoices and to whom to direct reports. These should be part of the printed form. If printed on the back of a small form be sure a reference to them appears on the front of the form. Avoid personal names in addresses unless the institution requires their use.

If a library conducts a large volume of business with a dealer, it may be economical to have forms for that dealer preprinted with address and any other details common to orders placed with the firm.

II. Placement of purchase orders

Send orders out regularly. Do not allow routine orders to accumulate for irregular periods and then send them out all at one time. This creates a bottleneck for the dealer and slows down all orders. Mail orders at least once a week, even if only a few items are involved.

When large groups of orders must go out together, as for reserve books, classroom collections, or an opening-day collection, discuss procedures in advance with the dealer. Be sure such orders are submitted well in advance of need, accompanied by a letter to the dealer explaining deadlines. In most cases he will require at least six to eight weeks in which to effect supply, depending upon the location of the publishers involved and on the dealer's own inventory.

Set up a separate "rush" procedure to cover urgent orders and special requests. Define *rush* carefully according to your own needs and do not overuse it. Explain to your dealers what you mean by *rush* and ask for their cooperation. If extra services such as airmail or special delivery are needed, be prepared to pay for them.

III. Claims

A. Before claiming unsupplied items librarians should:

1. Try to determine the publication status of a book; e.g. if it is known that the book has not yet been published, do not claim.

2. Keep a record of reports received from the dealer. Do not follow an "out of stock—ordering" report with a claim a week later.

3. Allow a waiting period. Librarians can reasonably expect receipt of books within the following time limits, and may, therefore, establish a system of claiming based on these times.

(a) U.S. commercial publishers
Supply within 30–60 days. At least 60% of orders should be supplied or reported on within 45 days. *Note:* Older in-print titles (i.e. books published three or more years ago) may take longer to supply from publishers, agencies, and dealers. An extension to 90 days is permissible for older titles, but at least 50% of such orders should be filled within 60 days.

(b) U.S. non-commercial publishers
Recent titles should be supplied within 90 days. For more obscure publications a reasonable time is 120 days. *Note:* Librarians can help greatly by providing the publisher's full address or by ordering directly from the publishers.

(c) Foreign commercial publishers
Most Western European titles should be supplied within 150 days. Books from other countries will frequently take longer. *Note:* Librarians should determine whether U.S. dealers are able and willing to handle noncommercial and foreign publications. In many cases the former are best handled by direct order from the publisher (a good dealer will so advise librarians); the latter through dealers in the country of publication or specialist dealers in the United States.

In determining how to handle such publications both librarian and dealer should be frank about expectations and capabilities. Nothing is gained by either party when a dealer offers to handle orders which he is not able to process effectively. Conversely, librarians should not entertain unrealistic expectations about service and the cost of that service.

Librarians should be able to expect supply within these limits, with the understanding that they are subject to modification if the status of the item has changed in the time between order placement and order fulfillment.

The item ordered or a report should reach librarians within these limits; librarians should then have the option of cancelling outstanding orders.

(d) Allow sufficient time between claims for two-way postal deliveries (i.e. between library and dealer and between dealer and publisher). In most instances this now means about four weeks for domestic correspondence. Air mail can be used to shorten this lag, but increases service costs. A second claim can legitimately be made after 30 days for U.S. orders.

B. Designate all claims clearly and include all necessary information concerning the items in question.

1. Separate letters or forms may be used, but copies of the original order prominently labelled or overprinted are recommended. Suggested wording is: FIRST CLAIM (date)—This is not an order.
2. The claim form must provide a space for the dealer's reply, with an instruction to return the form properly annotated.
3. If copies of the original order are not used, be sure to give dealer complete details about the item being claimed, such as order number, specific volumes of a set, or proportion of the number of copies ordered.

The best response to a claim is, of course, receipt of the book. If, however, a high proportion of supply comes only after the first claim or second claims become the rule, the librarian must investigate. If library procedures are at fault, correct them; then discuss the matter with the dealer. If there is still no satisfaction, the only recourse would be to change dealers.

IV. Cancellations

Set up regular procedures for cancelling orders in consultation with the major dealers. Cancel outstanding orders after a stated period of time, unless in the intervening period information has been supplied that the order is still active. Such cancellations should relate to the periods of supply outlined above. This routine allows regular reconsideration of orders and avoidance of a large accumulation of encumbered funds. It also discourages arbitrary cancel-reorder practices. A dealer is entitled to expect that a library will actually buy the books it has ordered, within the time period agreed upon.

Financial controls sometimes require the expenditure of funds by a particular date. To accomplish this, the library will have to cancel all outstanding orders to free funds tied up for unreceived books and spend the money elsewhere.

Mistaken or unintentional duplicate orders may be cancelled, but this action should be covered also by the agreement with dealers. The return of a book from the library to the dealer to the publisher is an expensive process. Occasionally a dealer will accept a loss to oblige a customer, but such a practice cannot be repeated frequently.

Librarians should consider the cost of returning a book and establish a cost level below which the item will not be returned. (This expense will vary among libraries but the paperwork involved in returns may well exceed $3.00.) If the number of unintentional duplications is high, there is probably something wrong in the searching and ordering process.

V. Returns

Decide on routines for handling returns in consultation with the dealers concerned. Incorporate all such routines in the procedures manual.

Accompany all returns with a dated explanation, stating fully the reason for return. This can be a form letter with the appropriate box checked, e.g.

_____wrong title	_____oversupply of copies
_____wrong edition	_____not our order
_____duplicate supply	_____defective copy

Include in each letter reference to the purchase order and invoice affected, and state how adjustment is to be made; e.g. invoice is being held awaiting receipt of correct title, or credit is to be issued.

A. Wrong books

1. When the dealer supplies a book which was not ordered, it may be returned automatically. When the error is caused by the library's order, a request for permission to return is required.
2. Return book unmarked. Library processing systems should postpone the marking and stamping of books until the checking-in procedure is completed.

B. Defective books

1. Defective books may be returned for replacement when received. Defects are not always discovered, however, until the books have been in use, and it is important not to confuse unfair wear and tear with defective craftmanship.
2. Determine from the dealer whether or not the return of the whole book is necessary. Some publishers will accept the title page only, with a note regarding defects. This procedure saves money for all concerned.
3. Specify the defects on the book-return form letter.

C. Invoice adjustments

1. Invoice adjustments must be determined by the requirements of the dealer, as well as by the library's bookkeeping procedures. See VI-B-5 below.

VI. Financial requirements

Keep requirements concerning invoices and payment procedures as simple as possible. Some states or local governments have statutory requirements but most regulations are institutional.

Librarians should be familiar with the accounting procedures of their institutions. In addition, it is strongly recommended that libraries point out to the appropriate officers that library purchasing is a continuous flow operation which does not lend itself to spot checking, batching, or time scheduling except within very broad limits. Order- or price-confirmation requirements are also undesirable except for very expensive items. Changing many invoices and other forms to a standard institutional form is time-consuming and counterproductive.

Many institutions use computerized accounting systems. There are usually clearly established time periods for payment and periods when the system is "down," particularly at the end of a financial year. There may also be set periods each month for the review and payment of particular types of invoices. Be thoroughly familiar with these and with "exception" procedures, and inform dealers about them. If any of these procedures work to your detriment, discuss them with the accounting office and attempt to establish better routines.

A. Invoicing procedure

Given the wide variety of institutional accounting systems, only a few general recommendations about invoicing procedures can be made.

1. Inform dealers clearly of the type of invoice required, whether it be separate invoices for each order or batched invoices covering several orders. In general, separate invoices should not be required unless special funds requiring different routines are involved. Such orders should carry a boldly typed instruction, "SPECIAL FUND— PLEASE BILL SEPARATELY." Do not set up a procedure which would require dealers to consult correspondence or other files.
2. Advise dealers if a machine accounting system imposes limits on the number of invoices that can be paid on one check, since it may affect their reconciliation records and result in superfluous requests for confirmation of payment.
3. When standing orders and subscriptions are processed separately

from book orders, inform your dealers and ask for their cooperation.

4. Keep addresses to which invoices are to be sent up-to-date. Use designations such as "acquisitions librarian" rather than personal names. Inform dealers promptly of any change.
5. Ask for the minimum number of copies necessary for handling the order. Three copies of an invoice should suffice for ordinary use.

B. Payment procedures

1. Make prompt payments to ensure preferential treatment. 30 days should be a general goal for most payments. Delays of 90 days or longer are undesirable and may carry penalties.
2. Inform dealers of time constraints outside library control. Do not compound these by delays in the library's own procedures.
3. Batch invoices only if arrangements have been made with a dealer to consolidate invoices biweekly or monthly, or if the library has so many invoices that significant cost savings can be made by collecting several over a short period, such as ten days.
4. Hold invoices for incomplete orders no longer than 30 days. While shipping delays may spread the receipt of packages over a two- or three-week period, all missing items should be claimed within 30 days and partial payment made.
5. Work out a routine for handling partial shipments, returns, and errors. Various methods are available. Check with each dealer on the most suitable one to use.
   (a) By credit note. This usually means holding the incomplete invoice until credit is received from the dealer.
   (b) By striking from the invoice. This requires that the dealer be advised which items have been struck off, usually by a copy of the amended invoice.
   (c) By requesting a corrected invoice. This may be the slowest method, but it is the most appropriate when a substantial portion of the invoice is affected or the necessary corrections are complicated.
   (d) By returning the invoice with the book(s), if no other items appear on the same invoice.
6. Remember to record action taken regarding credits and partial payments on orders or elsewhere in your records.
7. Include invoice number on the check or provide some other record of invoices paid with each payment.
8. Pay attention to special requests from dealers or publishers, e.g.

"Please return punched card with check." If the requests cause problems to the institution, discuss these with the dealer.

9. Be prepared to check statements from dealers, whether in the library or the accounting office. Invoice numbers and amounts should suffice to identify the invoices.

DEALER GUIDELINES

I. Forms to accompany books without library purchase orders

When, by prior agreement, dealers originate the supply of items for libraries (e.g. volumes in sets, series of publications, individual items supplied on approval, or under some form of standing order), librarians should receive full details about the item supplied. This procedure speeds up processing time and simplifies the handling of approval items.

Devise forms which supply the necessary information. These may be lists or individual order/invoices. In either case, include the basic data suggested above for library purchase orders in the entry for each item. Because the book is in hand, these can be simplified but codes and greatly abbreviated entries should not be used.

Librarians know that cataloging rules for corporate entries or for editors are complicated. Errors in corporate entries, while not desirable, are understandable, but the entry of an author's work under an editor's name causes problems.

Include in all correspondence or forms reference to the library's order number or to a letter or code indicating the reason for supply, e.g.: S.O. no. 66/2, or Approval Plan (letter of 7/1/70).

II. Order fulfillment

A. Waiting period

Librarians can reasonably expect receipt of books within the following time limits.

1. U.S. commercial publishers
   Supply within 30–60 days. At least 60% of the order should have been supplied or reported on within 45 days. *Note:* An extension to 90 days is permissible for older titles, but at least 50% of such orders should be filled within 60 days.
2. U.S. noncommercial publishers
   Recent titles should be supplied within 90 days. For more obscure publications a reasonable time is 120 days.

3. Foreign commercial publishers

   Most Western European titles should be supplied within 150 days. More time may be allowed for books from other countries.

B. Supply routines

1. Do not batch orders if this means a delay of more than two days, unless it is agreed by the librarian that shipments may be sent in a certain bulk.
2. Send "rush" orders immediately. Extra handling costs incurred may legitimately be charged to the library. Librarian and dealer should agree on the means of transport to be used.

III. Reports on unfilled or delayed orders

A. General

1. Make status reports clear and unambiguous.
2. Forward a status report on all unfilled orders to libraries by the end of the appropriate period of supply, as outlined above.
3. On all reports refer to
   (a) Library purchase-order number (and item number if on a list order) and date.
   (b) Brief bibliographic information, sufficient to identify the item.
   (c) The report itself and details of remedial action taken.
   (d) Date of the report.
4. If reports are on library claim forms, the items above may be suitably modified.
5. Both dealer and librarian must keep a record of reports and claims.

Note: Computer and other automated processes frequently depend on letter by letter accuracy for matching record files. Be careful, therefore, not to transpose letters or numbers.

B. Recommended reports

1. Reports arising from dealer-related activities

   (a) *Not yet received from the publisher* (NYR). This *must* mean that the dealer has actually placed the order with publisher or agent. Follow-up action must be under way.
   (b) *Out-of-stock, ordering* (OS ordering). This *must* mean out-of-stock at the dealer and that further copies have been or-

dered from the publisher. If possible, give an expected delivery date.

(c) *Claiming.* This *must* mean that the dealer is following up an active order.

2. Reports arising from publisher-related activities

(a) *Not yet published* (NYP). This should be based on information received from the publisher and checked against available records. The report should include the expected date of publication, if available.

(b) *Out-of-stock, publisher* (OS Publisher) and *reprinting/binding.* These form a joint report and should refer to the publisher's own statements, including an expected time of delivery. An additional status—"on order"—may be used where the source of supply to the dealer is an agency for one or more publishers. If the new supply date is indefinite, the order is best cancelled.

(c) *Out-of-print* (OP). These are usually true and acceptable reports, but when stock falls below a certain level, some publishers will supply only direct orders from individual customers and not dealers. Dealers should try to ascertain this and advise librarians accordingly. In the context of these guidelines, "out-of-print, cancelled" is the recommended report. *Note:* Librarian and dealer should settle on a routine for handling OP orders. If a dealer offers to search for such items, work out a suitable reporting procedure and specify a cut-off date. In general, most librarians and dealers prefer to handle such orders separately from in-print materials. If this is the case, librarians should accept such a report as a cancellation.

3. Miscellaneous reports

(a) *Not our publication* (NOP). This is a report received by a dealer from a publisher. The dealer should recheck the publisher's lists and investigate any discrepancy. When a dealer forwards such a report to a librarian, the order may be regarded as cancelled. If the librarian wishes to reorder the publication after finding more information, it will then be treated as a new order.

(b) *Wrong title supplied.* If a wrong title is supplied by the publisher or agent, send an interim report to the librarian, since it will explain the delay.

(c) *Defective copy.* Same as for wrong title supplied.
(d) *Wrong quantity supplied,* etc. If the wrong number of copies has been supplied, send them with a report to the librarian that the rest of the order will be supplied.

IV. Invoices

Make invoices as clear and precise as possible. Send to the library the original of each invoice and two other copies.

A. Invoice content

1. Name of dealer, with address to which payment is to be made.
2. Library purchase-order number(s) (and item number[s] when appropriate).
3. Bibliographical information on each item. Author and title constitute the minimum requirement. Use the form of entry on the library's purchase order. *Note:* Do not use coded abbreviations and numbers, etc. These delay checking and payment.

   If the publication is part of a series, the series information alone is *not* adequate.
4. Number of copies supplied. (If this differs from the number ordered, explain the difference.)
5. Number of volumes supplied, identifying them; e.g.: Vols. 1 thru 6, or 2v.
6. Price of each item, both publisher's list price and net price to library.
7. Service charges, tax, postage, etc.
8. When items are listed on more than one page, state clearly the amount brought forward on each page and specify clearly the final outstanding balance. Do not print the final total on a separate page; it may too easily become separated from the pages detailing items supplied, thus delaying checking and payment.

B. Cautions

1. Do not include status information on invoices. Invoices should list only items actually supplied.
2. Do not include monographs and serials or continuations on a single invoice. These publications are usually handled separately in libraries. Their inclusion on the same invoice may well delay payment.
3. Do not list too many items on one invoice. Invoices should correspond to single shipments.

4. Do invoice separately items being sent direct to a library by the publisher. If mixed invoices are used, an error in supply or failure to receive one item may hold up the verification and payment of the invoice.
5. Do not mix on one invoice items which had different supply addresses on the order. This treatment usually implies separate processing in the library.
6. Do be careful to invoice items separately when required, particularly when payments are being made from special funds. Sometimes this situation can be adjusted internally by the librarian but it frequently calls for re-invoicing.

C. Dispatch of invoices

Send invoices with the material invoiced. Where direct supply or several parcels are involved, the invoices may be sent separately to coincide as far as possible with the receipt of the shipment at the library.

Packages without invoices should contain packing slips. If these are duplicates of the invoices, they must be marked "duplicate" or "packing slip," to avoid confusion with the actual invoice and possible double payment.

State clearly on pro forma and pre-payment invoices what action is required.

D. Statements

Statements of outstanding invoices must be clearly distinguishable from the invoices themselves. Too many statements, particularly those produced by machine, look exactly like invoices and may cause double payment.

Remember that most librarians are not accountants and that the purpose of each form should, therefore, be made clear.

GENERAL GUIDELINES

The guiding overall purpose must be to achieve the best possible combination of service and cost. Cut-rate costs and first-rank services are incompatible; high costs and poor service, unacceptable. Librarians can and should expect to pay for good service, but they are then entitled to that service.

Librarians

Select your dealers carefully. Be sure that they understand what kinds of material you expect them to handle. Society publications, low-discount, and similar items pose particular problems to dealers who cannot be expected to handle them as easily and cheaply as regular trade publications. Be sure you understand and agree on discounts, service charges, and procedures. Abide by agreements you have made. Discuss your needs and problems regularly with your dealer and understand his problems.

Dealers

Librarians have problems, too. Do not promise more than you can perform. Discuss your problems openly with librarians. Remember that librarians are seldom in total control of a system, particularly of its financial aspects. They are, however, usually willing to see what can be done to effect necessary changes. Above all, keep communications open. Librarians must be able to explain to their patrons reasons for delays or other difficulties. Full information improves service and helps both dealer and librarian.

GLOSSARY

This glossary contains library and information science terms used but not explained in the text and others that an acquisitions librarian might be expected to know, especially those commonly found on invoices. Terms discussed in the text may be found through the index.

More thorough glossaries are in Mary C. Turner *The Bookman's Glossary* (4th ed.; Bowker, 1961); Anthony Thompson *Vocabularium bibliothecarii* (2d. ed.; UNESCO, 1962); Jerrold Orne *Language of the Foreign Book Trade* (2d. ed.; American Library Assn., 1962) and in the "Glossary-Definitions" of Robert M. Hayes and Joseph Becker *Handbook of Data Processing for Libraries* (Wiley, 1970).

abbonamento (It.); abonnement (Fr.); Abonnement (Ger.): subscription

accession record: a list of volumes added to the library in the sequence in which they are added; usually in book or ledger form, but may be on cards or sheets

agotado (Sp.): out of print

Angebot (Ger.): quotation

annuals: serials published once a year

Ansicht, zur (Ger.): on approval

antiquarian books: old, rare, and secondhand books

anular (Sp.): cancel

Auftrag (Ger.): order

Ausgabe (Ger.): edition

author entry: an entry of a work in a catalog under its author's name, usually the main entry. An author entry may be a personal or a corporate name or a pseudonym, etc.

back order: orders held for future delivery

backfile: issues of a periodical preceding the current issue

Band (Ger.): volume

Bestellung (Ger.): order

Buch (Ger.): book

Buchhändler (Ger.): bookseller

cambio (It., Sp.): exchange

card, punched: a card into which holes are punched and subsequently sensed electrically, mechanically, or optically

cartridge: a self-contained unit of film or tape that operates without manual threading

cassette: a tape cartridge that operates on small transistorized recorders

cathode ray tube (CRT): a vacuum tube for display of an image; a television tube is an example

cloth: bound in boards covered with cloth

code: a system of symbols for use in representing data; for computers they are machine-language instructions

collate: to examine a book or other publication to determine whether or not it is complete and perfect

commande (Fr.): order

compte (Fr.): account

computer: a machine that solves problems by manipulating symbols in a predetermined and self-directed manner

continuation: a work or part of a work issued in continuation of a book or a serial

conto (It.): account

corporate entry: a main entry or an added entry under the name of an organization, institution, or government rather than a person

cost accounting: the allocation of costs to tasks or processes for the purpose of comparing them with costs of alternative methods or standard costs

credit memo: a note issued by a vendor in place of a cash refund on orders unfilled or returned, to be deducted from the total charge on one of the vendor's invoices

cuenta (Sp.): account

data base: a file of data in machine language

descuento (Sp.): discount

desiderata: a list of books and other materials wanted but not immediately available

disc: a phonograph record

discount: reduction from list price

disponible (Fr., Sp.): available

document: a government publication

Drucker (Ger.): printer

edición (Sp.): edition

éditeur (Fr.): publisher, editor

edition: all of the copies of a work printed at one time; or the form of publication of a literary work with a changed text or notes or format

editor (Sp.): publisher

editore (It.): publisher, editor

edizione (It.): edition

Einband (Ger.); binding

ejemplar (Sp.): copy

embarque (Sp.): shipment

encuadernado (Sp.): bound

entry: a record of a book in a catalog or list

ephemera: material of temporary interest or value

épuisé (Fr.): out of print

erneuern (Ger.): renew
erschienen (Ger.): published
esaurito (It.): out of print
esemplare (It.): copy
exemplaire (Fr.): copy

facsimile: an exact reproduction of a book or other publication, usually made by a photomechanical process
factura (Sp.); facture (Fr.); Faktur (Ger.): invoice
fascicle: a part of a work that is being published in small installments, usually unbound and incomplete in itself
fascicolo (It.): part
fattura (It.): invoice
flow chart: a graphical representation of a sequence of operations
Folge (Ger.): series
Fortsetzung (Ger.): continuation

gebunden (Ger.): bound

hardbound: bound in boards covered with cloth or paper
Heft (Ger.): issue
herausgeben (Ger.): publish

impresor (Sp.): printer
imprimeur (Fr.): printer
imprint: the place and date of publication and the name of the publisher
in press: being printed
in print: available from the publisher
in progress: a work in parts, not complete
incomplet (Fr.); incompleto (It., Sp.): incomplete

inédit (Fr.); inédito (It., Sp.): unpublished

Kauf (Ger.): purchase
keypunching: to produce punched cards at a keyboard

Ladenpreis (Ger.): list price
laufende Bestellung (Ger.): standing order
legatura (It.): binding
librairie (Fr.): bookstore
library binding: a binding that is reinforced for library use. Library binding may be done after publication, called rebinding, or before the regular binding is applied in publication, called prebinding
libreria (It.); librería (Sp.): bookstore
libro (It., Sp.): book
lieferbar (Ger.): available for delivery
list price: the publisher's price for the retail trade, before discounts are applied
livraison (Fr.): part, issue
livre (Fr.): book
livre broché (Fr.): paperbound book

main entry: a catalog entry, usually the author entry, giving all the information necessary to the complete identification of a work
mensual (Sp.): monthly
monograph: a work on a particular subject

NOP: not our publication
NYP: not yet published

NYR: not yet received from the publisher

net: no discount

nouveau (Fr.): new

nuevo (Sp.): new

número (Sp.): issue, number

nuovo (It.): new

OP: out of print

OS: out of stock

on approval: material sent by a vendor that may be returned if not wanted

out of print: the publisher no longer has copies

out of stock: the publisher or wholesaler has no stock but expects to replenish it

packing slip: a slip sent with a shipment listing the items contained in the shipment

paper: a publication that is paperbound

paper tape: in automation, a strip of paper into which holes are punched and subsequently sensed electrically, mechanically, or optically

paperbound: a publication covered in paper

paraître (Fr.): publish, appear

pedido (Sp.): order

periodico (It.): periodical

periodique (Fr.): periodical

prebinding: *see* library binding

precataloging: the bibliographic searching done to gather pertinent data concerning -main or added entries, subjects, series, etc; may include preparation of descriptive cataloging copy

precio (Sp.): price

Preis (Ger.): price

prezzo (It.): price

prix (Fr.): price

pro forma invoice: an invoice sent before materials are sent and usually paid before materials are received, as in subscriptions

program: instructions to a computer to execute a desired task

pubblicare (It.); publicar (Sp.): publish

publié (Fr.): published

Rabatt (Ger.): discount

Rechnung (Ger.): invoice

recibo (Sp.): receipt

Reihe (Ger.): series

reissue: a reprint from the type of the original edition

relié (Fr.): bound

reliure (Fr.): binding

remainder: a publisher's stock of a title to be sold at reduced prices, usually through wholesalers and book dealers

remise (Fr.): discount

renouveler (Fr.): renew

renovar (Sp.): renew

review copy: a copy of a book sent free by a publisher for review or notice

ribasso (It.): discount

rilegato (It.): bound

rinnovare (It.): renew

sconto (It.): discount

service basis charge: a scheme under which a library is charged for subscriptions according to its income, circulation, or periodical holdings shelflist: a record of the items in a library arranged in the same order as they are arranged on the shelves

slide: a 35mm transparent, still photograph

soft cover: paperbound

Sortiment (Ger.): bookstore or book trade

standing order: an order to a vendor to send a serial as it is published unless otherwise notified

statement: a notice of unpaid invoices from a vendor

Subskription (Ger.): subscription

suscripción (Sp.): subscription

TOP: temporarily out of print

TOS: temporarily out of stock

tela (Sp.): cloth

tirage (Fr.): edition, printing

title: a printed publication that forms a separate whole, whether in one or several volumes

ungebunden (Ger.): unbound

vergriffen (Ger.): out of print

Verlag (Ger.): publisher

veröffentlich (Ger.): publish

Versand (Ger.): shipment

vertical file: material arranged vertically in filing drawers, usually pamphlets, clippings, and similar materials

videotape: an electronically reproduced visual image, usually with sound

volume: a physical unit of any printed work contained in one binding or portfolio

want list: see desiderata

Zeitschrift (Ger.): periodical

INDEX